GRAVEYARD OF CLERICS

Stanford Studies *in* Middle Eastern *and* Islamic Societies *and* Cultures

GRAVEYARD OF CLERICS

EVERYDAY ACTIVISM IN SAUDI ARABIA

■ ■ ■ ■ ■

Pascal Menoret

STANFORD UNIVERSITY PRESS

Stanford, California

STANFORD UNIVERSITY PRESS
Stanford, California

Printed in the United States of America on acid-free, archival-quality paper

Library of Congress Cataloging-in-Publication Data
Names: Ménoret, Pascal, 1976– author.
Title: Graveyard of clerics : everyday activism in Saudi Arabia / Pascal Menoret.
Other titles: Stanford studies in Middle Eastern and Islamic societies and cultures.
Description: Stanford, California : Stanford University Press, 2020. | Series: Stanford
Studies in Middle Eastern and Islamic societies and cultures | Includes
bibliographical references and index.
Identifiers: LCCN 2019040805 | ISBN 9780804799805 (cloth) |
ISBN 9781503612464 (paperback) | ISBN 9781503612471 (ebook)
Subjects: LCSH: Political participation—Saudi Arabia. | Political activists—Saudi
Arabia. | Islam and politics—Saudi Arabia. | Suburbs—Political aspects—Saudi
Arabia. | Saudi Arabia—Politics and government.
Classification: LCC JQ1841.A91 M46 2020 | DDC 322.409538—dc23
LC record available at https://lccn.loc.gov/2019040805

Cover design: Rob Ehle

Cover photo: Paul Stallan

Text design: Kevin Barrett Kane

Typeset at Stanford University Press in 10.5/14.4 Brill

For Mutti (1936–2018)

"Saudi Arabia is a graveyard of clerics
and a prison for preachers."

Abu Muhammad al-Maqdisi

Contents

GRAVEYARD OF CLERICS

PART I
THE ISLAMIC AWAKENING

■ ■ ■ ■ ■

Chapter 1   **GRAVEYARD OF CLERICS**

I QUIT SMOKING THANKS TO ISLAMIC ACTIVISTS.

I had been researching youth politics in Riyadh for about two years, chain-smoking between interviews but never during them, for Islamic activists—the bulk of my interlocutors—loathed tobacco.

Friends and interviewees were concerned about my habit and one of them recommended a religious charity that helped smokers. I drove there one day. Inside the building a volunteer greeted me with a grin. He looked like many religious activists in Saudi Arabia: with a beard, short white robes, a flowing headdress, and a boisterous sense of purpose. He took me to an office where he measured my lung capacity with a small device. Looking at the results, he praised the speed of my exhalation and said recovery would be easier than I thought.

He then led me to a large room where there was a tall transparent container, with a slot in the top, that looked vaguely like a ballot box. The container was filled with crumpled cigarette packs. A few others joined us there for an impromptu ceremony: the volunteer invited me to take out the pack that had been distorting the front pocket of my jeans, crush it, and throw it into the box, all of which I did, and they applauded. From there the man led me into a room of examination tables covered in clean sheets. The blinds were shut and the lights were dimmed; each table had a pillow and a pair of electrodes.

I lay down and he fixed the electrodes to the small flaps in front of my ear openings. He told me to relax and turned on a rheostat.

A mild electric current passed through my skull between my ears. I closed my eyes and focused on breathing. The buzz receded into the background; I dozed off to the swish of cars on the avenue outside. After about twenty minutes, the man came back, removed the electrodes, and told me to come back the next day.

As I left the building I inhaled the dusty air, filled with car exhaust and cooking scents. A man was walking down the street, a cigarette dangling from the corner of his mouth. He walked past and I caught a full whiff of tobacco smoke.

I thought I would be attracted to the smell, but what I perceived was an odor I had not sensed in fourteen years: it was acrid and unpleasant, not the seductive aroma I had grown to love. Cigarette smoke was now as alien to me as it had been before I started smoking. The electrodes had acted on my senses like a time machine.

The treatment was free of charge and lasted for a week, during which I did not touch tobacco. But after the electric treatments stopped, I started smoking again. I cursed the false hope the charity had given me, then forgot about it. My life as a researcher went on as before until one day, a few months later, I had to put out my morning cigarette after a couple of drags. This was very unusual. The day's first cigarette was often the best, but that one I found repulsive. I remembered the Islamic charity's electrodes and ran to the nearest pharmacy. I bought nicotine patches, vitamins, and magnesium—and I braced myself.

I told this story a few years later to a Saudi student in the United States, a social scientist who was closely watching the political scene in his country. He told me he regretted that Islamic activists had vanished from public spaces in recent years: they were now in prison, in hiding, or dead.

"Without them, we are left alone to face the Saudi state," he said. "They used to organize society in an autonomous manner. They created all kinds of institutions that were outside of the state's purview. Your addiction clinic is a good example of this."

That this chain smoker and amateur of strong cocktails missed Islamic activists was a testimony to their wide appeal. Smoking was so prevalent in the country that addiction clinics sprouted up in several cities. Like other behaviors that activists had constructed as sins, smoking was an opportunity for dedicated individuals to organize and collectively demonstrate their social utility.[1] The addiction clinic was not only a political tool, however, but also a site of transformation. There everyday smokers could reform themselves by submitting to the higher orders of meditation and electricity.

Addiction clinics were part of a nationwide network of charities, youth movements, women's groups, and activist organizations that emerged in the 1970s and were called, as a whole, the Islamic Awakening[2] or sometimes, simply, the Awakening. Awakening activists critiqued and protested the top-down modernization of the country by princes and experts, the Saudi-U.S. military alliance, Western arms sales to the country, and the repression of political and religious activism. They organized youth movements, provided a purpose to generations of Saudis, and helped members of the middle and the lower middle class gain in confidence and self-respect. And despite—or because of—their popularity, they were repressed and criminalized.

The eventual political crackdown was the outcome of long-term international cooperation. 'Abd al-'Aziz Al Sa'ud created the Saudi state in the first decades of the twentieth century. To fund his political projects, he sought support from the Ottoman Empire, then the British Empire, and eventually the United States. The Ottomans appointed 'Abd al-'Aziz's father *kaymakam*, local imperial administrator. The British made Central Arabia into a protectorate during World War I and helped 'Abd al-'Aziz conquer the vast territories that extend from the Red Sea to the Persian Gulf. In the 1930s, U.S. oil companies carved an informal empire out of the Saudi oil province, a territory east of Riyadh that was the size of Ukraine. Their corporate influence was soon formalized in a U.S. military protectorate over Saudi Arabia.[3]

U.S. Americans introduced wage labor, military air bases, economic planning, racial segregation, and suburban developments to Saudi Arabia. They powered the repressive apparatus of a state that grew more authoritarian as more Western experts joined it. Western modernity produced pipelines, asphalt roads, single-family houses—and torture chambers.[4] In oil-fueled, Western-powered Saudi Arabia, dissidents became traitors, and traitors could be tortured and disposed of.

'Abd al-'Aziz first cracked down on those who resisted his conquests. The fledging state banned political parties in 1932 as a way to help British and

Saudi forces fight the Free Hijazi Party, a movement that resisted 'Abd al-'Aziz's annexation of the holy cities of Mecca and Medina.[5] The next targets of police and military repression were the workers' movements that fought the U.S. oil company's racist, exploitative practices. The state banned unions and strikes and systematically suppressed public dissent.[6] U.S., British, and French experts trained Saudi officers. U.S., British, and French weapons manufacturers armed them. The Pax Americana was also a Pax Britannica and a Pax Gallica.

In 1976, the French intelligence head Alexandre de Marenches godfathered the Safari Club, an international coalition whose mission was to hunt down subversives in the Middle East and Africa. The Safari Club was made up of Egypt, France, Iran, Morocco, and Saudi Arabia. It soon organized counter-insurgency operations in Congo and Somalia and supported an Islamic insurgency against the new communist government of Afghanistan. When an armed movement occupied Mecca's Great Mosque in 1979 and lambasted the Saudi monarchy, the Saudi head of intelligence reached out to his French partners, and President Valéry Giscard d'Estaing sent in an elite unit.[7] Saudi and French forces killed between four and five thousand people during the siege of the mosque. The following year, a state-owned French development corporation started building a ten-thousand-unit suburb near Mecca. Political repression and real estate development often went hand in hand.[8]

The Saudi War on Terror has continued the Safari Club's counterinsurgency operations in the twenty-first century. In 2011 there were between twelve and thirty thousand political prisoners and prisoners of opinion in the country, some of whom had been personally processed by FBI officers.[9] Regulations enacted in 2013 and 2014 expanded the definition of terrorism to include the mildest forms of public speech. "Doubting the principles of Islam" became terrorism, as did "supporting or belonging to[…]organizations, groups, movements, gatherings, or political parties." Participating in a sit-in or a demonstration was terrorism. Attending conferences that "sow discord in society" was terrorism. The Muslim Brotherhood was a terrorist organization. Atheists were terrorists, too.[10]

Meanwhile, people kept disappearing into the black hole of the Saudi security system. When Salman bin 'Abd al-'Aziz, an aged son of the founding father, came to power in 2015, he found a perfectly greased machine. Salman's son, Muhammad bin Salman, lost little time before beginning to push its most gruesome buttons; brasher than his forebears, he did not bother to hide his actions. Saudi state brutality, which had been known to Saudis for decades, became international news.[11]

Far from being a haven for Islamic activists, Saudi Arabia has imprisoned them by the thousands since the late 1970s. "Saudi Arabia is a graveyard of clerics and a prison for preachers,"[12] the Palestinian writer Abu Muhammad al-Maqdisi wrote in 1989. The quip became proverbial, not least because of the prolific career of its author, one of the foremost ideologues of global jihad. Al-Maqdisi was born in 1959 and claimed Central Arabian ancestry; he lived in Kuwait and Saudi Arabia before joining the fight against the Soviet Union in Pakistan and Afghanistan in the 1980s. But this scholar did not really know how to use firearms: his weapons of choice were writing and teaching. While in Pakistan he penned a relentless critique of the Saudi political and religious establishment under the title *The Clear Evidence of the Irreligion of the Saudi State*.[13]

The state uses clerics, he wrote, "as a fig leaf and a smokescreen." Clerics "play a more important role than the army, the National Guard, the Royal Guard, the U.S. bases, the AWACS aircrafts, and all defense and security agreements: they anesthetize the people, put them to sleep, and deceive them." Saudi Arabia is a "morgue of clerics" and true believers should leave the country, lest they end up behind bars, beaten, and tortured.[14]

A few years after al-Maqdisi, the Yemeni activist Muqbil al-Wadiʻi used similar language. Born in the 1930s, al-Wadiʻi spent several decades studying religion in Saudi Arabia, where he joined the movement that occupied the Great Mosque of Mecca in 1979. Arrested, imprisoned, and finally deported to Yemen, al-Wadiʻi deplored the fact that Saudi money and state brutality had stripped clerics and preachers of their independence. "In Saudi prisons today, there are around five hundred preachers," he wrote in 1992, on the eve of a campaign of repression that would see hundreds more rounded up. "Many preachers wish to escape to the United States or Sudan, for their country has become a graveyard of clerics."[15] A few years later, al-Wadiʻi also went to the United States; but it was to undergo cancer treatment, paid for by one of Salman's brothers.[16]

Al-Wadiʻi may have been inspired by the history of his country, too. In the nineteenth century, Yemenis used to say that their country was "the graveyard of the Turks," a place that resisted imperial projects and where the Ottomans went to die. Some Yemenis saw the Ottomans as corrupt wine drinkers who had sex with small boys and exploited the poor; despite their pretensions to lead the Islamic community they were barely Muslim, and therefore fighting them was allowed.[17]

Neither al-Maqdisi nor al-Wadi'i, however, thought that Saudi clerics were corrupt, wine-drinking pedophiles who exploited the poor and were scarcely Muslim. They both had enormous respect for prominent Saudi clerics. What they mourned was the fact that clerics had been deprived of their freedom, buried alive in a bureaucratic maze or, if they tried to break the fetters, thrown in jail and tortured. Saudi Arabia was not the Islamic utopia it claimed to be, but an irreligious dystopia where state violence ruled supreme.

Most of the activists I have studied were either Islamic Awakening preachers or their followers and managed to organize in the rare spaces of freedom they had carved out amid intense, often spectacular repression. These activists rarely called themselves *Islamiyun*, Islamists, except when contrasting their positions to those of the liberals[18] or the secularists,[19] whom they saw as a broadly pro-Western current of thought, influential in the press and among decision-makers. Instead of "Islamists" they preferred to speak of "Islamic youth,"[20] "Awakening youth,"[21] or, perhaps to oppose their own vitality to the gerontocracy of the Al Saʻud royal family, simply "youth."[22]

We in Western countries often call "Islamists" those we want to frame as exotic criminals, prone to violence and mired in medieval ways of thinking. I actively refrain from using "Islamist" or "Islamism" here. *Islamisme* is a neologism Voltaire crafted in the eighteenth century to name Islam on the model of the French words *Judaïsme* and *Christianisme*. The word was then abandoned, along with *mahométanisme*, in favor of *islam*, only to reappear in Western scholarship after the 1979 Iranian revolution to describe movements that, more radically than Arab nationalisms, questioned Western hegemony.[23] Politicians and pundits now use this neologism to criminalize generations of activists, cast doubt on their political claims, and help suppress the movements they created. That activists kept organizing in the graveyard of clerics is a feat that, pace terrorism and security studies, deserves understanding and respect—not the rehearsing of uncertain Eurocentric stereotypes.

I first landed in Riyadh a few days after September 11, 2001, to teach French in a small institute near the Imam Muhammad bin Saʿud Islamic University, in the northern suburbs of the city. I became fascinated by Riyadh's physical and political landscape, with its modernist superblocks and its persistent expressions of political defiance. I started jotting down observations and chatting with whoever would talk to me. I was already conducting ethnographic research without knowing it. In the end I abandoned my graduate studies in philosophy to study Saudi youth politics. I joined a program in Middle East Studies, obtained a research visa in 2004, and moved back to Saudi Arabia, where I lived until the summer of 2007. I had a small stipend from the French Center for Archaeology and Social Science in Sana'a, Yemen, and the King Faysal Center for Research and Islamic Studies, based in Riyadh, lent me an office for the duration of my stay.

Studying political activism in Saudi Arabia is no easy task. I could only conduct field research with men, because gender segregation was pervasive in the 2000s; there are dynamic female Islamic activists, but hanging out with them was nearly impossible for me.[24] My own identity as a French researcher was also an obstacle. Everywhere I could see the heavy footprint of Western experts and other social scientists who had come since World War II to help keep the Saudi population in check. Many interlocutors looked through me toward an international system that had suppressed political life in their country. They assumed I was a spy, because I could very well have become one: one day, two French intelligence officers, after plying me with copious amounts of food and wine, asked if I would keep tabs on French converts living in Riyadh. I could have said yes, and no one would have been any the wiser.

Few anthropologists "go native," Talal Asad writes in a recent text, because their "deepest feelings are truly at home" only in their own society.[25] I confess to the opposite. For a set of complicated reasons, when I moved to Riyadh in early 2005 I thought of myself as an immigrant to Saudi Arabia, not an expat passing through. I actively tried to assimilate. I lived outside of the gated communities where most Westerners lived, learned to speak Arabic with a Riyadh accent, and would listen to Saudi and Iraqi music, watch Saudi television, and eat Najdi, Hijazi, Yemeni, and Iraqi food.

One day one of my closest friends told me to stop wearing jeans and buttoned-up shirts, "like an Indian," and start "dressing like a man"—as if immigrants from the subcontinent were less than human. He dragged me to his tailor and walked me through all the tiny decisions governing *thob* elegance: what type of cloth, what collar, what length, how close to the body. For more than a year I wore a long, white, tailored *thob* and often sported a *shmagh* and a *'igal*, the red-and-white-checkered headdress and the black double rope that so elegantly complete male Saudi silhouettes.

I was proud of "passing." When the man sitting next to me on a domestic flight asked if I was from Jeddah, I beamed with pride and later boasted about it to my friends in Riyadh, who had arabized Pascal into Basil and sometimes added their own tribal name to my first name. At times I thought I would stay and become Saudi, like a Yemeni friend who, after several years and many interventions, had been granted the citizenship.

"Whatever happens, you will remain a Westerner," an Islamic activist said to me one day. Despite all my efforts at "passing," my being there was predicated on a system of power that, from my French scholarship to my link with the King Faysal Center, excluded him by definition. How could I understand his experience and his perspective? How could I put myself in his shoes? This conundrum has kept me busy for some time. One of my political and epistemological goals in the past years has been to not remain a Westerner, even if, ultimately, I conducted field research as one.

"It is one thing to try to understand 'the native's point of view,'" Talal Asad writes in the same text; "it is quite another for the anthropologist to approach 'the native' with the possibility of learning something important for her own form of life that might help to transform how that life is understood."[26] My encounter with Islamic activists durably changed my "deepest feelings" and altered my idea of what a home should be. I not only understood "how it is that the language of Islam has come to apprehend the aspirations of so many people"[27] across the world; I also lost the sense of centrality and superiority that my elitist French upbringing had impressed on me.

This transformation was not only intellectual and political: it also passed through an alteration of my body itself. Perhaps the fact that Islamic activists helped cure my addiction to tobacco, and that I let myself be literally shocked by them, did something to disrupt my structural position as a Westerner. Or perhaps this is the story that I like to tell myself, after having had all things Saudi impressed upon me for almost twenty years. It remains that, more than ten years after visiting the Islamic charity, I am still tobacco-free. Islamic activists may have helped me live a longer, healthier life. They have certainly helped thousands of others to live better lives—or maybe just live—in an extremely repressive context.

The graveyard of clerics only authorized fleeting, subtle political life, what my interlocutors called Islamic action,[28] an expression that, contrary to the Western notion of "Islamism," is dynamic and points to practices, not texts and doctrines. I am not interested here in religion as a doctrinal tradition and do not study how individuals cultivate themselves within it.[29] There is definitely "too much Islam in the anthropology of Islam" and also, certainly, too much anthropology of Islam in the study of contemporary Islamic movements: just as most believers are not dedicated activists, most activists may not be committed believers. Studying Islamic activists should not be confused with an analysis of what Islam "does," but it should allow us to better understand the complex relationships between activism, reform, and repression. My project therefore is to examine the ambiguities and contradictions that are inseparable from the daily lives of ordinary activists.[30]

Saying that Saudi Arabia is a graveyard of clerics does not only mean that the state, by instituting an official religion, has forced its clerics and preachers into a narrow straitjacket. It also implies an intimate relationship between the nation and graveyards. Saudi Arabia as a nation was born through the act of destroying the tombs of saints, prophets, and martyrs.[31] In the 1920s, after ʿAbd al-ʿAziz conquered the holy cities of Mecca and Medina, his army demolished the al-Muʿalla and al-Baqiʿ cemeteries, where close relatives of the Prophet Muhammad were buried. The destruction was thorough and spectacular. A European passing through Medina in 1926 wrote that its "wilderness of ruined building materials and tombstones" showed the graves had not been "ruined by a casual hand, but raked away from their places and ground small."[32] Saudi Arabia had become a graveyard of graveyards.

Modern Saudi graveyards are walled off and empty: no tombstones, no inscriptions, only gravel or sand or dust and, to mark each tomb, two bare stones. In some cities, municipal services clear out the tombs every two years to make space for new bodies; in Mecca, bodies are pushed aside and mixed with older bones every year. Being buried near the Great Mosque has become a prized commodity.[33] Like the cities that surround them, Saudi graveyards are transient and subjected to the market. In Riyadh, tombs are marked electronically[34] and soon, even the two stones that mark each grave might be entirely replaced by digital records and the graveyards swept clean, the mere reflection of datasets kept elsewhere and accessible only under certain conditions.

A graveyard is a place where the dead are cast away, pushed toward the periphery of the city. But growing cities now surround graveyards, and the peripheries have become central. Graveyards have become places of mixing, where old bones mingle with yet older ones as fresher corpses are brought in and interred.

That Saudi Arabia is a graveyard of clerics means that clerics are constantly subjected to the threat of metaphorical or actual death. The state has suspended them in a state between life and death, condemned them to "the status of living dead."[35] It also means that the place is awaiting a revival, that its politics need to be re-enchanted. No wonder the main social and political movement in the country called itself the Awakening. There was much to awaken in the death-world the Al Saʿud family created, beginning with the very streets of Riyadh, which had been put to death by princes, planners, and developers.[36]

Chapter 2 **LA MUBALA**

"IN THE BEGINNING IS THIS: THERE IS BASICALLY NO COLLECTIVE action here. No student movement. Nothing."

Nawwaf[1] spoke fast and then stood silent for a while, looking at me with wide, intense eyes. Behind the shut window, the hum of Riyadh: car engines droning, construction tools rattling, a honk here and there.

"Has it changed lately?" I asked.

I had known Nawwaf for years and we often chatted about the lack of a political life in the country. He had participated in several banned demonstrations and knew what it meant to defy public order and run away from the police. Why had he and others decided to march in a context where demonstrations and protests were violently repressed? What did their rebellion say about spatial politics?

He looked at me without a word, and then he spoke.

"The situation has not changed, really. People's nature has changed. People have become indifferent. They don't give a fuck anymore.

"Al Jazeera TV was among the things that could bring awareness to politics. When it was created in 1997, no network dared ask the kind of questions we hear now. You would hear these new questions and think, 'No way. Is this Arab TV? Qatari TV?' Their debates, their audacity enlightened me. But I mean, I was asking tough questions even before Al Jazeera. Where did I get this audacity from? Was it from my self-assurance? No: it was from my apathy."

La mubala. Not-giving-a-fuck-ness. The study of protest movements often looks at what triggers the transformation from apathy to outrage and to politicization.[2] The assumption is that apathy alone does not lead to action. But it is only after Nawwaf became more indifferent that he became more audacious, more self-confident, in a word, more politically active. Apathy was a form of creative emptiness. It was not numbness, but the silence in which one could find one's self and muster the courage to do something. Apathy was repressed political desire. It was the calm before the great passion.[3]

"See, the problem is that the government created that atmosphere," Nawwaf said. "It gave people the illusion that the secret police are everywhere, that walls have ears. But it is not true. So I would tell people, 'It is a lie.' You see? 'Do not believe any of it. We created our own fears.'"

In the violently repressive Saudi context, people who engaged in banned political action had to numb themselves to the reality of the public sphere and stop worrying about repression, the secret police, informers, or the consequences of their actions. But this self-inflicted blindness was puzzling: how could one forget about the reality of arrests and prison, torture and pain?

Young Saudis often said they were *tafshan*, an adjective beginning with an emphatic *t* and expressing disappointment and frustration. Sociologists often translated the related noun *tufush* into "vacuum" and "boredom," but there was something more to it. *Tufush* was the subtle despair that gripped young Saudis when they understood that they were powerless in the face of the political forces shaping society.[4] According to another interviewee, if boredom "means a vacuum, non-existence," *tufush*, in contrast, "is what drives you to do anything and everything. It is what pushes you to become a *'arbaji*, a hooligan."[5] Nawwaf's *la mubala* was close to *tufush*, which other interviewees described as the rage of having to witness political injustice, either inside Saudi Arabia or worldwide, without being able to act on it. Activists I interviewed often told me how enraged they were at the idea that Saudi Arabia, through its military alliance with the United States and Western Europe, participated in the misery of Muslims everywhere.

"My goal is for the situation of Muslims to get better," Nawwaf said. "If Ibn Sa'ud was working toward this goal, I would probably stay silent, but he is not: there is neither progress, nor reform. Ibn Sa'ud will not change."

Ibn Saʿud was what opponents sometimes called the king, the core princes, or Al Saʿud as a whole: this massive social group that, immensely powerful, awarded itself many privileges.

"There is no other way but to grab Ibn Saʿud, like this, and to compel him to change, by force. Indoor whispers are useless."

"What is the solution, then?" I asked.

"The solution? It is this."

Nawwaf pointed to my tape recorder, set on the desk between us.

"Part of what I am telling you, I hope you will publish it," he said. "Part of what I say is part of the solution; it is a harassment strategy.... If I talk to you, it is not to fulfill *your* desire. It is something *I* want, something *I* decided."

At the outset of our interview he had told me, "Say: 'In the name of God, the most gracious, the most merciful,'" before enjoining me to "ask my questions." Nawwaf made it clear that *he* was the one conducting the interview and that my desire for knowledge came second to his will. The fact that we were in my office at the King Faysal Center for Research and Islamic Studies, a quasi-governmental institution headed by the former director of the Saudi intelligence, did not seem to bother him. To him, our interview itself was political action: let the walls listen to what he had to say. He was too apathetic to care, anyway.

So he told me how, in the fall of 2003, the Islamic Awakening activist Saʿd al-Faqih, from his London exile, had called Saudis to march against political repression, and how he himself had joined the march. Al-Faqih, born in 1957, was an opposition figure who in the early 1990s had protested the U.S.-Saudi alliance and the Gulf War. He had dodged arrest and gone into exile in London, where in 1996 he created the Movement for Islamic Reform in Arabia. He communicated with his followers inside Saudi Arabia through Radio Reform, his movement's satellite radio station.[6]

Saʿd al-Faqih had planned the demonstration for October 14, 2003 near the Mamlaka Tower, a skyscraper where the interior minister, on the same day, was chairing an international human rights conference. Al-Faqih wanted to tell the world that the peculiar mix of reform and repression that the Saudi state had been brewing since 9/11 was not acceptable. Saudi political elites had engaged in their own version of the War on Terror. Random arrests and unlawful detentions were already part of the domestic arsenal; packaging these as a Saudi campaign against terrorism, its ideologues, and its funders was a sure way to avoid being targeted by the U.S.-led War on Terror. Meanwhile, the council of ministers had promised municipal elections, but Sa'd al-Faqih was determined that these should not divert international observers from the reality of the dictatorship.

"Even Saddam Hussein had elections," al-Faqih told the *New York Times*. "But without freedom of expression and freedom of assembly, they are worthless."[7]

Another exiled activist, 'Abd al-'Aziz al-Khamis, wrote from London that Saudis refused to buy into "tiny, timid" municipal elections.[8] Nawwaf was on the same page.

"With their elections and voting booths, they try to improve their image in the foreign media," he said to me. "You see, the simple actions of selecting a name and putting a ballot in a box mean a great deal to foreign journalists. But if the truth of the municipal elections is to silence us, then there is a problem.

"I was constantly listening to Radio Reform.[9] I told my friends about the march and I asked them to join. One of them is jobless and I told him, 'Come and express yourself. Say publicly that you are jobless.' But none of them did; they were weak and scared. I tried to convince them, but they were not ready, they were frightened, and they did not know what to do. I told them, 'There will be victims; there will be arrests. Change does not come easily. You may sit and wait for a smooth change, but this will not happen.' Change can only be deadly, at least in part. So I got in my car before the afternoon prayer, I turned the ignition key, and I put on Radio Quran."[10]

Unlike Radio Reform, Radio Quran was an official state media outlet, which featured pro-government voices and embodied Al Sa'ud's control over religion. If Saudi Arabia was a graveyard of clerics, then Radio Quran was the voice of the undertakers.

"Some government sheikh was speaking. As I drove I saw cars headed in the same direction. There were many police patrols, too. I witnessed the great number of cars and the traffic jams at intersections, and something snapped in me. Could it be possible that the state had become weak? That the punishing cane could hit the state's own fingers?[11] On the radio, the sheikh talked about the corruption of society, and said it was a sin to disobey the ruler."

He paused.

"Our meeting point was the mosque south of the Mamlaka Tower. You would pray there and then start walking. But I did not pray there; I prayed elsewhere and I drove there. I knew the place would be shut down and I drove through the back streets."

The meeting point was smack in the middle of the capital's business district. The Mamlaka ("Kingdom") Tower, which looked like a bottle opener with its wide, elliptical hole, was Riyadh's tallest building. It stood in the middle of a long line of towers and luxurious constructions squeezed in between two straight, parallel highways: King Fahd Road and 'Olaya Avenue. This long, linear neighborhood was designed in the late 1960s by the Greek urbanist Constantinos Doxiadis to free the center of Riyadh from congestion. Doxiadis had observed most cities grew around a central core that was gradually choked by overuse and traffic. His model of a linear city followed a central spine that could be extended indefinitely and serve as the political and economic lifeline of the community. The Doxiadis axis now linked the historical center of Riyadh to the beige and grey desert of Banban, some forty kilometers north of the city. But high land prices in the business district had slowed development, so that the linear neighborhood had become a patchy collection of towers, shopping malls, and undeveloped dust.

"We were initially supposed to march toward this empty lot, between the Mamlaka Tower and the mosque."

He drew a map in my notebook.

"The mosque was full for the afternoon prayer. People went out and headed toward the empty lot. But the security services had the same information, and they locked down the whole area. How do you get in? People were blocked here, here, and here. The mosque is not that big, and the police had been there since the morning. Because the demonstration had been publicized weeks before, by Sa'd al-Faqih's radio. When the people exited the mosque in procession, they were arrested right away."

Al-Faqih's instructions were now obsolete, and so marchers improvised alternative routes. They were forced out of the grounds of the tower, and what should have been one procession ended up being "a demonstration broken into pieces. . . . Three marches, and here the mosque."

A first group of protesters marched on King Fahd Road. A second one walked along 'Aruba Avenue, a road perpendicular to King Fahd and 'Olaya. A third group walked on 'Olaya. All groups were headed toward the tower. Nawwaf started walking on King Fahd Road, near the 'Obeikan bookstore. His group followed the road to the intersection with 'Aruba Avenue and then made a right toward the Mamlaka Tower. The closer protesters got to the tower, the more onlookers they encountered.

"We wanted to walk as one group until the end of 'Aruba, so that passers-by could join the procession. The more people there were in it, the more protected the group would be. It is easy: join us to protect yourself. Protect others by joining us.[12] This was the idea. . . . But there was no organization, no coordination on the ground. The demonstration happened in a haphazard way. . . . For instance, we were very thirsty and needed water; we did not know we had to carry water. . . . When you march, you need water, especially in our region. . . . I, on the other end, was prepared. I was ready from the get-go. I even put on shoes, to be able to run easily."

In October it was still very warm, and the leather sandals that many Saudi men were in the habit of wearing in the summer were slippery and could get you caught.

"I was prepared, but I had not readied myself for the possibility of being arrested."

La mubala, again. The government press would later use the marchers' lack of preparation against them. The day after the protest, an eyewitness, talking to the pro-government daily *Al-Sharq al-Awsat*, claimed that he, with others, had staged an impromptu counter-demonstration to give the police a hand.

"Most protesters found themselves surrounded by us," he said to the press. "We chanted our refusal of the way they expressed themselves. . . . Some of them carried signs demanding the release of some detainees. . . . Others had Qurans in their hands. . . . We persuaded the police to disperse them and arrest them, because they offered a repulsive sight. The way they protested was artificial and silly."[13]

The eyewitness report was inane; according to Nawwaf, there had been no counter-demonstration. The police did not need to be persuaded by law-abiding citizens to arrest protesters; it was following orders and was ready to crack down. *Al-Sharq al-Awsat* was eager to show that arrests of protesters were not evidence of state violence but a mere service the police had extended to concerned citizens. The newspaper made it sound as though a mob had set out to free criminals serving lawful sentences. But the detainees whose relatives had taken to the streets were political prisoners who had been disappeared by the security services.

"Our main slogan was: Allahu Akbar, God is the Greatest," Nawwaf said. "Nobody can ban us from saying: God is the Greatest. . . . On 'Aruba Avenue, some people were holding signs saying, 'Free the prisoners'. . . . We were not very many, maybe two, three hundred people in our group. But the action was scattered; it was not a collective action. Some people came only to gawk. Put in your head that if you come, it is to join in, not to gawk. . . . But many people came, saw the police presence, and thought it was not worth it. Some people were coming and going, between the march and the sidewalks.

"And then someone got hit by a cop. One of the things that I really liked is that a marcher with a camera started filming the scene. You can really embarrass the government with this. What, a peaceful march, and you respond to it with violence and repression?"

The protesters did not square up against the police like two armies on a battlefield, however. This was no pitched battle, but rather a series of micro-scenes that expressed not only hostility and violence but a whole range of emotions, some negative and some positive.

"The cops . . . looked at us with respect: 'You're powerful'; with fear, with a lot of different emotions. . . . Several weeks after the demonstration, I met a cop who had been there. At that time I was working in the area as a security agent, and we worked alongside cops. And I would speak a lot. I told a few of them, 'You see, I was one of the 'Olaya protesters,' and that cop said, 'I like what you did. I like you.' He was happy I participated, although he is a cop. He was one of those who were making the arrests. . . . They arrested many more than a hundred people. . . . That cop told me they arrested maybe four hundred people."

Right after the demonstration, the interior minister, Prince Nayef, said that 150 protesters had been arrested. The Interior Ministry later revised his figure, saying that 271 protesters had been arrested, of whom 188 were freed a week later, "after proving that they had been drawn into the crowd and acted out of curiosity". According to the Kuwait News Agency, "no official estimates were given as to the size of the demonstration."[14]

"But even the state was poorly prepared," Nawwaf said. "Cops were catching people walking near their vans, but they had small vans, which could not hold all the people. So cops were pushing protesters away, saying, 'We do not want them. We are full.'

"Judging by their appearance, most marchers came from villages and small towns. Most looked like average people. A friend of mine recognized a rural judge. . . . They said women marched, too, but not in massive numbers. I did not see any of them."

Nawwaf did not see any women, but he heard about Umm Sa'ud, a female marcher who became famous on that day. The security forces had disappeared her husband in the 1990s. Then "her son, the apple of her eye,"[15] was arrested after Al-Qa'eda reportedly bombed three gated communities in May of 2003. The police arrested more than six hundred people in the spring of 2003, of whom a hundred and ninety were released after a few months, eighty were prosecuted, and hundreds remained in jail, where they were probably still being interrogated and tortured.[16] The security forces had certainly disappeared many more and held them outside of any legal procedure. Families were rarely notified and had to move heaven and earth to track down loved ones. And then, in September of 2003, a fire ravaged the al-Hayer political prison, killing Umm Sa'ud's son and sixty-six other political prisoners.[17]

After the al-Hayer fire, people started meeting after Friday prayers to demand justice for the dead and the release of their relatives still in jail. Week after week, a group of protesters occupied the plaza in front of the lavish al-Rajhi mosque, in the capital. Sa'd al-Faqih had capitalized on this wage of anger to organize the October 14 demonstration.

Umm Sa'ud "brought her Quran and her prayer mat and headed toward the site of the march. As young protesters ran away from the regime's thugs, she stopped and shouted at the top of her lungs, 'O, woe is me, o Sa'ud. Where are you, where did injustice carry you away?' "[18] She was carrying a photo of her son and asking that his body be returned to her.[19] Yet "the officer did not listen to her; he rained blows on her, and threw her fragile body into a van filled with female protesters."[20]

"Honestly, I would be ashamed to grab an old lady like this and throw her into a police van," Nawwaf said. "By God, for a monthly salary of three, four thousand riyals [seven hundred and fifty to a thousand dollars], grabbing a woman and throwing her like this? Not for anything. It upsets me when I think about it."

Activists presented the march as a duel between Umm Saʿud and Ibn Saʿud, between the mother of Saʿud and the son of Saʿud, between "a woman of the Qahtan tribe, a Saudi woman who patiently endured the injuries of time, the arrogance of men, the ignorance of politicians, and the narrowness of all minds,"[21] and the royal family, whose power depended on public service wages and on the type of repression Umm Saʿud was a victim of.

From London, ʿAbd al-ʿAziz al-Khamis explained that women and the young, these two forgotten halves of Saudi society, had opened "a new era in Saudi political history." They had "stifled their own fear of the regime" and shown that "the weak, the women, the young, could enter into dissidence through their contentious action."[22]

"I marched for maybe two hours, maybe a little less," Nawwaf said. "The demonstration was supposed to last from the afternoon prayer to the sunset prayer. After that, I got in my car, I stopped somewhere to perform the sunset prayer, and I went home to watch the news on Al Jazeera, but there was nothing about the march. . . . My goal was to embarrass the government and to win some concessions. To say: the time of moderation is over. The time of, 'You are always right, everything you do is fine,' all of this is over. The demonstration did not target the state or the ministers. It targeted the royal family itself."

And the royal family responded. A few weeks after the march, the interior minister, Prince Nayef, declared, "if democracy means justice, equality, and freedom, then we are all democrats." The president of the supreme court, Sheikh Salih al-Luhaydan, said that "demonstrations [were] an obvious deviance."[23] Umm Saʿud was jailed in Riyadh's infamously crowded and violent Malaz prison, where she was beaten and tortured.[24] On December 9, thirty-six protesters, including Umm Saʿud and two other women, were sentenced to three months in prison.[25] In the following years, protesters kept marching and asking for the release of political prisoners, but the state's response was the same: more repression, more bans, and more political prisoners. If the common repertoire of protest—marches, public declarations—was forbidden, how then could activists make their voices heard? And how did the Islamic Awakening survive repression, recruit new members, and impose its cultural and political hegemony?

Chapter 3   HOW CAN THE STATE TORTURE CLERICS?

UNLIKE OTHER ACTIVISTS, NAWWAF HAD NEVER BEEN A REGULAR member of an Islamic group, yet his socialization took place in the context of the Awakening. How did he become politicized in the larger environment created by the Islamic movements?

Nawwaf was a white-collar employee in his mid-twenties when I interviewed him. Neither tall nor short, he was handsome yet unremarkable. His white robes were spotless and ordinary. He did not wrap his checkered headdress in any particular fashion. He simply folded its right extremity on his left shoulder, which gave him a no-nonsense, down-to-earth air. He drove a secondhand Lexus, which compounded this first impression: he knew material things were of little worth and refused to pay a steep price for them. His job was perhaps the least ordinary thing about him: most employed Saudis worked in the public sector, but Nawwaf worked for a private company, which was both a more demanding and a less rewarding career path. (Private companies usually paid less than the state.)

Because of his limited means and the housing crisis in Riyadh, Nawwaf still lived with his parents, whose "love and support for the government" he no longer shared. His father was a blue-collar employee who had recently retired from the Ministry of Education. Nawwaf knew his father was "not educated," just like his mother, a homemaker who had brought up three sons and two daughters. Nawwaf was the last child, "the last thing," as he said, and his ideas started diverging from theirs when he was in middle school, "to the point that I stopped asking my dad for money." Nawwaf was slowly becoming his own man.

His teenage years were a time when state clerics considered satellite television sinful, but he bought a satellite dish and brought it home. His parents and brothers tried to stop him, arguing that religion was threatened and that a dish on one's roof was a mark of shame. *Share' 'Iblis*, the Devil's Alley: this is how Riyadh residents had renamed the stretch of the Sulaymaniyya street where one could buy satellite dishes. Nawwaf did not budge, and his relatives stopped resisting his purchase.

The Gulf War broke out when Nawwaf was in middle school. Saddam Hussein's Iraq invaded Kuwait. The Saudi royal family, convinced by the U.S. vice-president, Dick Cheney, that Saudi Arabia was next, allowed a coalition of Western militaries to use the Saudi territory as a launch pad for their war on Iraq. From 1991 to 1994, a group of intellectuals, clerics, preachers, professors, doctors, judges, and civil servants publicly criticized Al Sa'ud for calling on Westerners for military help after they had spent billions of dollars on U.S., British, and French weaponry. Where had all that money gone, they asked, if the country was now unable to defend itself? Other grievances followed. The newly formed opposition was linked to the wider Islamic Awakening movement. Its leaders demanded wide-ranging reforms, including the creation of a parliament, the independence of the judiciary, and the protection of basic rights. They also wanted an end to the special relationship between Saudi Arabia and the United States, which had resulted in more repression and fewer freedoms.

Sheikhs, professors, doctors, judges, engineers, and students signed petitions and organized demonstrations and sit-ins. But there was no legal way to institutionalize the protest movement, and hundreds of activists and religious sheikhs were arrested. High-profile arrests became occasions for more protests, especially in the Qassim region, northwest of Riyadh, where the city of Burayda witnessed what has since become known as the "Burayda Intifada," led in particular by the sheikhs Salman al-'Ouda and Safar al-Hawali, two prominent Awakening activists who were arrested in 1994.[1]

"It deeply shocked me: these are sheikhs," Nawwaf said. "Sheikhs here are dignified, and people respect them. Especially the state, which says all the time, 'We respect clerics.' They have a privileged status. Why, those are clerics. How can the state throw them in jail and torture them?"

Nawwaf's father and uncles, despite their religious feelings, however, were unfazed. "Old people looked at these activists and said, 'These people studied in the West and were influenced by the West; they are secularists who came back here carrying Western ideas and Western influence.'"

For more traditional Saudis, asking for the independence of religious institutions marked you as a secularist and a Westernized spirit, even if you were a sheikh or a cleric yourself. The Islamic Awakening was so deviant a phenomenon that it had to stem from the West.

"Old people are not educated," Nawwaf said. "Westerners often believe that our elders are venerable sages. Let me tell you: those in their fifties, sixties, or seventies, when they were young, they used to work really hard, they worked tough jobs, in construction. . . . They worked from sunrise to sundown and then went home to sleep. And again, from morning to night, to earn a crust. And then the oil era began, they became civil servants, they got money and new houses. They thought these things were gifts from the government. They thought they had to be thankful. That is how they see their lives: I had to toil, and then I could rest. Life was tough, and then it became easy. When some old guy buys a car with his own money, he ends up curtsying to the royal family. He thanks them for the car, even though *he* bought it.

"So Saʿd al-Faqih and the other Islamist exiles, those who criticized them used to say, 'The government paid for your education. It paid for your U.S. or English or German PhDs. How dare you not be grateful?' That is what the media and the elders said, as if that money was the private property of the prince. As if, when the state gives you money, it is out of the goodness of the princes' hearts, and not out of duty.

"Look, in our society, the elders love the government. Those who come after them, much less so. Many even started hating the government. And the third generation has inherited something from this second generation. Today, people my age or younger love to insult the government. It is something we have inherited. Do not pay attention to what the media say: the revolt will not calm down. It will not vanish.

"Why do you think I liked to read the pamphlets of the opposition? Because they were banned. Why did I like to listen to BBC Arabic? Because it was banned. There was no other alternative. . . . I joined Islamic groups in school for a very short period of time because of what they were offering: they had desert trips, excursions, activities. Then I left them. I also joined a Quran memorization circle at the mosque; I stayed about a month and did not continue. I did not really adhere to Islamic groups. I do not think they are actual organizations."

Nawwaf was a free spirit who had been moved by the Awakening's protest movement of the early 1990s and shocked to see its sheikhs and leaders arrested, one after the other. He came of age politically during the repressive 1990s, when the main Awakening activists were behind bars and the movements they had fostered were being cracked down on. But Awakening groups were not the only spaces of debate. Suburban homes featured semi-public spaces, and this is where Nawwaf experienced his first political disappointments. A typical middle-class house was made up of a semi-public and a private zone. The courtyard, behind a gate frequently left open, often featured a fireplace[2] or an annex[3] that were the house's most public spaces, where the household head received his friends, colleagues, and neighbors and could hold any conversation he saw fit. Inside the house, the men's sitting room[4] and a restroom were semi-public as well and could also be used for public or familial functions.

As a teenager, Nawwaf often sat in his parents' sitting room among "people older than myself, people who know better, from my family, from the neighborhood, friends. And I often found their conversations naïve and disappointing. I did not like to sit around people who talk about music, culture, soccer, mundane topics. I preferred to chat about politics and political legitimacy." He started to listen to Radio Reform and developed his political consciousness by listening to the exiled Awakening activist Sa'd al-Faqih. Nawwaf himself was not an Awakening activist, but he had grown up, intellectually and politically, in the large shadow cast by the Awakening movement.

The Islamic Awakening relied on three main structures, two of which operated year-round, while the third was seasonal. Islamic awareness groups[5] in middle and high schools and Quran memorization circles[6] in mosques were the permanent structures, organized by teachers and college students. Summer camps[7] were seasonal activities offered by several institutions during summer holidays.

The problem faced by the Islamic Awakening was how to rally in punishing circumstances. Political indifference might have helped Nawwaf mobilize; but the Islamic Awakening sought to fight the very apathy and powerlessness that Nawwaf and others so eloquently described. Islamic awareness groups were typically started by middle and high school teachers and offered extracurricular activities, from sports to theater and from camping to religious culture. The Arabic word for awareness[8] literally meant "conscientization," and activists called on students not only to embody religious tenets in their daily lives but also to become political actors and fight social and political evils.

Their counterparts in local mosques were Quran memorization circles. Quran memorization was encouraged by the state and could pass as an innocuous activity—yet it was crucial to the Islamic Awakening. Islamic awareness groups in schools attracted a broader constituency and they were not as noble, in the activists' eyes, as Quranic circles. Because they emerged in the shadow of two state institutions, the Ministry of Education and the Ministry of Islamic Affairs, however, Islamic awareness groups and Quranic circles were at constant risk of being choked.

The Islamic Awakening was the result of a myriad of individual and small-scale endeavors to re-enchant public life. Everyday practices were key to the movement: going to school, joining small study circles, picnicking in the desert, and hanging out with friends all became politicized practices as young activists turned them into weapons against police and intellectual repression.[9]

After the Islamic Awakening supported the protests of the early 1990s, the Ministry of Education tried to rein in Islamic activities. Mosques were no longer able to be the open spaces they had been in the 1960s and 1970s. The Islamic challenge prompted the security services to tighten their grip: the Interior Ministry planted informers among worshippers, and the mosques were now closed between prayers lest they serve as recruiting and organizing grounds.[10] In response, Islamic activists became even more secretive.

"Nobody broadcasts that he is working in this field," a local Awakening organizer said to me. "The only thing that is visible to society is the activities: mosque circles and school activities." Of course, the security services knew what was going on inside the Islamic movements, more or less, and secrecy was no longer a way to protect oneself. It had become more cultural than functional. "The state knows about these movements in detail," the organizer continued, "but society does not know a lot. . . . The state does not officially acknowledge the existence of organizations within Saudi Arabia, but it lets them work. . . . The state does not want these organizations to go public, and within the movement there is an unwritten understanding that going public would scare away society."

There was an implicit contract between Islamic movements and the state, in other words, whereby activists were complicit in their own silencing. As long as they behaved as if their organizations did not exist, the state kept its distance, allowing members of society to be recruited and join without fear. Repression struck when activists went public and announced the creation of political institutions, as happened in the 1990s with the Committee for the Defense of Legitimate Rights and again in the late 2000s with the Association for Political and Civil Rights. Both organizations were shut down and their members imprisoned.[11]

As a result of this secrecy, students who joined mosque or school activities were not necessarily aware of their connection to a particular Islamic organization, whether it be the Muslim Brothers or the Salafis. "You are aware from the get-go that you are engaged in some action, but you cannot clearly picture it in your mind," the organizer said. "You intuitively know that you are in the midst of a huge group, engaged in one action, behind one leadership. You feel it when you are with the youth, because you are in the same summer camps and you see the same activities in various youth groups and in different mosques."

It was only later, after they had become more intimate with the movement, that new members would understand that they were part of a given organization. This realization typically took place during a formal rite called "revelation."[12] "After you stay with a certain group for a while," the organizer said, "they pick some of the members, and they take them to more private sessions, with intellectual debates, books, readings. . . . They tell them, 'We are such and such a group; we have an organization and a history.' They tell them what the other groups are."

Because of this careful organization, the Islamic Awakening was very fragmented. The notion of an organization does not really describe what was going on within the Awakening: it was more a movement of movements than any kind of top-down, hierarchical structure. The Awakening lacked stable leaders, a known ideology, a defined program, or regular slogans.[13]

Despite this fragmentation, activists often distinguished between two main trends within the Islamic Awakening: the Muslim Brothers and the Salafis. Since the 1950s, the Muslim Brothers had formed several organizations in the country and had mobilized youth within the Ministries of Education and of Islamic affairs, where many of them worked. Salafis had a reputation for being stricter. They were often more interested in understanding the scriptures than in engaging in social and political action.

"Salafism is an intellectual methodology before being a movement," the organizer said, "whereas the Muslim Brothers are a movement before being a way of looking at the texts."

Saudi Salafi activists emerged in and around the Islamic universities that Al Sa'ud created beginning in the 1950s. The term "Salafism" came from the word "ancestors," *al-salaf*: those contemporaries of the Prophet who had a living memory of his actions and sayings. Their consensus was the basis of Sunni Islam and the bottom line to which they aspired. Salafis were characterized by their insistence on scholarship; Salafism, as already noted, was therefore an academic milieu before being a social movement.[14]

The Muslim Brotherhood also emerged in universities and schools starting in the 1950s, but its members thought of it as a social reform movement, not primarily as an academic enterprise. Prominent Egyptian, Syrian, and Iraqi Muslim Brothers had taken refuge in Saudi Arabia from the repression that struck their movements in the 1950s and 1960s. The Egyptian activist Manna' al-Qattan was one of the first Egyptian Muslim Brothers to arrive in Saudi Arabia in 1953; he started teaching at the capital's Sharia College and later became the dean of the new Islamic University of Riyadh. Foreign-born Muslim Brothers were closer to the circles of power. It was they who convinced King Sa'ud to create the World Islamic League in 1962. In the 1960s, they advised King Faysal on his Islamic policies, including the creation of the Islamic Development Bank in 1975 and, from the 1970s onward, the publication of religious curricula. Muhammad Mahmud al-Sawwaf, a prominent Iraqi Muslim Brother, became King Faysal's adviser and his informal ambassador to African nations.[15]

"Today, you cannot find anywhere a single copy of Sayyid Qutb's *In the Shade of the Quran*," the local organizer said. "At the time of Faysal, they were given away for free."

The Saudi Muslim Brotherhood was not a centralized institution but rather a loose network of movements with a strong regional base. There were at least three main Brotherhoods in the country: the Hijazi Muslim Brothers; the Najdi Muslim Brothers, based around Riyadh; and the Zubayr Muslim Brothers, based in the Eastern Province and in Riyadh and named after the Iraqi town of Zubayr, where many Najdi families had emigrated before the discovery of oil. These three movements were divided, in turn, into sub-movements and branches.

"The nature of the Muslim Brothers' thought does not require an organizational link between the different groups and the mother ship," the organizer said. "It is a thought that allows you to work even if you are all alone. It is a decentralized thought."

"Ideas do not play a role" in mobilization, he continued. Since Islamic movements had to remain secret, they did not attract recruits through political exposés or ideological programs, but through the activities they organized.

"Teachers come to class," he said, "and advertise for their activities and their group. I remember joining because, in my first year of high school, a teacher came who represented the Muslim Brothers of Zubayr and said, 'We have activities, theater, and we go out every other weekend to play soccer.' I worshipped soccer at the time, and I did not know where to play. I talked to other students and we joined. I went there for soccer."

Fun played an important role in the Islamic movement; it was by offering entertainment and sports that Muslim Brothers and Salafis attracted new members. Because of this lack of a defined ideology, the difference between Muslim Brother and Salafi networks had more to do in the end with personalities and historical circumstances than with ideas. The line between the two movements was often blurred.

"In the end, the logic of the Brothers, when they look at Islamic texts, is Salafi," the local organizer said. "From this perspective, the Brothers are Salafi. And they say of themselves, 'We are a Salafi group, we belong to the Salafi mission.'"

Salafis were often seen as being more indigenous to the Saudi context, even though they also were the product of complex international migrations; Muslim Brothers on the other hand were often seen as a foreign implant, even though by the 1980s they were fully indigenized. Salafis borrowed from the Muslim Brothers their notions of organization and the very idea of a political movement. And to recruit Saudi members, the first Muslim Brothers who set foot in the country showed allegiance to Salafi methods.[16]

The Muslim Brothers' interest in Salafism was not only tactical. After the repression of the 1990s, many Muslim Brothers found it safer to focus on the study of religion, keeping their distance from public preaching and social action. This also allowed them to expand further and become a truly hegemonic movement.

Islamic Awakening intellectuals had thought a lot about the difficulties of organizing in Saudi Arabia. Muhammad al-Duwish, born in 1963 in Central Arabia, taught at the Islamic University of Riyadh's college of education and supervised a network of Islamic awareness groups in the city's high schools and colleges.[17] I attended a lecture he gave on "Social Institutions and Youth." Right before the event, eight middle school and high school students demonstrated a few tae kwon do forms under the watchful eye of their instructor. I was seated near a Syrian-Saudi man and his teenage son, who was a member of his high school's Islamic awareness group. The atmosphere was relaxed: there were green coffee, red tea, and cookies on a table, and children were quietly playing in the back of the room.

"Why talk about social institutions?" al-Duwish asked his audience. "Because the Islamic world suffers from an excess of individualism. Institutions do not work well. At the state level, for instance, power is personalized. There is no continuity in government. . . . Even the institutions of preaching are limited, and when they succeed, this success is due to individuals. Our society is governed by individualism. Even in families, it is an individual, the father, who governs all the other individuals."

Al Sa'ud had fought communal mechanisms and embraced a divide-and-rule strategy. Authoritarianism, to al-Duwish, was an extreme form of individualism.

"We lack a culture of collective action," he said, "even though many Islamic sayings stress the importance of the community. To be religiously valid, for instance, prayer has to be collective; the same goes for fasting. Legislation is also a group endeavor that has to be carried out by the community of believers, even when the ruler is unjust or ignorant. The Prophet compared Muslims to a unified body: people often read this saying superficially and say that, if a problem arises, the Prophet simply asked us to stick together. This is a superficial understanding: sacred texts are deeper than that."

Contrary to what state clerics said, citizens did not have to obey their rulers, especially if these were unjust or oppressive. Against the consensus of establishment clerics, al-Duwish also considered legislation to be a collective endeavor.

"Collective action is the foundation of the community of believers," he went on. "It is also the type of action that works best when applied to life, from the economy to preaching. Youth, like laws, are everybody's business. They bring an energy that we often mistake for a problem, but which is in reality a wonderful opportunity for the whole society. The young are ready for everything, they are energetic, malleable; let us not mistake their energy for a catastrophe, because we can really turn it into a chance."

For al-Duwish, youth and the law would come to shape the future of society and needed to be managed collectively. Youth could be heaven and hell, resource and curse, energy and catastrophe. It was not a self-evident idea that youth was a specific period in the life of men and women, between childhood and adulthood, between the age of dependence and immaturity and the age of independence and maturity. That childhood and adulthood should be separate ages was not, either.[18] And the notion that the law should be a collective matter was totally foreign to the Saudi context.

Al-Duwish was daring, but his audience was sparse and his barely veiled criticism of the personalization of power was met with silence. In front of him, middle-aged family men were attentively following his reasoning, nodding here and there. Al-Duwish presented his expertise as apolitical, as the informed opinion of an educator who held back from meddling in politics and was weary of generalizations. The day before, during another lecture, he had said that his "political interests" were "limited by [his] job as an educator." In this lecture, too, political comments were coated in specialized, technical speech about education and management. These neutral topics allowed him to talk about politics, often in a trenchant tone, without shocking his audience.

It was often by appearing as detached and apolitical as possible that Islamic Awakening activists were able to talk about politics. Muhammad Nasir al-Din al-'Albani, a Syrian cleric who had had an international career, between Syria, Saudi Arabia, and Jordan, used to put it this way: "The best politics is to leave politics behind."[19] This paradox exemplified the complex ways Islamic activists engaged with a locked-up political sphere. In the face of state repression, they had to cultivate indifference and apathy to reach another level of political consciousness. This was not calculated deception; it was the cultivation of an ethical (and political) attitude of detachment from the state and the political sphere. Political indifference (*la mubala*) was the paradoxical condition for autonomous politics.

Saudi Islamic activists started seeing youth as a resource in the 1960s, at a time when the progress of higher education had made references to the social sciences, in particular Egyptian and European sociology, more generally accessible. Islamic activists saw youth as teenage vitality and social resource. This idea had emerged during the late industrial revolution as a way to integrate young adults into the labor and consumer markets and into the budding European and Middle Eastern party systems and to enroll them in various wars.[20] The generalization of waged labor in an era of high oil prices and public sector growth had also given birth to the idea of leisure, empty time that needed to be filled, occupied, exploited. Islamic Awakening activists wanted to seduce youth, to harvest their energy to reform society.

The Saudi state elites, meanwhile, were wary of the youth. They wished to enroll them in the economy and to keep them away from protest politics. But this official attention had the effect of politicizing youth: it transformed an age group into a site of political action. The Saudi state created the General Presidency for Youth Patronage[21] in 1974, a year after the oil boom sent the Saudi economy into an upward spiral. The Presidency, which was renamed the General Sports Authority in 2016, organized collective sports and managed soccer clubs and public swimming pools. Since the 1979 occupation of Mecca's Great Mosque, the Saudi state has been eager to control its youth and to provide them with carefully regimented leisure, under the benevolent patronage of the royal family. The Saudi elites did not hesitate to send the most energetic youth to Afghanistan. It is perhaps no coincidence that the notion of youth as both a resource and a curse took flight during a time of war, as Saudi Arabia was investing money and young men in the Afghan resistance against the Soviet Union.[22] Crushing collective action and entertaining the youth were crucial to the survival of Al Saʿud. Boredom and the great passions it could give rise to were not to be tolerated.

Chapter 4   # GET IN YOUR CAR AND DRIVE

SAʿD AL-FAQIH TOLD THE *NEW YORK TIMES* THAT, BEFORE THE October 14, 2003 demonstration, he "thought it was too early to call Saudis into the streets, that people needed their confidence built up to face the regime. . . . Since our culture is not one of demonstrations and vigils or opposing the government in a public manner, I never imagined they would appear in such numbers."

Police crackdowns, however, were why people came out en masse, and for that reason, the police presence could not deter them from marching.

"For most of them, it was their first collective experience," al-Faqih continued. "They had come only with Qurans in their hands and mats to kneel on, and they found themselves being treated very harshly. They are very angry about that. . . . Before October 14, even people who agreed with us thought we were talking about things that were impossible in Saudi Arabia, and they called me impractical and unrealistic. But now I am confident to say that the downfall of the regime is an inevitable result of what has started."[1]

For Nawwaf, this was empty talk, and al-Faqih had "started from the end: a full-fledged demonstration." The exiled activist had forgotten that, "in terms of preparation, we were all virgins."

"The thing is," Nawwaf said, "you can talk all you want about demonstrations, but nobody knows what they are. In a demonstration, you need a group;

you need leaders to show the way; and somebody needs to give a speech, so the security forces understand what is going on. Because cops are Bedouins, they do not understand what the protesters want. 'There are people fighting the government. They want to overthrow the government.' That is all they understand. Well, no: protesters have claims; listen to what they are talking about."

Nawwaf came from a sedentary background; he often expressed prejudice against Saudis with a nomadic ancestry. He thought the Bedouins who manned the security forces were both loyalist and unrefined and needed to be schooled by protesters.

"You know, that cop I met when I worked as a security guard?" Nawwaf said. "He told me he did not look down on the protesters. He was on their side. He told me, 'Their message was strong; their message was powerful. These are things that can turn your head, they were convincing.' So you need a plan with clear steps: one, two, three, four. . . . It would have been better to start at the beginning and tell them, 'Guys, on that day, a month from now, get in your car and drive toward this avenue, at 9 pm.' That is it. 'Do not stop or congregate. Just drive there, that is all.' In order to gradually get used to activism. It is only then that you organize gatherings. Little by little."

"Get in your car and drive": in a city of highways, driving is one way to escape police repression. Joyriders knew it: night after night, they organized high-octane automobile shows; they swerved cars, creating complex choreographies, to the applause of large crowds of followers; they regularly dodged the police, so much so that the police sometimes sought to learn from them to improve their own driving techniques.[2] Joyriding, this car revolt, had been around since the 1970s, and continued unabated well into the 2010s. Police repression could be ducked, provided that one invested in speed and collective tactics.

The next demonstration al-Faqih organized was a clear failure. "They wanted to continue the protests," Nawwaf said. "And there was the December 15, 2004 march, a few months ago: they called us to march and I came out, but marching was impossible. The security forces were well prepared."

For this demonstration, nicknamed "the big drift"[3] and organized in Riyadh, Jeddah, and a few other cities, the mobilization was uncertain. In Jeddah, the police shot at the crowd and killed at least one protester. In Tabuk and Ha'il, in the northwest of the kingdom, processions marched through town without major incident. In Riyadh, the riot police locked down the city in advance.

"People came from various regions," Nawwaf said. "The day before the December march, all the cheap hotels were full. The police set up checkpoints on the highways. If they saw a group of men in a car, they would stop them from getting to Riyadh. A guy alone in his car was fine. But a bunch of guys would get arrested. And even if they passed the checkpoint, they could not get where they wanted to go. So nothing happened in the end, because the security forces were well prepared.

"I tried to join the movement. . . . The beginning of the demonstration was set for after the midday prayer, at 1 pm. I drove off, but the avenues were totally empty. There were very few cars, and the situation looked normal. But I followed the movement on the radio. There was a demonstration in Jeddah, some action. The fact that the security forces were prepared tells you that the government does not trust the people at all. . . . We always hear that the government is fostering people's allegiance. . . . How many newspapers do they own? How many TV channels? They spend so much on communication, and you, with only one march, you manage to create a demonstration of cops. They do not trust the people, do they?"

The fact that he had publicized his demonstration projects meant that Sa'd al-Faqih was sending his troops into a predictable defeat. Joyriders were usually more astute and avoided the Internet: they generally organized through text messages and phone calls. Unlike al-Faqih, they stayed away from public platforms and used surprise as a weapon. Political activists could definitely have learned from joyriding: on this and other things, they were lacking in strategic acumen.

So that I might better understand the relationship between activism and repression, Nawwaf recommended that I meet with Sheikh 'Abd al-Ilah, who had been central to the 1990s protest movement. In 1991, Sheikh 'Abd al-Ilah was a recent college graduate. During the mobilization against Saudi participation in the Gulf War, he noted that a majority of activists refused to protest if they did not get a green light from state clerics. But this was something that could not happen, because state clerics, by definition, supported the existing order and, like Sheikh Salih al-Luhaydan, called any form of protest "deviant."

Sheikh 'Abd al-Ilah was eager to convince his fellow activists. He spent months researching what he called the jurisprudence of demonstrations:[4] what jurists had said about protest action. He found only five occurrences of demonstrations in the corpus. He had come to the conclusion that, because state clerics had eradicated the very idea of peaceful protest, his fellow activists were torn between submission to the state and violent revolt: they had no notion of what a pacific opposition could look like, but they improvised and protested until 1993, when the state eventually cracked down. Sheikh 'Abd al-Ilah himself was arrested and spent five years in a prison cell.

Nawwaf could name dozens of activists who had either been killed or landed in prison. During my field research, I came to realize that almost everybody I knew had at least one friend or relative who was jailed or had been disappeared for political reasons. Many jailed activists were tortured. Some were compelled to repent publicly. A few received sentence reductions if they agreed to collaborate with the security services. The interior minister himself had summoned senior activists to negotiate their liberation in exchange for their allegiance. Some joined the circles of power, while others refused and stayed in prison much longer.

"I am always amazed at those who repent," Nawwaf said. "I find it bizarre. I think tenacity is part of victory. Victory does not mean reaching a particular goal. Only a minority will hold fast and will stick to their principles. For instance, Muhsin al-'Awaji had a very strong stance; why did he turn his coat?"

Muhsin al-'Awaji, who was born in 1961, was an agricultural science graduate who became, along with Sa'd al-Faqih and Sheikh Salman al-'Ouda, a leader of the 1991–1994 mobilization against the monarchy. Arrested in 1994, he was tortured in prison and freed in the late 1990s. He was arrested and let go a few times in the 2000s and 2010s.

"Some people have no patience," Nawwaf said. "Not like Sheikh Sa'id bin Zu'ayr, who perhaps committed a few mistakes, but pleased people through his tenacity."

Born in 1950, Sa'id bin Zu'ayr was a university professor who also signed the 1991–1992 petitions to the king. Arrested in 1994, he was freed in 2003, then thrown into prison several times more. Activists considered him one of the oldest political prisoners in the country. In the early 1990s, Talal Asad compared one of bin Zu'ayr's taped lectures, "Religion Is Integrity,"[5] to Immanuel Kant's writings on the public usage of reason. Kant viewed political criticism as a *right* patiently acquired by a few philosophers, against states that had become powerful thanks to absolutism and centralization. This right to criticize did not include a right to disobey: as Jeremy Bentham put it, a good citizen had "to obey punctually; to censure freely."[6] The liberal political tradition was based in part on a refusal of civil disobedience.

Saʿid bin Zuʿayr, by contrast, saw political criticism as a *duty*—and not only a right—incumbent on *all* believers who witness mistakes, oppression, or injustices. He and other Islamic Awakening activists revived the tradition of gently advising rulers for their own good, of offering moral and political advice.[7] Depending on the political situation, this advice could range from supplication through public criticism to direct action, as shown by a famous saying of the Prophet: "Whosoever of you sees an evil action, let him change it with his hand; and if he is unable to do so, then with his tongue; and if he is not able to do so, then with his heart—and that is the weakest expression of faith."[8]

"After nine years in the shadows, bin Zuʿayr refused to sign any repentance," Nawwaf said. "He swore and said, 'I will not lay a drop of ink on your paperwork.' They had just asked him to sign. 'I was jailed without a reason, this is an insult to human dignity.' His parents even met with the interior minister, Prince Nayef. 'Just tell us why he was jailed,' they asked him. 'Why nine years? Tell us why.' And the prince responded, 'If he signs, he gets out.'"

"What a mark of intransigence," I said.

"Yes. You will find many marks of intransigence and toughness today."

Nawwaf stood silent for a short while, then looked at me with anger.

"Did you think he would live a peaceful life? You, before you go to sleep, the security services inspect your bed before you lie in it. Are you happy like this? Before you sit on a chair, you fear there might be something under it. What intransigence? What toughness are you talking about?"

Nawwaf now seemed beside himself.

"This is not cool. You've heard of ʿOmar bin Khattab? He slept under a tree...."

ʿOmar bin Khattab, the second caliph of Islam, had such trust in the justice of his estate that he was known to nap under a tree without a single guard in sight.

"Do you know anybody who would do that?" Nawwaf asked. "Checkpoints and arrests do not create any security."

He pointed to a penholder on my desk.

"That penholder, there, because of checkpoints, can become a bomb."

State violence shaped the public sphere and conditioned activism in ways that I was only starting to understand. Nawwaf had protested outside an international conference on human rights held by the interior minister, who ran the very institution that disappeared activists and imprisoned dissidents. Saudi repression was a liberal enterprise that painted its enemies with a wide brush and claimed they were "radicals,"[9] "extremists,"[10] enemies of reason and of moderation.

But to many of my interlocutors, including Nawwaf, repression and liberalism were not two opposites but one and the same thing. It was for liberal reasons that the Saudi state cracked down on all manner of political activity: Al Sa'ud and its allies systematically labeled activists as extremists or terrorists. It was for liberal reasons that the United States and its allies had invaded Afghanistan and Iraq, for liberal reasons that the European Union and the United States were aiding some of the most repressive regimes on earth. Liberal repression and repressive liberalism were Saudi activists' daily reality, which triggered both their rage and their apathy.

Repression was not only a police operation but also an intellectual project. Beyond the activist's body, the Saudi state targeted the hearts and minds of the general population. 'Adel was an Islamic activist I befriended early in my fieldwork. Younger than Nawwaf, he was a college student and belonged to two different Islamic groups: one, more radical, that he had joined while in high school and the other, more political, that he found at the university. But he had a complex relationship with the Islamic Awakening.

"I was one of its victims," he joked when I interviewed him. "But it was really very helpful, really very, very helpful. And I guess that, had I not gone with them, I wouldn't have become the 'Adel you know today, even if I disagree with many of their ideas. . . . I would have become very dull; I would be up for anything and nothing. . . . If I had not gone with them, I would not have any goal."

The Islamic movements awakened him to himself and gave him the practical and intellectual means to act in his everyday life. But he still liked to describe himself as an observer, even though, like Nawwaf, he had joined Sa'd al-Faqih's failed December 2004 demonstration. When he saw the overwhelming police presence that day, he recoiled in fear. He summed up the situation later by saying, "Glory to God, Sa'd al-Faqih succeeded in organizing a cops' demonstration."

To 'Adel, police repression was not sui generis, but it originated in an intellectual repression of sorts, which to him was the work of secularists, a visible lobby in Saudi politics in the mid-2000s.

"They are old," 'Adel said of them. "Poor guys, they might still have young bodies, but they have old minds. This is what happened to a lot of people among us, especially the elderly. As for the young . . . there is an awakening of the youth. There is new awareness. But for the elderly, there is no hope they might be convinced by new ideas. . . . Most fathers, when their sons talk to them—and these are sons who studied, who understand, whereas their fathers, in most cases, have not studied beyond primary school and are peasants—when their sons come to them and say, 'Dad, I studied agronomy, and you ought to do this and that; I know this is none of my business, but you would be better off doing it this way,' most fathers will respond, 'What do you know? Yesterday we were bottle-feeding you, and today you want to teach us life?' "

In 'Adel's mind, secularists were an older generation, those who held on to positions of power and looked up to the state to protect them from Islamic activists, who were younger in mind and spirit.

"In high school my Islamic group held a literary competition. You had to write a poem or a short story, and I won the first prize for short stories. . . . My short story was about the newspaper Al-Riyad. We considered all newspapers to be secularist, and we had declared a war on that one in particular. My short story was called, 'The Wolf's Teeth. . . .' It is the story of a man who goes to work in the morning, a large grin across his face. He gets in his car and drives to the newspaper headquarters, where he works from morning to night. Two hours before the end of the workday, somebody phones him and wants to publish an opinion piece; he agrees. Then somebody else comes to his office and wants to publish another opinion piece, a very different one, which I thought was on the right side. But the journalist refuses to publish it. The editor in chief then comes in, and what is amazing is that he and the journalist have exactly the same smile, an immovable rictus, the same, from morning to night. The editor in chief tells him that the meeting has begun, and they all convene in a meeting room, where everybody has the same large grin. After they all sit down, the editor in chief removes his mask, and they all do the same. That is when you see their wolf's teeth."

'Adel laughed. He found his old high school self slightly embarrassing, at least compared to the 'Adel he had become after going to college. He had become a religious activist by opposing secularists. His Islamic group leader in high school tried to steer him away from unilateral thinking, but 'Adel was too enraged at the power of secularism to take heed of the advice.

"Most tapes I listened to were Islamic," he said. "By Sheikh Muhammad al-Munajjid, for instance, or Salman al-'Ouda, Nasir al-'Omar. . . . Of course, I listened to their tapes when they were in prison . . . because what is forbidden is desirable. They said these had been banned, so I thought they would be special, and I wanted to know why they were banned. These tapes were useful; they are full of good things. Especially Salman al-'Ouda's tapes, for instance 'The King of Clerics, al-'Izz bin 'Abd al-Salam,'[11] which was a revolutionary speech of the first order."

Al-'Izz bin 'Abd al-Salam was a thirteenth-century cleric who had publicly condemned injustice and criticized the Mameluke rulers of Syria and Egypt. "They say he was a seller of kings, and he actually sold princes, he sold them in the market, he auctioned them," 'Adel said.

The Mamelukes were slave soldiers who had become members of a ruling caste. When he was chief judge in Egypt, al-'Izz bin 'Abd al-Salam refused to swear allegiance to the new sultan, Baybars, who was not only a slave but also the slave of a former slave. Al-'Izz bin 'Abd al-Salam thought he could give these aristocrats a taste of their own medicine and treat them like the slaves they still (legally) were.[12] Al-'Izz bin 'Abd al-Salam published a legal opinion saying the Mameluke princes had to be removed from public office and should be auctioned off in the marketplace.[13] Sheikh Salman al-'Ouda used the story of the "seller of kings" as a model of political virtue and public criticism after the 1990 Gulf War. It did not seem to matter that Saudi princes were not slaves, but actually owned the country that was named after them.

"The Mamelukes thought Islam could be their slave," 'Adel said, "but they ended up selling themselves. Thanks to his religious authority, al-'Izz bin 'Abd al-Salam was able to rule over politics."

Secularists and princes were the new Mamelukes that Islamic activists had the mission to dethrone. "Islamic" in this case meant not only adhering to a set of rules and dogmas but also being able to speak truth to power and act in the face of political danger. Islamic action was a way for activists to affirm their own agency within a political and social context that they thought needed an intervention.

A police operation and an intellectual project, repression was also a spatial setting and the outcome of decades of expertise, urban planning, and infrastructural investments. As Nawwaf and 'Adel understood when they came out to demonstrate, the space of Saudi cities, crisscrossed with oversized highways and burdened with long, low-density residential blocks and wide, sun-drenched avenues, was not conducive to public gatherings. Riyadh is not a city of squares, streets, or street corners. It is a city of walls and highways,[14] of palisades and overpasses, gated communities, interchanges, fortified enclaves,[15] and tunnels. In its older neighborhoods, streets, street corners, and squares died long ago because of car traffic and the proliferation of such indoor spaces as shopping malls and office buildings. Riyadh is a realization of Le Corbusier's somber prophecy of the "Death of the Street."[16]

The Islamic Awakening relied on the transportation infrastructure to shake up the dead public spaces of Riyadh. The organization of the Islamic movements was evidence of the centrality of space in the minds of activists. In Egypt, the smallest unit in the Muslim Brotherhood was the family,[17] which was supposed to be the ferment of the future society that the Brothers were creating. In Saudi Arabia, there were also families in the Muslim Brotherhood: they were groups of ten to twenty people who regularly met under the guidance of a supervisor.[18] But the smallest unit of any Islamic group was the car.[19]

Each Islamic family, in a very suburban manner, was divided into a number of cars. Each car was composed of four activists and one supervisor-driver, generally older and slightly higher up in the organization. Cities were spread out and cars were therefore crucial to activist groups. Quran memorization circles were few and far between, and older students with cars—often college students—were needed to ferry the rank and file, who were generally high school students. As for the Islamic groups in schools, they tapped into a pool of students who were already on site, but they still needed cars for weekend activities and other trips. The car war the basic, moving cell of the Islamic Awakening.

For Islamic activists, cars were not mere vehicles, and mobility was much more complex than a simple translation in space. "A car"—the metonym for "a car group"—stuck together. Its occupants held "car activities" to fill their commute time: they listened to sermons, read texts, or organized small competitions. "A car" went out to dinner or to the desert *as a car*: four activists and their supervisor-driver. Cars could be accused of individualizing mobility and society, of separating people into distinct, quasi-private spheres, hermetic extensions of their bodies; but activists turned these atomizing tools into bonding devices.

"We have that saying, that car activities are the most important activities," a twenty-year-old Muslim Brother told me. "They are the most important because a Quran memorization circle is a vast, composite thing, with many moving pieces: individuals, families, cars. . . . When you count everybody, you may find yourself among forty people. So when you sit in a circle for a lecture, for instance, the amount of benefit will not be that great. It is not like car meetings, where four people debate and invite each other to religion. That is how you maximize profit. . . . The subdivision of Islamic groups into families and cars is very useful from an educational perspective."

Just as Islamic Awakening leaders often talked of youth as a resource or an energy to harness, so their flock talked of the Awakening as a good investment of their time. 'Adel had acquired self-respect and goals in the Islamic movement; this young Muslim Brother thought car activities were the most beneficial because of the intimate connection among their members. Cars were also instrumental to internal promotion within the Islamic groups. Ordinary members usually ascended to their first supervising position when they went to college and bought a car: they could then become "university students" in charge of a car, the first step toward becoming group supervisors. The hierarchy of the Islamic movement was predicated upon the ability to drive through suburbia and to bring together individuals who lived scattered across vast expanses of land.

It is perhaps not a coincidence that the Islamic Awakening emerged in the 1960s and 1970s, during the very time when Saudi cities spread out in all directions and turned into massive, car-based suburbs. To understand this transformation and the functioning of Saudi spatial politics, we need to go back to the founding of the state and to examine the complex relationships between activism, repression, and urban planning.

PART II
SAUDI SUBURBIA

■ ■ ■ ■ ■

Chapter 5   **ARAMCO'S LEVITTOWN**

A FEW WEEKS AFTER WE FIRST MET IN SEPTEMBER, 2001, ʿADEL picked me up and drove me to a rest house in the northern suburbs of Riyadh, where his friends from the Islamic group were spending the evening. We passed empty freeways and deserted roundabouts. ʿAdel occasionally used the handbrake and steering wheel to make his car swerve and produce a loud screeching noise. Looking at me out of the corner of his eyes, he seemed to enormously enjoy my reactions. He was not only a mosque enthusiast, but also a bit of a joyrider.

We arrived at the rest house. ʿAdel's friends were seated at the edge of a soccer field, outside a tent-like structure. Rest houses[1] were walled-in gardens built on the outskirts of the city. They often featured a sitting room, a fireplace, and a sports field and ranged from small, scraggy pens to massive, country-club-like structures with several sports fields, dining rooms, and a swimming pool. Riyadh residents bought or rented them to spend evenings and weekends away from the strictures of family life. There they engaged in communal hobbies, from cinema to soccer and political activism.

"We talked about September 11th," ʿAdel remembered when I interviewed him a few years later. "It was right after the events, and the Saudi people could not hide their joy ... Imagine you have a very obnoxious neighbor ... a neighbor who constantly insults you and treats you in all kinds of poor ways."

'Adel loved allegories.

"Now imagine that people from your family, folks you have not seen or heard from in a while, come and beat him up so badly that they do not leave one single vein connected to another in his body. When this happens, even though you know they have done something terribly wrong, it is still natural that the situation, somehow, makes you weirdly happy: someone has just avenged you. Well, this was Saudi society at that time: people were rejoicing over September 11th."

As I sat in the rest house on that evening of October, 2001, a friend of 'Adel's asked me what I thought of Osama bin Laden and al-Qaʿeda. I mumbled a few confused sentences. Somebody else asked me to explain the Holy Trinity. My uninspired response was not very convincing. A tall guy with an inviting face asked if I wished to convert to Islam. I tried to dodge the question. Was it the theological bent of the conversation? The uncanny feeling of the rest house, with its row of lavatories near a soccer field? It all felt like the Sunday school in my parents' parish, where I had spent most of my free time as a child watching cartoons, reading comic books, playing soccer, and experiencing my first amorous commotions. Even the salacious jokes—"during Ramadan, we can fuck only after sunset"—sounded familiar.

'Adel was born in the southern suburb of Suwaydi. *Suwaydi* means "bitter soil" and was a reference to the infertile grounds on which the neighborhood grew in the late 1970s. Its soil was so rocky that people joked you did not need to dig foundations to build a home. Located on the right bank of the Wadi Hanifa, across the riverbed from the center of Riyadh, Suwaydi attracted middle-class families who had left their cramped quarters downtown. With its superblocks, its straight streets, its villas enclosed within high walls, and its legendary soccer clubs—al-Hilal and al-Nasr—Suwaydi was a model suburb, dedicated to residence and leisure. In the 1980s, its many schools and mosques became one of the strongholds of the Islamic movement. Some residents nicknamed it "the Fallujah of Riyadh," or "the Sunni triangle."[2]

'Adel introduced me to the peculiar ecology of greater Riyadh, with its ubiquitous walls and fences, its large highways, its patchy developments, its rest houses, and its trash tumbling around. Most people in Riyadh lived in neighborhoods that, like Suwaydi, had been planned and developed in the previous forty years, since the 1973 oil boom had revolutionized the economy.[3] People who had grown up in the city's older areas still remembered their old neighborhoods and some-times went there on pilgrimages. One of my friends, who was born in old Riyadh, would often take me there with him. We would drive around al-Margab, Harat al-ʿAbid, or Shumaysi, stopping for cheap, plentiful Yemeni food and touring the ruins of a lost existence: narrow, shadowed lanes; mud-brick and cement houses; gardens tucked away behind small mosques.

Many Saudi families had deserted downtown in the 1970s and 1980s. They had fled congestion, traffic, labor migrants, and racialized minorities, in par-ticular Afro-Saudi descendants of the slaves who had been freed in 1962. The middle classes headed toward the newly developed areas of the north, the east, and the south. The west was reserved for the royal palaces and the diplomatic quarter, a gated neighborhood designed in 1982: the centers of power had been suburbanized, too. Some owners had converted their homes downtown into boarding houses for migrant workers, cramming foreign bodies into small, overheated rooms and making an extra dime on the backs of underpaid labor-ers. In the old Riyadh, several families had often lived under a single roof and shared the semi-public space of the street, where children played and women visited each other. In the new Riyadh, most families now lived in separate houses. Fathers discouraged their children from roaming the streets. Women could not drive and lived somewhat reclusive lives hidden behind high walls, or had to bother a male relative to take them where they wanted to go. Female mobility was a constant source of worry.[4]

The old Riyadh, with its once elegant avenues, stately courtyard houses, and palm groves along the Wadi Hanifa, had been the center of the country. It was now marginal to the life and imagination of its inhabitants. The suburbs of yore, these massive areas developed after 1973, had become the city itself, and the notion of city center was now obsolete.

Suburban growth had atomized society, fragmented families, and scattered networks of solidarity. It had created monotonous residential areas dotted with gas stations and shopping malls. Parks were few and far between; there were no movie theaters; leisure spaces were exclusive and expensive. Highways were everywhere, and cars ruled. In the mid-2000s, Riyadh was a city of more than five million inhabitants without a public transit system (a bus and metro network was planned to open in 2020). In 2000, Riyadh residents used cars for 98% of their trips across the city. There were approximately five million daily trips. Of these, 93% of them were taken by private car, 5% by taxi, and only 2% by collective transit, mostly privately owned minibuses.[5]

When the Greek architect Constantinos Doxiadis planned Riyadh in the late 1960s, he envisioned a city where, by 2000, anyone could drive anywhere within twenty minutes.[6] But in the 2000s, Riyadh drivers regularly spent hours stuck in traffic. Instead of making Saudis free, individual cars had killed mobility. The Doxiadis plan promoted car mobility, but produced unintended consequences. How did Saudi cities come to embody the transition from public spaces to private cars, which is characteristic of the city planning of the past century?[7] How did Riyadh become the capital of the twentieth century, with its highway system and its far-flung suburbs? How did cars become so central to Saudi society and politics that even Islamic activists mobilized around them?

In 1933, a year after the creation of the Kingdom of Saudi Arabia, King 'Abd al-'Aziz granted an oil concession, covering more than half the Saudi territory, to a subsidiary of Standard Oil of California. Harry St. John 'Abd Allah Philby midwifed the agreement. Philby was a former British political agent in Riyadh who had converted to Islam and become 'Abd al-'Aziz's advisor and Ford Motors' agent in Arabia. Renamed the Arabian-American Oil Company (Aramco) in 1944, the U.S. corporation was for several decades far wealthier than the Saudi state and employed many more people.

Cars were key to Western imperialism in general and to colonial power in Arabia in particular.[8] The revolt of the Ikhwan militia, a nomadic army that 'Abd al-'Aziz enrolled in the 1910s to conquer the peninsula, was crushed in 1929 thanks to British armored cars and warplanes. No wonder the Ikhwan saw "automobiles as the invention of the godless, if not of the devil" and thought "planes flew contrary to Allah's will."[9] Cars would ultimately become emblematic of the Saudi state, with "gold Cadillacs" in particular standing for Al Sa'ud's lavish spending in the 1950s. But it is the growth of car imports and services in the 1970s that turned the 'Ali Rezas, the Juffalis, the Jumaihs, and other merchant families into an oligarchy.[10] The informal U.S. empire triumphed not through titles, durbars, or military marches but thanks to car sales, maintenance contracts, and spare parts monopolies.

Aramco established itself in the hills of Jebel Dhahran, at a distance from the old urban cores of al-Qatif and al-Hofuf. King 'Abd al-'Aziz also left his crowded Riyadh quarters in 1938, the year the U.S. oil company first struck oil in the country. He built his Murabba' palace one mile north of the city wall and connected it to Riyadh by a concrete road. Crown Prince Sa'ud and Prince Faysal also built palaces in al-Futa and al-Badi'a, north and west of the walled city. Cars, which became the only way to get around in Riyadh,[11] were central to the exercise of state power. The king was a motorist; he rode through town, from the old castle downtown to his new palace on the outskirts. State bureaucracy began as a car commute.

Aramco started building a California-style suburb for its senior staff in Dhahran in the 1940s. Senior employees were almost exclusively U.S. citizens, and their newly built quarters sat at the top of Jebel Dhahran, a system of hills a few miles away from the coast of the Gulf. The Senior Camp, nicknamed "American Camp," exhibited single-family houses, tree-lined streets, cul-de-sacs, conveniences stores, swimming pools, and movie theaters. The contrast between this manicured suburbia and the squalid conditions of the General Camp downhill was stark. The General Camp, or "Saudi Camp," was made of palm huts, tents, and brick barracks; it lacked running water, sewers, and electricity. It was unfenced and separated from the American Camp by the Intermediate Camp, built for technical and clerical employees, mostly from Palestine, India, and Italy.[12] Saudi workers were kept out of the white man's paradise by a set of Jim Crow rules.[13] There were separate restaurants for U.S. and Saudi employees and separate cinemas (the Arab cinema was open-air, without air conditioning). Saudis were given an employee I.D. number that, according to a former Aramco worker now in his eighties, "controlled your whole life," and were banned from swimming pools. They did not have the right to go to the beach, either.[14]

Another Saudi retiree told me that the company "taught us everything without ever humiliating us." He was also quick to remember what it meant to cross the color line in the 1960s. Once he tried to drink from a fountain reserved for Euro-Americans, the *fonten hag al-khawajat*.

"This water is for the Sahibs, go drink outside," a U.S. employee told him.

A basin outside was reserved for Saudi workers, which U.S. Americans demeaned by mobilizing repertoires that harked back to both U.S. racial segregation and British imperial habits. The retired worker told me later, "Americans obviously came to rob our country of its riches, and never wanted to spend them on Saudis."[15] If this was the opinion of a pro-U.S., mid-level employee, what must anti-U.S., unskilled workers have thought?

"We walked to Dhahran in search of a job," an eighty-something-year-old from al-Qatif told me in the late 2000s. He had joined the company right after World War II. "We were dirt-poor. Landowners exploited us, and we tried to escape them by joining Aramco . . . We were given a number on a metal plate. Americans were interested in the bodies of the applicants. They lined us up like cattle on a large plaza, under the sun, under the Dhahran hills. They looked at our teeth and at our eyes. Then they brought us to Dhahran on a flatbed truck for medical exams."

Laborers were housed in the General "Saudi" Camp, in barastis (palm-frond huts) that were later replaced by equally miserable prefab houses. But becoming a coolie, as Saudi workers were called, was still considered desirable.

"Coolies had the best social standing in the region," said another ex-Aramco worker, a slim man in his late seventies. He explained that Aramco had destroyed feudalism and the power of landowners.

"Not intentionally," he said, "for capitalists do not care. But the result is the same: feudalism has disappeared." Aramco policies were only slightly better. "The elders were treated like cattle until 1967," he added. "It is the strikes that brought changes in food, housing, and wages."[16]

In 1945, thousands of Saudi oil workers went on strike, followed by the Italians, who were " 'fed up' with being treated 'just like the Arabs.' "[17] In 1953, Saudi intermediate employees petitioned the company and demanded an end to racial segregation. They also asked for better housing, safer working conditions, and higher wages. The company refused to negotiate and had the workers' representatives arrested. Oil workers went on strike, and the state and Aramco sent in the army.

The Saudi state ordered weapons and armored cars from the United States. According to U.S. diplomatic cables, these were "needed urgently" to quell "riots and civil disturbances in Dammam area, which includes major Aramco installations."[18] In 1955 and 1956, workers organized a bus boycott, stoned cars, attacked fences, and petitioned the king again, this time to demand an end to military cooperation with the United States. Mosques became nodes of mobilization and workers targeted cars and buses as symbols of segregation.[19]

In 1947, the governor of the Eastern Province asked Aramco to draw up plans for Khobar and Dammam. These twin cities, located between the oil wells and the company's landing pier on the Gulf, had grown quickly. Shantytowns around Dhahran were demolished and their inhabitants rehoused. Aramco planned the two cities along a gridiron pattern and, in doing so, turned away from local architecture and urban patterns that were more appropriate to the harsh climate. The importation of U.S. urban solutions revealed Aramco's contempt for Saudi culture.[20]

In Riyadh, too, labor unrest accelerated urban sprawl. Two thousand workers demonstrated in 1942 on a construction site near the Shamsiya Palace, asking for shorter work hours. Strike leaders were beaten and imprisoned.[21] The municipality created New Manfuha in the late 1940s along a gridiron street pattern similar to the one Aramco had implemented in Dammam and Khobar.[22] New Manfuha was subdivided into tiny lots of about seven hundred square feet each, along perpendicular streets that were easy to police.[23]

In the Eastern Province, Aramco created the Home Ownership Program for its Saudi employees in 1951, which further removed the Saudi and Arab workforce from the immediate proximity of Dhahran. Employees received free lots in the newly planned, gridded developments and could get free construction loans, provided they built recognizably suburban villas, one story high, set back from the street. The company pulled the rug from under the unionists' feet and disciplined the workers by way of loans and red tape. Dammam and Khobar's "workers' towns" were an outcome of this policy, as well as the new towns of Rahima, near the oil port and refinery of Ra's Tanura (Cape Brazier), and Abqaiq, about fifty miles inland.[24] Suburbanization did not cater to workers, but it prevented conflicts to "speed the flow of oil to an industrial civilization."[25]

Aramco operated at a time when U.S. elites viewed home ownership, cheap loans, and mass consumerism as a powerful alternative to communism. It was suburbanites living in northern Virginia and commuting to the suburban campuses of the CIA and the Pentagon who conducted U.S. foreign interventions, engineered coups, overthrew regimes, and fostered the creation of large, consumerist, individualist economies. French and British colonizers had built cities; the U.S. empire would be suburban.[26]

Aramco's Home Ownership Program dulled the once diverse scenery of the Eastern Province, with its ancient walled towns, vast palm groves, and endless beaches, into a flat landscape of wide roads and single-family villas. "Aramco's Levittown" was met with uneven enthusiasm. Rahima, planned in 1953, remained half empty. Most refinery workers hailed from close-knit communities nearby and preferred not to move into single-family villas placed under the inquisitive gaze of the company.[27]

Suburbanization leaped forward after state agencies and ministries moved from Jeddah to Riyadh in 1953. The Finance Ministry planned the suburb of Malaz, or New Riyadh,[28] to house civil servants and their families.[29] No doubt fully equipped kitchens and gleaming bathrooms helped lure civil servants from multicultural Jeddah to Riyadh, a city they considered provincial and hostile. Planned in 1957 on the model of Aramco's workers' towns, New Riyadh featured 754 single-family villas sold to Saudi civil servants on long-term payment plans and 180 apartments rented on a permanent basis.[30] Two-story, single-family houses built in the middle of their plots and set back from large, straight streets, financed by state-guaranteed loans, and linked to the city center by large highways, were becoming the norm.

New strikes, boycotts, and demonstrations took place in the oil province in 1964, 1966, and 1967. In 1967, between one and two thousand Saudi workers occupied the U.S. airbase in Dhahran and destroyed cars, a movie theater, a bar, and a bowling alley, markers of suburban culture and racial privilege. A smaller group entered the Aramco Senior Camp to smash cars and loot houses.[31]

In the later 1960s, wary of unrest, the ruling family commissioned Greek and British planners to manage urban growth and to try to limit rural migration to big cities, including Riyadh and Jeddah. European planners proposed modernist solutions and introduced regional planning to keep cities as small and orderly as possible. In Riyadh and other cities, Constantinos Doxiadis and his team designed large 2km-by-2km superblocks, organized in a grid at a distance from existing settlements. Each superblock was meant to function as a semi-autonomous, village-like community built around a central square with a school, a market, and a civic center. At the core of each superblock, a mosque was to become "the focal point of the community."[32] Mosques were central to Doxiadis's imagination of what a Saudi city should be. "We have been happy to find out that the overall topography has allowed us to direct [Riyadh's] main streets toward Mecca," Doxiadis wrote King Faysal in 1973, adding that these "Mecca-oriented roads" would make of Riyadh "a symbol for a Moslem city."[33]

Superblocks would enable "people to feel as much at home in them as they do inside their own houses." They would hopefully shield them from what Doxiadis believed were toxic political ideas.[34] In Islamabad and Baghdad, the Greek architect had designed superblocks that mimicked rural life and were meant to prevent the formation of crowds. Superblocks were not a new invention: in the early twentieth century, the Scottish planner Patrick Geddes had planned urban villages around similar blocks in Indore and Tel Aviv during the British colonial presence.[35] In both cities, he had designed pedestrian suburbs inspired by English garden cities and arranged around superblocks. Each superblock was a square doughnut whose center was reserved for community services or gardens.[36] The British planner Jacqueline Tyrwhitt was one of Geddes's disciples and a close collaborator of Doxiadis's. She popularized the ideas of self-contained blocks and self-built housing in British, Indian, and U.S. urban planning.[37]

Doxiadis had a knack for frontier planning and believed village-like communities could save modern cities from congestion and revolutions. He wanted cars to stay at the periphery of the superblocks, which would remain pedestrian. But cars soon reached far into each nook of Riyadh, and the pseudo-rural communities he had designed turned into a vast car-based suburbia. Instead of being quiet, depoliticized communities, these new suburbs became sites of mobilization and, sometimes, dramatic unrest.

Chapter 6 **BLESSED ARE
THE STRANGERS**

AL-HARRA AL-SHARGIYYA (THE EASTERN LAVA FIELD) IS A
neighborhood of Medina, northeast of the Prophet's mosque. Built in the 1950s,
this early suburb sits right outside the old city and was named after the vast
volcanic plain that borders Medina to the east. Its western part, closer to
the mosque and the old city, is not planned, and its winding streets follow
organic patterns. Its eastern part, in contrast, is organized around a series
of superblocks whose centers are community facilities: gardens, schools, a
supermarket, a soccer field, a hospital, and a social service center.

When Al Saʿud expanded the Prophet's mosque in the 1950s, demolish-
ing parts of the old city in the process, people living in the city center were
displaced to the periphery. Construction workers who had moved to Medina
in search of jobs built shacks and cement houses for themselves in al-Harra,
where they competed for space with bureaucrats and developers.[1]

Students of religion who had migrated from the steppes of the Hijaz and
Najd also settled in al-Harra. Students enrolled at the Islamic University of
Medina and the city's various religious institutes often clashed with the urban middle class. In 1965 students started removing fashion photographs and
mannequins from shop windows, arguing that the reproduction of animate
beings was religiously forbidden. Clashes with the shopkeepers ensued and
the police arrested the students and deported the foreigners among them.

After their release, a small group of students sought official protection from such crackdowns and decided to create a religious group under the umbrella of the Islamic University of Medina. According to a former member of the group, they met Sheikh 'Abd al-'Aziz bin Baz, president of the University, and told him that "corruption was becoming widespread, and that there was a need for preachers who invite people to come back to God according to the method of the pious ancestors."[2]

Bin Baz was no stranger to political opposition. As a young judge, he had opposed an agricultural project the U.S. oil company was planning south of Riyadh in the 1940s. He had argued that King 'Abd al-'Aziz could not give lands to U.S Americans who would use it "as if it was not the Muslim's territory." The king summoned the judge and confronted him with high-ranking clerics who argued that the Prophet himself had hired non-Muslims. Bin Baz was unconvinced, and 'Abd al-'Aziz had him jailed for threatening the public order.[3] This former radical gave the Medina students his blessing. He suggested that they name their movement The Salafi Group that Commands Virtue and Combats Vice,[4] became their spiritual guide, and paid the rent on their first house in al-Harra al-Shargiyya. He also allowed the group to use a mosque in al-Harra that had been entrusted to him by its founder.[5]

The group members called themselves the Brethren.[6] Their house looked like a monastery and was built around a central courtyard, like traditional Najdi houses. It could house about fifty students in sixteen rooms. A former group member explained how senior members lived in "self-built houses on lands they had encroached upon. People would build at night, away from the prying eyes of municipal employees. And if the latter started looking into illegal constructions, people would hand them kickbacks to silence them."[7] Sometimes "municipal agents checked the walls: if they were fresh and wet and no kickback had been paid to them, they would have the house demolished." For this reason, members of the Salafi group "covered the wet walls of their houses with dry mud, to give the impression that the house had been around for a while."[8]

Self-built houses "protected people's intimacy and featured walkways and back doors that allowed suspects to flee and prevented sudden intrusions. You could hide for years without being discovered."[9] Besides the street network, a system of back alleys allowed women to visit neighbors or run errands without being seen. The activists prevented the sale of tobacco and banned smoking in al-Harra. They slowly turned the area into a Salafi suburb, made of self-built houses where self-taught scholars and students tinkered with municipal regulations and religious doctrines. To them, Islamic action was a form of direct action.

The Brethren counted hundreds of members by the mid-1970s. They encroached on informal settlements in Mecca, Riyadh, Jeddah, Ta'if, al-Hofuf, and Ha'il. The edges of big cities were cheaper and less controlled than central areas; as in Medina, they were open to self-building and informal planning. In Mecca the group's members lived in Hawd al-Baqar, the "Cow Pen," a slum next to the cattle market, separated from the Great Mosque by a mountain range.[10] In Riyadh, their first house was on Khazzan Street; they then moved to the southern suburb of Manfuha, near the Ruwayyil mosque.

The group attracted young Bedouin who had migrated to the cities in search of employment or education; Saudi emigrants to other Gulf countries who returned home after the 1973 oil boom; and preachers or pilgrims from Yemen, Palestine, Syria, Egypt, Pakistan, and the United States.[11] According to a former member, the "Bedouin element," which had been repressed in the making of the modern state, was central to the worldview of the group, which "was one of confrontation between the city and the Bedouin." By joining the group after fleeing their families and hometown and migrating to big cities, its members entered "a state of revolt."[12]

Core members of the group followed the teachings of Sheikh Muhammad Nasir al-Din al-'Albani, the Syrian cleric who renewed the meaning of Salafi activism and taught for a while at the Islamic University of Medina. What made the group Salafi was not only its emulation of the three first generations of Muslims but also its radical questioning of the traditions that, according to its members, had obscured revelation. Al-'Albani made popular the critique of the transmission and reliability of the Prophet Mohammad's sayings, the hadith. The Brethren also took into their own hands the religious education of society, publicly criticizing widely accepted doctrines.

"These views were new to the public," and the clerics of Medina "were not prepared for the questions [the Brethren] asked. Perched on Hanbali jurisprudence, they were far removed from the sayings and actions of the Prophet. It was rare to find a cleric who could master the tools required to edit and establish the hadith."[13] The Hanbali School, one of the four Sunni currents of jurisprudence, is dominant in Saudi Arabia. By revisiting the textual foundations of religious authority, the Salafis critiqued the four currents of jurisprudence and undermined the credentials of state-appointed clerics, who were mostly Hanbalis. The group members were not only reclaiming urban spaces but also repossessing the religious culture that the state had turned into a tool of control.

"Some members of the group would never ask a sheikh's advice without also asking for the evidence. If the sheikh quoted evidence from the hadith, they would ask: is this hadith truthful, or is it weak? Their questions annoyed the sheikhs. . . . The Salafi Group broke the obstacle of respectful fear that separated the legal experts from the masses. Legal science had until then been the monopoly of clerics and of students of religion; the Salafi Group vulgarized it. It instilled in the masses the spirit of controversy. . . . Clerics had once monopolized mass influence; now the masses were moving clerics toward their own goals."[14]

A Pakistani sheikh who was affiliated with the group taught the writings of the eleventh-century Andalusian philosopher Ibn Hazm in the Great Mosque of Mecca. Salafis liked Ibn Hazm because he refused to distinguish between the four currents of jurisprudence, including the Hanbali and Hanafi schools, and called on Muslims to follow the letter of the scriptures. The former member of the group told me that the Pakistani scholar "got carried away. Near us there was a study circle from Bukhara that was studying Hanafi jurisprudence. And of course, Ibn Hazm used to write impossible things, for instance, that Hanafi Muslims were 'effeminate jurists.' So our teacher raised his voice and shouted in their direction, 'Look at these faggots. They abandon the hadith to study their Hanafi books. Faggots!'" Students complained about the Pakistani sheikh, who was invited to teach less divisive material.[15]

But the Brethren kept discussing politics. In their houses in Mecca, Medina, Riyadh, and Jeddah, this international group of radical students would debate hadith, Quran, religious jurisprudence, and political and social issues.[16] Soon the group members "were subjected to heavier surveillance from a majority of clerics."[17]

Things went south around 1976. The residents and clerics of Medina "no longer wrote to Sheikh 'Abd al-'Aziz bin Baz" to complain about the young Salafis.

"They wrote directly to the authorities, to King Khalid and to the governor of Medina. . . . One of the clerics wrote a report saying that the Salafi Group was gathering weapons." Clerics were getting angrier at these "young students who sat in their classes and, whenever they would say anything, would ask, 'What is your evidence?' And if they quoted a hadith, the students would ask, 'Who edited it?' They cornered the clerics, who decided in turn to make a scandal."[18]

The accusation of possessing weapons was a futile claim in a society known for high weapon ownership. But Juhayman al-'Otaybi, the leader of the group, also insisted on "the obligation to resist the Saudi government," which was considered a much more serious crime. Juhayman thought the government allowed usury, was in the hands of a corrupt royal family, and forced its citizens to swear allegiance to the state instead of letting them choose their ruler.[19] Juhayman al-'Otaybi was born in Central Arabia in 1936 to a family that belonged to the 'Otayba nomadic confederation, a once powerful tribal alliance. Juhayman had been a cigarette smuggler and a National Guard before dedicating his life to religious learning and to political activism.

Al Sa'ud "took the allegiance of the people, not by the hand and the heart, freely and by choice, but by force and constraint," Juhayman wrote in one of the letters that were published in 1978 by a left-wing Kuwaiti publishing house. "We live under an oppressive rule, where Muslims no longer choose the caliph: it is the caliph who imposes himself on them and forces them to pay allegiance to him."[20] Juhayman's argument was politically and religiously potent. To the state's religious claims, the Salafis opposed the right to resist oppression and freely choose their ruler.

The ire of the group was directed at the state clerics, who were "flatterers, mercenaries, salaried, and obedient." According to a hadith that was dear to Juhayman, the Prophet feared those "misguided imams" as much as the Antichrist. Juhayman criticized even Sheikh 'Abd al-'Aziz bin Baz, who "denounces a sin only when he is asked to, but never ventures to criticize anything by himself, because he is a pillar of the state. . . . He is now a civil servant and they deceive him by calling him 'our father' and 'our sheikh.' "[21]

The Salafi Group's capacity for mobilizing a transnational youth movement and agitating was a direct threat to Al Sa'ud, which placed the group under police surveillance. Juhayman thought that the police had infiltrated the movement and made it clear that none of his followers should work for the government, not even as teachers, imams, or soldiers. He banned ID cards and passports and told his followers to stop studying in state schools. In the mid-1970s, the police arrested several dozen Brethren and deported the foreign group members. Juhayman snuck out of his house and escaped through the back alleys of al-Harra.

"These were the first collective arrests of this nature in the country: no Islamic group or Islamic organization had been cracked down upon before. But the young Salafis, oddly, exulted. They were proud to have experienced prison, which until then had been a monopoly of the [Egyptian, Syrian, and Iraqi] Muslim Brothers. One of the members said, 'The Muslim Brothers are not better than us. They went to prison, but some of us were thrown in prison, too.' "[22]

The imprisoned members were released after promising they would not assemble again or create a party. The remaining brethren went into hiding as a result of the state's repression, and they started to prepare themselves for a final confrontation. Juhayman's followers acquired more weapons and learned how to better use them. "Prison turned them into heroes and magnetized the Islamic public: all were attracted to them, and even those who were not convinced by their ideas followed them out of curiosity."[23]

As repression intensified, the young Salafis embraced millenarianism. Juhayman "would say that the end of time was near, that the Messiah was coming, that the rule of deceitful King Khalid would end."[24] In one of his letters, Juhayman wrote, "We left behind the civil servants, who grab the tail of the state and, alone, we faced truth, which is always strange, and in front of which we are condemned to remain strangers. But the hadith says, 'Islam began as something strange, and will come back as something strange. Blessed are the strangers.' "[25]

Juhayman identified his own brother-in-law as the awaited Messiah. Millenarianism was not unique to Saudis or Salafis. From the United States to Pakistan, other protesters were adopting millenarianist beliefs in the second half of the twentieth century. The Cold War itself was placed under the sign of the apocalypse. The threat of the atomic bomb had "put the globe at stake in the practice of politics, by dividing it into two rival hemispheres" and by forcing people "to conceive of its destruction and abandonment."[26] Millenarianism allowed Salafi activists to both accept the state's corruption and rebel against it. "Corruption increases at the end of time,"[27] the Salafis would say, but in the end comes the Messiah who wins over the tyrants.

In the early morning of November 20, 1979, several hundred supporters of Juhayman entered the Great Mosque of Mecca with their wives and children. Some went to the mosque's basement, returned with weapons they had previously hidden, and distributed them among their comrades. At the end of the dawn prayer, one of them grabbed the microphone and demanded the abolition of the monarchy, the severing of military ties with the United States, and the expulsion of Western experts.[28]

Al Sa'ud sent the army and the National Guard, which bombed the Great Mosque, destroying several walls and five of the seven minarets. After a failed chemical attack by the CIA, Al Sa'ud then turned to France's Gendarmerie Nationale, which flooded the basement with polluted water and used CS gas, a potentially lethal riot-control gas. The French had brought a ton of it, "enough to poison an entire city."[29]

The Saudi government claimed that the campaign resulted in 135 deaths. Officers of France's Gendarmerie Nationale said that four thousand insurgents, pilgrims, and military personnel had died. French investigative journalists reached a figure of five thousand deaths.[30] After questioning and torture, 180 young Salafis were executed in secret on January 5, 1980. On January 9, 63 more insurgents were executed, this time in public, in eight different cities of the kingdom.[31] Cities had become the scourge of Al Sa'ud. Princes no longer needed urban planners, not because they had given up on controlling society but because they no longer believed in cities. What Al Sa'ud needed after Juhayman al-'Otaybi's adventure was more construction crews, more developers, and more security providers. The goal was to get rid of urban centers and to encourage the dispersion of populations.

Chapter 7 **SUBDIVISION FRENZY**

AFTER THE 1973 OIL BOOM, REAL ESTATE INVESTMENT, CONSTRUCTION contracts, and car imports soared and Riyadh expanded well beyond the limits fixed by the master plan for the city. According to the former deputy mayor of Riyadh, "the original Doxiadis plan designated a city area of 304 sq. km. and did not foresee the exponential growth of the city's population and the concomitant channeling of enormous financial savings into the real estate market. By 1977, the subdivision frenzy surpassed the original Doxiadis plan boundary of 300 sq. km. to cover a total area of 700 sq. km., resulting in unprecedented urban sprawl."[1]

A second master plan was needed. The Ministry of Municipal and Rural Affairs hired the French state-owned Société Centrale pour l'Equipement du Territoire International (SCETI) in 1976 to revise the Doxiadis plan. SCETI had been created in 1959 by the Caisse des Dépôts et Consignations, a French state financial institution that had managed the massive debt France forced on Haiti after the country's independence as a compensation paid to slave owners for their loss of human chattel. After France's African colonies became independent in the 1950s and 1960s, the Caisse des Dépôts organized French neocolonial intervention in the guise of development expertise.[2] "The crossing of the desert is over," one of SCETI's CEOs told his employees in 1983. "We are atop Mount Nebo, and the conquest of the Promised Land is about to begin: our grand scheme of intervention abroad."[3]

The French planners started working in Riyadh in the late 1970s. They endeavored to "define a very strict zonning [sic] on the Brasília model," and to create "functional ghettos" to separate Saudis from labor migrants. The SCETI project manager thought that "strict zoning" was "in the Muslim tradition (the Melha of yore, today's compounds),"[4] and that colonial compounds, which had been introduced into Saudi Arabia by Aramco, were somehow the heirs of a tradition that started with Moroccan Jewish ghettos.

The French planners were often young engineers who wanted to work abroad but were not paid enough to be overzealous.[5] They soon clashed with the Riyadh municipality on several issues. Like Doxiadis, the French wanted to create limited commercial zones, but the municipality, "to treat all landowners on an equal footing,"[6] was turning all large avenues into commercial districts. Las Vegas had but one commercial strip; Riyadh, by decree, had dozens of them, lined with vast parking lots and an abundance of palm trees.

The French worked with the Ministry of Municipal and Rural Affairs, but the Riyadh planning authority was under the authority of Prince Salman, who was trying his best to avoid paying the planners. The French gradually came to understand how land changed hands in and around the city. "All lands are the king's property," the project head wrote in 1979. "Moreover, all lands that did not have a clear owner in early 1978 (within the 1971 master plan) became municipal property. . . . The king gives away gigantic properties to princes and collaborators. These are sold by chunks, progressively, to citizens or real estate agencies. . . . Lands are then parceled out following the specifications of the Doxiadis plan, whether they are within the 1971 master plan or not."[7] Land was political, and many in government did not wish to see foreign experts encroaching on their land-granting politics.

To better control the work of the French planners, the Ministry of Municipal and Rural Affairs appointed an inspector who was a graduate of al-Azhar University in Cairo. The inspector started enforcing daily prayers in the French office and counting mosques in the newly planned suburbs, making sure that each house was less than 250 meters from a mosque.[8]

In the end, the French added a second axis to Doxiadis's central spine and legalized the superblocks that had been informally built by investors and speculators. The French experts seemed to believe that all Saudis were repressed Bedouin and that urban sprawl was the continuation of nomadic customs. "The city's explosion is an established fact (some approved subdivisions are more than 25 km from the city center). It is the outcome of ancestral mobility habits that the advent of the automobile only multiplied. It seems highly uncertain that the city's expansion could be limited through regulation."[9] For French experts, suburbs were the infrastructure of Bedouin mobility.

Other observers were not as culturalist. A French ethnographer who worked in Riyadh in the 1970s observed how princes, investors, and realtors cooperated after the 1973 oil boom. He saw their alliance becoming the backbone of the Saudi political structure, whereby political acquiescence was rewarded with business opportunities and land deals. The ethnographer showed that women and children bore the brunt of suburbanization. The liberation of middle-class Saudi men by the automobile actually meant less mobility for their wives, daughters, and children. "Women may go out only by car, which subjects their comings and goings to the control of their husbands, the family chauffeur or society." Cars were tools of control, not of freedom. "In fact, more than half the Saudi population of Riyadh suffers from the extreme growth of the city and the subservience of urban planning to the needs of the automobile."[10]

No wonder the city kept expanding. In a militant article urging municipal authorities to stop suburban sprawl, a Saudi geographer wrote in the late 1980s, "the built up area of the city increased from 4,238 hectares in 1976 to 45,197 hectares in 1987, an increase of more than 1000%, while the city population increased by about 100%." During the same ten-year period, "the city overall population density dropped considerably, from 140 to 29 persons per hectare."[11] Car ownership was the capstone of the suburban system; it was crucial to the definition of Saudi citizenship. In 1989, there was "nearly one car for every 2 persons, compared with one car for 48 persons in 1971."[12]

Meanwhile, "average dwelling size increased from 100 sq. m. in 1969 to 600 sq. m. in 1980. People in the modern affluent society of Riyadh wanted spacious houses with larger rooms to accommodate the modern furniture, gardens, garages, swimming pools and other amenities." Less wealthy people tried to follow the same trend and went into massive debt. They soon realized that suburban living also came with a social price. "People there drive longer distances for work as well as for obtaining services. Friends and relatives are too far away to visit and the time will come when travel will approach the maximum of human endurance."[13] Society turned into a collection of consumers, drivers, and passengers. In this world of citizen-commuters, property values became key to how people saw themselves and related to others.

All attempts to curb sprawl failed. In 1985, the council of ministers ordered a two-year freeze on new urban projects in the country. In 1989, it implemented an Urban Growth Boundary Policy to put suburban sprawl in check: this policy established clear urban limits outside of which development was strongly discouraged. To prevent developers from building outside of municipal boundaries, cities transferred the costs of basic infrastructure to those developers, who had to finance and build roads, electric networks, and street lighting.[14]

The new policy actually fostered what it was meant to stop. Landowners and developers were not deterred by the extra cost and kept building outside of the plan. In an ironic twist, they threw the Doxiadis and SCETI plans out the window but fully adopted Doxiadis's vocabulary of superblocks, central plazas, and straight highways. Far from the city proper, developers and builders followed "Doxiadis' 2 sq. km. superblock structural framework to lay out the major arterial street network"[15] in the hope that their informal but planned subdivisions would one day be legalized. This was a good calculation: in the end, municipalities usually granted legal recognition to these new developments.

Most cities followed the example of Riyadh and became far-flung, flat, monotonous grids of perpendicular avenues organized in superblocks and lined with single-family houses. Everywhere in the country, powerful and well-connected landowners and developers turned empty land around old cities into quick and easy sources of wealth. "Lenient municipal ordinances could not stop greedy powerful landowners from the continuous proliferation of subdivisions.... Suburbanization [was] achieved at the cost of sustainability in the wider meaning of the term."[16]

Municipalities had sacrificed urban governance on the altar of capital accumulation. By scattering people across vast subdivisions, they rendered society both weaker and less governable. The transformation of dense cities into vast, shapeless urban spaces was most dramatic in parts of the country where political protests had happened. In November 1979, during the occupation of the Great Mosque of Mecca, another protest movement unfolded in the oil province, where workers and Shiʿa Islamic activists demonstrated against discrimination and economic marginalization.[17] Shiʿa Muslims in this part of the country had been subjected to state violence and discrimination since the conquest of their territory by ʿAbd al-ʿAziz Al Saʿud in 1913. In 1979, residents mobilized in the tight urban spaces of the old walled city of al-Qatif to organize and dodge repression. They used a maze of narrow passageways[18] to hide and move from building to building. In the aftermath of the "Intifada of the Eastern Province," the state razed the walled city of al-Qatif to the ground and relocated its inhabitants.

The state claimed that urban renewal, by fostering real estate investment, would ultimately respond to the protesters' demands, including better housing and investment opportunities. But the center of town remained barren until the late 2000s, when it was converted into a huge, circular parking lot. In the 1980s and 1990s, the areas surrounding al-Qatif became suburban subdivisions; millennial palm groves were uprooted and land was reclaimed from the sea. The Portuguese had built a fort on neighboring Tarut Island in the sixteenth century; the British had signed a protectorate agreement with Al Sa'ud there in 1915. Tarut Island was now encased in a glacis of superblocks à la Doxiadis, with single-family homes and traffic islands.

Urban destruction was not limited to Shi'a areas. The state also razed the old cities of Mecca and Medina to the ground between the 1980s and the 2000s and then allowed them to be progressively rebuilt. In Mecca, the very landscape of the city, made of dramatic hills and valleys, was flattened by subcontractors in preparation for the extension of the Great Mosque and high-rise developments, including a six-hundred-meter-high replica of Big Ben.[19] In Riyadh, urban renewal projects in the old city pushed out vulnerable populations and forced them to relocate to the inner city or the inner suburbs.[20] Al Sa'ud hollowed out cities and disposed of them by force, market penetration, or both. Everywhere developers built sprawling suburbs and sold villas to middle-class wage earners, whom they expected to behave like responsible homeowners, repaying their loans and living quiet, dull, controlled lives.

Suburbanization replaced horizontal solidarities with vertical links between citizens, financial institutions, and the state. But suburban sprawl, based on a state-sponsored celebration of private property and individual transportation and visible through the proliferation of villas and cars, did not deter politicization. It is precisely in the suburbs of Riyadh, Jeddah, and other Saudi cities that Islamic activists organized all through the 1980s and 1990s.

Chapter 8 **THE GENIE WAS
OUT OF THE BOTTLE**

SHEIKH 'ABD AL-ILAH, THE CLERIC WHO IN 1991 HAD STUDIED
the jurisprudence of demonstrations, was born into a religious family in the
1960s. He joined a Quran memorization circle when he was six. At that time,
these circles were traditional institutions, "without any hint of Awakening,"
he said. The sheikhs running them taught children to memorize the Quran,
no more, no less.

The members of Juhayman's group renamed the circles "libraries" in
the 1970s to insist on the academic dimension of their religious experience.
They gathered hadith collections and legal books in a room or a corner of
the mosque. Their study circles became research groups exploring religious
knowledge and legal resources and making them available to worshippers.

"Juhayman's followers . . . used to meet in Riyadh in the Skirina neighborhood," Sheikh 'Abd al-Ilah told me when I interviewed him about his career
in the Islamic Awakening. "Other neighborhoods got very excited about the
idea, and many libraries emerged at that time. They were not centralized so as
not to arouse suspicion, but they all belonged to specific cultural or religious
coalitions."

Mosque libraries aimed at religious revival and transnational Islamic solidarity and were linked to one another. But contrary to what their detractors said, the
libraries did not come from Egypt and had not been imported to Saudi Arabia by
the Muslim Brothers: they were a Saudi variation on a classical theme.

"We once had a library in Riyadh where state clerics would meet, near the house of the mufti," 'Abd al-Ilah said. "It was not the National Library—this one was created for the liberals—but the Religious Library. And it still exists today, within the House of Fatwas.[1] It was where students in religion and the more political clerics would meet. They would talk about the removal of King Sa'ud from power, about dissent within the royal family, etc. I imagine that the idea of the library developed either from there or from Skirina."

King Faysal deposed his brother Sa'ud in a palace coup in 1964, with the support of the chief clerics and of their Religious Library. Juhayman's disciples democratized the exclusive institution of the library, which had shown its political power during the coup, by replicating it in many neighborhoods and opening it to commoners. This politicization was inconspicuous at first. Libraries tended to open in new mosques, built in the recent suburbs. Far away from city centers and state institutions, libraries were pioneering new spaces.

"Young activists started inviting me to events," Sheikh 'Abd al-Ilah said, talking about his high school years. "Around 1976, they also invited me to join a library . . . that had just been created in a nearby mosque. The mosque was brand new. A Quran memorization circle had opened there for a short period, then they had put up a sign saying 'Library.' That is where the young Islamic activists met in the late afternoon, and students would gather around them. They taught them the Quran and organized lectures. And these lectures were, obviously, about activist topics. They called for cooperation, mutual support, brotherhood; they taught you a culture of collective action. And they told you about the misfortunes of Muslims to exhort you to a common belonging and a shared adhesion."

But 'Abd al-Ilah's father cut his visits to the library short.

"I stayed with them for Quran memorization, but I did not like to sit in the other meetings, because my father . . . did not want me to get in trouble. It was around the time when Juhayman started having problems with the state. There were confrontations between the state and activists. The elderly were anxious; they feared for their safety. People had just lived through King Faysal's repression of nationalist and leftist movements. I went with the library only once. . . . And then my dad forbade me to join any activity outside of school. . . . Like all paternalist fathers, my dad was afraid of the issues arising with secret organizations": denunciation, arrest, jail, and potentially torture. 'Abd al-Ilah kept to himself after that, reading works of literature and philosophy. He was 16 when Juhayman and his group occupied the Great Mosque.

"Our professors warned us against dissent. . . . Two of my maternal uncles were thrown in prison at that time. One of them had given financial support to Juhayman's group. He did not follow the news and did not really know what he was doing. He was politically far away from their positions, but he gathered donations and would send money to charitable causes. . . . My other uncle was inside the Great Mosque on the day they occupied it. He managed to escape but was accused of being one of them. They questioned him for a long time and he was not imprisoned, but put under house arrest."

The designation of "library" faded away in the early 1980s because of its association with Juhayman al-'Otaybi, but the Quran memorization circles continued. Sheikh 'Abd al-Ilah introduced me to other activists and I grew closer to one of them, Thamir, who taught religion in high school and had created an Islamic awareness group. Thamir told me why the name "library" was still used in some provinces of the country while it had fallen out of favor in others.

"In some regions, it became harder to call an Islamic group a 'library'; it was too odd," Thamir told me. "Why 'library'? parents would ask. They did not accept this new term; it was too strange, too modern. As for those running the libraries . . . 'Who are these guys?' parents would say. 'Two young men? Our kids go to school, who are these older guys who hang out with them all the time?' So Islamic activists looked for more acceptable activities, and they found them in the Quran memorization circles, which had been around for a longer time. . . . Mobilizing students through the circles was not as suspect; nobody would question their goals or be worried to see them together."

To survive repression after 1980, Islamic activists also had to join the state campaign against Juhayman's influence.

"This was a period of sudden withdrawal," 'Abd al-Ilah said. "But what served some Islamic activists well, at that time, was their clear position against Juhayman. They were part of the movements that the state supported against revolutionary Salafism.

"The Muslim Brothers were very loyal to the state. Of course, twenty years later, we found out that there had been communication channels between the

security services and some Muslim Brothers who lived abroad, which strengthened the alliance between them. . . . The state adopted the Islamic ideal and
considerably bent its own modernizing course; it then managed to contain the
Islamic wave, because it had become part of its own values. . . . Meanwhile,
the politicization of the Islamic Awakening was postponed by about ten years.
This confiscation of the Islamic Awakening prevented Islamic activists from
openly declaring any negative position vis-à-vis the state."

But Islamic activists kept organizing in mosque circles, schools, and universities. 'Abd al-Ilah studied sharia in the early 1980s and kept his distance
from what he called "a vociferating polarization" between various political
groups. It is around that time that he stumbled on Immanuel Kant's *Critique
of Pure Reason* at the university library and was "stunned by its immensity."
Despite his theoretical interests, he also kept his finger on the political pulse
of the country.

"Students were simmering across the kingdom," he said. "They were angry
at the prodigious corruption that we were witnessing at the time. We would
read booklets and pamphlets denouncing corruption and the illegitimate
deals" between Al Sa'ud and Western nations, in particular arms deals. "People
were extremely angry. . . . We would talk to a number of sheikhs and ask them,
'Why do we not do something? Why do we not speak up against corruption?'
But nobody could say anything; there was no way you could appear on the
public scene. The media were repressed; any movement was shut down, especially when it came to politics. Those who had political aspirations could
not move in any direction.

"Four or five years after Juhayman's events, the climate got calmer at the
Sharia College, and we witnessed new cultural phenomena, lectures, and clubs.
The Janadriya Festival started around that time."

The Janadriya Festival was launched in 1985 by the National Guard in a
northern suburb of Riyadh to feature the openness of the regime while building a top-down national heritage out of scraps of traditions and historical
shrapnel.[2] The festival's military origins did not prevent it from becoming a
political scene of sorts; it is there that a culture war was waged, which Saudi
activists and intellectuals nicknamed the "battle of modernity."[3]

Two groups in particular fought each other at the festival: the "modernist
youth" and the "Islamic youth." Saudi modernists had become a literary trend

in the 1960s. In the mid-1980s, unable to criticize the government directly, Islamic activists protested the link between the state and the modernists, while modernists pointed at the public funding of religious institutions. The "battle of modernity" was a turning point in 'Abd al-Ilah's career. "It marked my practical entry into the Islamic Awakening," he said. What was true of 'Abd al-Ilah was probably true for other students, too: the audience of the Islamic movement grew exponentially in the mid- to late 1980s.

Suburban Janadriya became a recruitment and training ground for the Islamic Awakening. Activists refined the art of the "oral intervention" at the festival. After public lectures, they would ask questions that snowballed into heated speeches while other activists heckled the lecturers. They perfected other modes of action as well.

"[We had] countless lectures, roundtables, and house meetings, to create a block, to gather ourselves, to cooperate, to set the clerics and the people in motion. Preachers gave sermons, they spoke out—they became activists. There were very brutal oral interventions during talks at Janadriya. . . . There were visits to the decision makers. Of course, this was a common practice at the time: petitions to the decision makers, petitions to state clerics to ask them to protect us during confrontations."

Activists mobilized everyday resources, from the private space of the house to the public spaces of the mosque, the lecture hall, and the royal palace. Like Juhayman's followers ten years before, they were also preparing themselves for later confrontations. In 1988, in an effort to put an end to the battle and avoid the attacks of Islamic activists, the Ministry of Information banned the word "modernity" from all written and broadcast media.[4]

"No modernist remained standing," 'Abd al-Ilah said. "Their social and media image was broken. Even their families were under fire. They were so-cially dead."

But state elites punished Islamic activists, too. A popular religious sheikh, 'A'id al-Garni, was accused of pedophilia by a powerful prince and imprisoned. Al-Garni "had gained his popularity and his followers in the streets, with a group of young sheikhs whose popularity was growing at the time and that included Safar al-Hawali, Salman al-'Ouda, etc., who competed with state cler-ics and were becoming religious figures," 'Abd al-Ilah said. An "unbelievable social movement" came out in support of al-Garni. "Hundreds of people visited him. Clerics and students mobilized. They created powerful committees to conduct an inquiry and clear his name."

The networks that Islamic activists had created at the Janadriya Festival were now directly pushing back against an Al Sa'ud prince.

"This was a new battle, against the state this time, and no longer against modernist intellectuals," 'Abd al-Ilah said. "People held meetings and created coalitions; there were many sessions with the sheikhs to discuss the issue and mobilize hundreds of participants. The idea emerged that grassroots coalitions were possible, that we could create quasi-institutions around the activist clerics who opposed the state."

Another step toward popular mobilization was taken in 1989, when Sheikh 'Abd al-Muhsin al-'Obeikan created grassroots committees to monitor public spaces, command virtue, and combat vice in Riyadh. To command virtue and combat vice: this Quranic principle was the motto of the ubiquitous morality police (the Committee that Commands Virtue and Combats Vice). Created in 1926 by 'Abd al-'Aziz Al Sa'ud, the Committee that Commands Virtue and Combats Vice had turned what might elsewhere have been an individual or communal duty into a state monopoly.[5] Such Islamic activists as Sheikhs 'Abd al-Ilah and al-'Obeikan were of two minds over the morality police: they saw its work as essential to the making of a religious society but did not believe that the Quranic principle should be appropriated by the state.

Thousands of people attended a public meeting Sheikh al-'Obeikan organized at the Jawhara mosque, on Khazzan Street, and activists agreed on the urgency of organizing collective action. But Prince Salman nipped the people's committees in the bud. He summoned al-'Obeikan to his office and ordered him to keep quiet. The sheikh kept organizing, and the prince asked Sheikh 'Abd al-'Aziz bin Baz to convince him to stop organizing.[6]

"Opposition in itself was an event and a good piece of news," 'Abd al-Ilah said. "My colleagues and I wanted to infiltrate these committees to lead them toward something more important than women's veils or public morality in shopping malls. I attended one of the meetings and told them that the issue was not only this, but also how state money was spent."

The Quran described the Islamic community as "the best nation produced as an example for mankind," a nation that "commands virtue and combats vice."[7] Islamic activists insisted that virtue and vice were not only individual, but also collective, and that commanding virtue and combatting vice had to encompass state affairs, too. In their sermons, for instance, the sheikhs Safar al-Hawali and Salman al-'Ouda articulated religion, morality, and politics. They became the spearhead of the Islamic movement by shifting the general conversation from the battle of modernity to the reform of the state and from morality to politics.[8]

"When the Gulf War happened, we knew who the activists were," 'Abd al-Ilah said. "During the first ten days, we could not understand what was going on. Then we started to consult people, to meet friends we had made during the battle of modernity and at Janadriya."

A few weeks after the invasion of Kuwait, the sheikhs Safar al-Hawali, Salman al-'Ouda, and Nasir al-'Omar publicly denounced state clerics and condemned their support for the Gulf War.

"The genie was out of the bottle," 'Abd al-Ilah said. "The state was weakened; it was unable to fight on all fronts."

'Abd al-Ilah joined a loose coalition of sheikhs, Islamic intellectuals, and young activists to put pressure on the government. Just like Juhayman had done in 1965, Islamic activists tried to recruit Sheikh 'Abd al-'Aziz bin Baz to their cause.

"Sheikh al-'Obeikan visited Sheikh bin Baz [late 1990] and asked him, 'How can you stay silent when the king is a hesitant, vile spendthrift who wastes the state budget, leads the country to bankruptcy, and misleads people?' 'Abd al-Ilah said. "Bin Baz asked him, 'Well, what do you want?' 'I want to write a constitution and impose it on the king,' al-'Obeikan said. Bin Baz told him, 'Write a constitution, gather the sheikhs and have them sign it, and we will impose it on the king; we will ask the king to implement it.'

"Al-'Obeikan called us. Of course, he did not know how to write a constitution; he barely knew what a constitution was. . . . And we told him, 'No, if you say 'constitution,' the state clerics will withdraw. They will tell you that our constitution is the Quran, and this will create a secondary front where you will be defeated.' He asked, 'What do we do, then?' We responded, 'Write down the legitimate principles of government. Write a concise text, do not dwell on or get sidelined by secondary questions, which would allow the state to sow discord among us.'"

This platform became the Letter of Demands,[9] discussed and publicized in 1991 through suburban networks in dining rooms, mosques, and rest houses.

Activists sent the Letter to King Fahd in May 1991. The list of signatories "triggered a massive shock in the state apparatus," 'Abd al-Ilah said. "Later, when we were in prison, they told us during interrogations, 'The worst thing you did was to separate the state from its most trusted men.'" By mobilizing important religious clerics, the Islamic Awakening was shattering the state monopoly on religion.

The first arrests took place the same month. The following year, Islamic activists sent a more detailed petition to the king: the Memorandum of Advice.[10] Arrests became more frequent, which prompted a transformation of the Islamic movement from a reform movement to a movement of self-defense.

"When somebody was arrested," 'Abd al-Ilah said, "we would rejoice, because these were opportunities to march in the streets. In the Eastern Province, they organized a huge march when one of their activists was arrested. And in Riyadh, too, hundreds of people. We gathered in a mosque; we were between five hundred and a thousand people. And we demonstrated. We chanted for reforms. We shouted our demands."

For a while, activists turned repression into a political resource. Demonstrations gave birth to grassroots committees "with an elected president, a budget, a secretary general, secretaries who would write meeting notes; they would meet every week, plan precise actions" to defend the rights of those arrested and gather donations in their name. Activists would sometimes reach the gates of the royal palaces. Once Prince Mish'al, a brother of the king, slapped a sheikh in a shopping mall. This incident, too, was an occasion for mobilization.

"They rendezvoused with people at a mosque near the Riyadh governorate, and around three to four hundred people stormed Prince Salman's office."

At first these incidents emboldened Islamists, but after a certain threshold was passed, activists understood that they were now facing down something much more serious and terrifying than before: mass arrest and torture in prison. After another round of arrests in 1993, a handful of prominent activists launched the Committee for the Defense of Legitimate Rights to advocate for the rights of the detainees.[11]

"[It] would be a human rights association, not a political party or an opposition group," 'Abd al-Ilah said. "It would defend anybody subjected to unlawful detention or a rights violation. There was a huge ambiguity, of course, because the Committee confronted political injustices. But . . . we did not want the Committee to confuse political confrontation with humanitarian, rights-based demands. We wanted it to be politically neutral, if that expression means anything. . . . It had to appear neutral and defend the victims of repression."

As Islamic activists were organizing in Riyadh and the Central Region, a rival Islamic trend emerged at the Islamic University of Medina. 'Abd al-Ilah called them "state Islamists" or "government Salafis." These students in religion were sometimes nicknamed "Madkhalis" or "Jamis" after the sheikhs Rabi' al-Madkhali and Muhammad 'Aman al-Jami, who led the movement.

By 1994 the leading Islamic activists were in prison. 'Abd al-Ilah was arrested, too, and incarcerated in the al-Hayer prison. Saudi guerrilla fighters coming home from Afghanistan in the early 1990s probably thought that they would be celebrated for defeating the Soviet Union. But several thousands of them were also detained. The failure of the reform movement and the repression that followed bolstered those who, like Osama bin Laden, advocated for a violent takeover.

"I met bin Laden twice," 'Abd al-Ilah said. "Once in 1991 in Riyadh, and the other time in 1992 in Jeddah. He was more receptive at our first meeting, and seemed to accept the idea of peaceful reform initiatives. But the second time we met, he was less optimistic and less encouraging. He no longer supported us. He refused to associate himself with us and said he believed more in armed action than in peaceful reform. . . . I invited him to sign the Letter of Demands, and he refused. At that time, al-Qaʿeda only targeted the Soviets in Afghanistan. It was still a legitimate organization, and the Saudi state supported them. We wanted to benefit from their contacts, to win their troops to the reform project, to help our action spread in the kingdom. . . . Bin Laden thought peaceful action would not yield any result, and said we were wasting our time."

In retrospect, Sheikh 'Abd al-Ilah said, he thought bin Laden had been right.

"Prison strengthened the partisans of armed action; it confirmed their notion that guerrilla action was the solution. It also confirmed everything they had said about the failure of peaceful reforms. Prison legitimized the idea of armed confrontation. It became the only alternative: you either get randomly arrested or choose to attack the security forces on your own terms, because you choose the place and the time. . . . Al-Qaʿeda was fueled by the idea that only confrontation would work, and that peaceful reform was an illusion."

A wide spectrum of activists, students of religion, sheikhs, intellectuals, professors, lawyers, and guerrilla fighters experienced unlawful arrests, detention, and torture in the 1990s. Some died; others were released.

"Back in the 1930s and 1940s," 'Abd al-Ilah said, "there were opposition voices; there was some movement; people were taking positions; we had a media; there was repression of course, but it was limited; it was not that bad. . . . Severe repression came with the Cold War and security alliances" with the West. With repression, "another crucial aspect became clearer. What Islamic militants had been saying all along was true: confronting the regime was too dangerous, since its priority was to be on good terms with the Americans and the West in general. This gave birth to the project of attacking America and waging war on the Crusaders, as they called it at the time. Because in the end, America and the West protect the security apparatus, support security operations, and allow for something unprecedented in the history of Islam: the repression of free speech. There is no precedent for the repression we have experienced for the last thirty years."

It is in this unprecedented situation that, in the mid-2000s, Islamic activists ran for office in the main cities of the Kingdom. The electoral drama would play out, once again, in and around Saudi suburbia.

Chapter 9　**WE COULD USE
THE PORK RIND**

SALEH WAS A TALKATIVE BUSINESSMAN IN HIS FIFTIES WHO
professed a belief in mysticism and sometimes took non-Muslims on tours
around Mecca. The Holy City was officially forbidden to non-believers, but
Saleh believed that Mecca was a gift to the whole world and thought all hu-
mans were innately Muslims. On the day we met, he offered to drive me to
the Ka'ba. I would have to convert to Islam, but this was a formality, he said,
and my conversion would be swiftly dealt with thanks to a sheikh he knew. I
declined the offer, much to Saleh's disappointment. I also told him that I was
interested in the municipal elections, and he invited me to come observe
the vote. The municipality had appointed him to manage a polling station in
a suburb of Jeddah. If I couldn't see the Ka'ba, I would at least visit another
Holy of Holies.

I arrived around noon on Election Day. The polling station was a series of
tents in an empty lot. Behind them, a new development climbed up the hills,
its winding streets lined with cement villas. Saleh assigned me a folding chair
at the high end of the tent. From there I had a commanding view of the scene:
the entrance behind a wooden screen; the sign-in table; five white plastic
ballot boxes; seven voting booths; and the exit behind another screen. I was
seated near the observers, journalists, and members of the candidates' teams,
whose numbers reached eight in the afternoon. Including Saleh there were

seven Saudi employees in the station, plus six policemen right outside the door and three South Asian janitors in yellow overalls. Voters often came in small groups of friends, relatives, colleagues, or neighbors; sometimes their children were with them. Saleh told me that most of the neighborhood's residents had recently migrated from the mountains or the steppes.

Saleh spent his day directing voters, offering instructions, and even leading some by the hand. He wanted the vote to succeed and worried voters would behave incorrectly, which could lead to the invalidation of the election. Saleh also worried about the voting in a country whose last polls dated to the early 1960s, before Prince Faysal, then prime minister, abolished the municipal elections.[1]

Cell phones were an issue. Saleh told me that voters had used their phones inside the station. Some had sold their votes and taken photos of the ballot, which they would later trade for payment. Others circulated cheat sheets behind the booths. In some stations, organizers had turned the voting booths to face the room, allowing the organizers to monitor what was going on in them.

Early in the morning, Saleh had decided not to ban cell phones at his station; he had given voters his number and told them to text him if they saw something. But after an hour, the turmoil was such that he finally banned phones after all. Now he had an employee walking around the booths to remove cheat sheets and make sure people did not use their phones while voting.

Nobody asked who I was or why I was there. The employees knew I was Saleh's friend; the voters were transient and barely lingered; the cops were outside. Saleh would often stop by my chair and comment on the vote. He asked my opinion when an old man who could not read came to vote. Saleh asked me what they did in similar cases in Riyadh. He knew I had observed the elections there two months earlier (the elections were held in three different sessions: February for the central province, March for the east and south, and April for the west and north). I told him that electoral agents would walk into the booth with illiterate voters and fill out the ballot with them.[2] He sent an employee in to help the man, and things seemed to work fine.

Many people showed up without being registered, and employees had to remind them of the rules. A few tried to vote anyway; others walked off, grumbling against the system. Disoriented by the three different election days, a man from Najran, in the south, who had missed the polls there in

March asked if he could vote here. One of Saleh's employees sent him away politely, but firmly.

Many more voters showed up around four, an hour before closing. They lined up at the entrance, behind the booths, and around the ballot boxes. A middle-aged man dragged a folding chair into a booth, sat down, and pulled out his cell phone. His double black rope pushed back on top of his headdress, his reading glasses perched on the tip of his nose, he was going from the tiny backlit screen to the ballot in front of him, checking off candidates' names one after the other. A few minutes later, a large bearded man joined him, followed by a younger man and a man with a stubble and a short moustache. All four of them were behind a single booth, at times conversing, at times trying to properly handle their ballots, which were long, seven-page pamphlets with hundreds of names on them. The man in the chair was handing out advice with the authority of an old-timer.

Other people were gathering and chatting while filling out their ballots. Witnessing the mayhem, Saleh called the policemen inside. Unsure what to do, the cops stood awkwardly in the middle while groups formed around them.

After much shuffling through their ballots, the three men who had been standing in the booth in front of me slowly walked away. They lingered a few minutes between the booths and the ballot boxes, chatting and comparing their votes right behind an oblivious cop. They then walked to the boxes, put their pamphlets into the tiny slot, and left with barely a nod. The man in the chair eventually stood up, walked to a box, and let go of his ballot, too.

Saleh's was not the only polling station whose manager called in the police. In Nazim, a Bedouin-majority neighborhood in the east of Riyadh, the police walked into a polling station to organize the vote, tame what a journalist called "anarchy," and disperse groups of voters.[3] In Hafr al-Batin, a military town on the Iraqi border, "the anarchy" was such that the election was interrupted in two of the city's eight polling stations, where groups of voters "attacked the stations and opened the ballot boxes."[4] In one station, people "tried to influence voters during the election, and voters clustered in the voting booths" while "candidates were trading votes in public, and an employee of the polling station tried to influence elderly illiterate voters to modify their vote."[5] Voters assaulted employees. Throughout the melee, a candidate was shouting into a megaphone outside the station, urging people to vote for him. The police intervened and the vote was canceled. It resumed the next day, but inside a municipal building and under heavy police surveillance.

The press spoke of ballot-trafficking Bedouins. "Illiteracy, tribalism, the environment, the lack of police, and bad management were the main causes for electoral anarchy,"[6] a journalist wrote in the capital's daily paper, *Al-Riyad*. In the public imagination, the Bedouin were thought to be backward and subjected to local notables: they were bad voters, and people who wanted to vote well were eager to distance themselves from them. "The people are influenced by propaganda, deceived by appearances, bought with money, and thus cannot choose the best,"[7] a journalist wrote in the pages of *'Okaz*. To journalists and pundits, the Bedouin tribes defeated the project of creating a rational and atomized voter in the isolation of the booth and through the sovereign act of voting. Was it tribalism, Bedouinism, and "the environment," or was something else going on? Was "electoral anarchy" fueled by illiteracy and propaganda, or was it the sign of another way of doing politics?

During his years with the Islamic Awakening, 'Adel had become interested in politics yet had adopted the position of spectator toward the movement. This distance brought him closer to my own perspective, that of an outsider who wanted to understand how political action had emerged within a highly repressive environment. 'Adel was a good ethnographic ally because he was at times able to walk away from his own group, not in order to leave it behind but to have a better look at it. But 'Adel had registered as a voter, because he did not want to leave even this tiny part of the political game to secularists, who he thought would rally en masse behind the electoral idea.

The council of ministers had promised municipal elections in 2003, on the eve of Sa'd al-Faqih's demonstration. People did not show much interest at first: women were barred from running for office and from voting, half the municipal council members were appointed by the Ministry of Municipal and Rural Affairs, and the municipal councils were consultative bodies with no real power. A few days after the beginning of the electoral campaign, Riyadh offered the uncanny sight of dozens of political billboards lining streets and boulevards. The billboards were not glued on walls or in designated electoral areas but displayed in street advertisement light boxes that usually featured luxury watches, perfumes, or jewelry. There were also cops everywhere, helicopters in the sky, and foreign journalists checking into the capital's best hotels. They were covering an International Counter Terrorism Conference that government media presented as "the first" in the history of the country.[8] Riyadh had experienced bombings since 2001, and Al Saʿud was playing the rewarding role of terrorism victim. One of the conference's recommendations was more public participation to prevent terrorism: as Saʿd al-Faqih had predicted, the elections were but one episode in the War on Terror.

An old friend invited me to a dinner at his manager's new home, in the opulent northern suburbs. We were seated on the carpeted floor, dipping our hands into a fragrant plate of *kabsa*. None of the guests had registered to vote.

"Elections are a joke," the manager said; they are "half-elections" because only men could vote; "quarter-elections" because half the council members were appointed; and "eighth-elections" because the municipal councils had no executive or legislative powers.

After dinner I rinsed my mouth in a long washroom near another guest who whispered, "The government did everything it could to make the experiment fail." We walked back to the living room, sat down, and started sipping sugary red tea. My friend's manager, who for an abstentionist showed a keen interest in all things electoral, told us that a camel had escaped an electoral tent in Suwaydi. The animal was about to be slaughtered by a candidate to feed his potential voters.

"This was an anti-democratic camel," somebody said. "No," our host replied. "This was a victim of democracy."

"I registered in order *to not* vote," ʿAdel told me a few days later, when I interviewed him about his participation in the vote. He had solid reasons for keeping his distance. He thought that elections were "both important and unimportant. Unimportant, because they are preposterous, because *they* think that society as a whole is minor, that we are in need of tutelage, and that this tutelage should come from them, the government. That is why they appoint seven councilors, and let us vote for the seven others. Which means that we do not even have the capacity to vote for who is going to represent us. . . . Elections are preposterous. But, on the other hand, they are important, because they are a way to promote our ideas, us, the society, to say who we are, what we think, who are the people that we want as representatives."

It was precisely because the electoral code revealed royal tutelage that society had to make its voice heard. In other words, elections were important precisely because they had been made unimportant, as a way to talk back to a paternalistic government. When he understood this dialectic, 'Adel changed his mind. He decided to vote for those Islamic activists who, in the end, won the election in Riyadh and in most big cities.

"Why did I vote for the Islamists? Not because I saw that, by God, they have the required competencies and skills to realize the interests of believers and country, no. . . . The main reason is that I wanted to say, 'Secularists do not belong here. We are not a secularist people, we are a religious, Muslim people, and we do not think anything but Islam should be our religion.' That was the idea. . . . Sixty-five percent of registered voters did not vote. . . . And only 10% of those who could register did register. . . . Which means that only 6.5% of Riyadh's people went to the polls. . . . I consider this a strike, in all the meanings of the word. . . . As if they wanted to get this message across: 'Elections are nothing, but we will still show you who deserves to represent us.' Whatever the means, even if there were no elections, even we only wanted to show who we think are the best people around."

In Riyadh, 86,462 citizens registered for the vote, and 56,354 of those actually voted. If one estimates the total number of eligible voters in Riyadh at around nine hundred thousand, then the voter turnout was indeed around 6.5%.[9] 'Adel described abstention as a blockade mobilization, as if voters were saying, let us register, but not vote, to bring down electoral participation and disqualify the operation. Yet he and thousands of others ultimately voted for the seven Islamic candidates who won the elections. How and why did they change their minds?

Voting operations were complex. The Saudi government had appointed a German consultant, Erhard Hruschka, to assist the Ministry of Municipal and Rural Affairs. Hruschka was a statistician from Hamburg who had organized polls in post-Soviet Eastern Europe and was an election observer in several Asian countries. The Ministry and Hruschka had decided that urban municipalities would be divided into several electoral wards, while rural municipalities would count only one ward each. Urban voters would have to vote not only in their own ward but also in each of the others, electing as many councilors as there were wards.

The principle of "one man, one vote" was valid only in rural areas: the German consultant and his clients were clearly fighting the specter of the "tribal vote." In Riyadh and Jeddah, cities with seven wards each, voting would be guided by the principle "one man, seven votes." In each city, voters would elect seven councilors, while the seven others would be appointed by the state. The business of voting was made harder by the staggering numbers of candidates: no fewer than 645 candidates—92 per ward on average—were competing for Riyadh's seven elected positions.

It was a challenge just to be informed about the candidates. But as if things were not confusing enough already, and as if to echo the 1932 ban on political parties, the Ministry and Hruschka also banned coalitions of candidates and electoral lists. Article 2 of the code stated that "electoral campaigns are individual endeavors and any agreement between candidates to form unified electoral lists for the municipal elections is prohibited, as is any direct or indirect cooperation between them." Article 4 prohibited any "link between electoral campaigns, and the direct or indirect mention, in any campaign material, of any cooperation between candidates, of mutual assistance between candidates, or of their association."[10] The authors of the law seemed to fear that the vote would be politicized, "tainted by ideology,"[11] or used by Islamic activists to advance their cause.

The Ministry of Municipal and Rural Affairs had created a disciplinary mechanism that atomized candidates and voters. Every candidate had to present himself individually to the voters; voters in turn had to vote as sovereign individuals. The voting booth embodied this atomization: this globally recognized infrastructure, as banal as a highway ramp or a fire hydrant, would isolate voters in order to physically ban collective decision-making.

Journalists decried any hint of collective behavior around the voting booths as "Bedouin." But electoral regulations and the architecture of the polling stations often failed to produce the desired individual voters. In Saleh's polling station, group voting was possible when voters had access to their phones or around closing time, when they were left to their own devices and could assemble to decide what to do. The scene I had observed in Jeddah showed that the abstract, individualized voter was by and large a fiction.

"When I got my voter ID," 'Adel said, "I thought, if there is no electoral agreement, I will not vote. . . . By God, I thought, I hope the Islamic candidates pass an agreement. And then I read in *Al-Riyad* that elections came with strings attached and, tsk tsk, that electoral alliances were forbidden. I stood there, wondering: what on earth is this backwardness? We want the whole gig, we want people to be able to form alliances, we want political parties. . . . It just broke my heart, when I read this. It is a stupid rule. And then I thought, I hope they pass an agreement, but under the table, you see."

For 'Adel, it was not society that was backward for trying to vote as a collective. It was the state that was backward for denying voters the basic tools that were electoral lists and political parties. By praising arrangements made "under the table," 'Adel implied that to vote "well" was to vote badly. His budding voting career was typical of the chiaroscuro of voting practices in general and of the election debate among Riyadh's Islamic activists in particular. In the beginning, 'Adel did not know anything about electoral machinery.

"When they announced the elections," he said, "I thought, it is all smoke and mirrors. . . . [12] And then I thought, let us give them a chance, they might do something good." He laughed: "God may use them for the right purpose. Ha, I felt we could use the pork rind."[13]

The electoral beast, this impure animal whose consumption was religiously prohibited, could be taken advantage of, no matter how superficially.

"I waited patiently," 'Adel said. "And we know what happened. . . . Even my grandmother is better at organizing polls. . . . "[14]

'Adel decided to vote without yet knowing exactly how. He set out to find information on the candidates, and he learned about the elections thanks to activists around him; his individual decision hinged on collective networks. It is by interacting with other voters and with the candidates' teams that 'Adel eventually learned how to participate in a cosmetic, incomplete, patronizing democratic experiment. His knowledge of the electoral machinery became finer. His understanding of the political vocabulary became broader, too. During the electoral campaign he acquired the means to participate in what was going to be a full subversion of the elections.

Chapter 10 **MAKE THE WAY NARROWER FOR THEM**

WHEN I ARRIVED AT SHEIKH ʿABD AL-ʿAZIZ AL-TURKI'S CAMPAIGN site, a young Egyptian named Husam greeted me, responding to my "*al-salamu ʿalaykum*" (peace be with you) with a clipped "*wa ʿalaykum*" (and with you). Courtesy suggested he add the word "*al-salam*" (peace), saying "*wa ʿalaykum al-salam*." Islamic activists often omitted it when greeting me, the non-Muslim coming from a land at war with several Muslim-majority countries. The presence of an Egyptian volunteer also reminded me that foreign workers were essential to the functioning of Saudi society, even in its promotion of local democracy.

Al-Turki's campaign site was a vast yellow tent planted on an empty lot along Riyadh's southern Ring Road in Suwaydi, ʿAdel's childhood neighborhood. Many candidates, inspired by Kuwait's thriving electoral scene, set up tents that resembled wedding pavilions, or rented wedding halls for the duration of the campaign.[1] The nuptial metaphor was sticking to the campaign, from the slaughtering of camels to the long lines of retainers who formed to greet the candidate, this unwedded hero of a lonely feast. Islamic candidates both adopted this familiar repertoire and tried to subvert it.

Husam slipped a flyer into my hand featuring al-Turki's program, his biography, and reproductions of letters of endorsement from five prominent clerics, including the sheikhs ʿAbd Allah al-Jibrin and Nasir al-ʿOmar. Many of these letters were handwritten and generally said what a good person and knowledgeable scholar al-Turki was, and what a good deed it would be to vote for him. On that night, Sheikh Nasir al-ʿOmar himself was coming to give a public lecture.

Just as Islamic groups were called "libraries" or "memorization circles," political rallies were called lectures[2] and adopted the format of a formal academic presentation, followed by a question-and-answer session. In general, the use of an academic vocabulary certainly had something to do with the necessity of disguising political activities. In this case however, political participation was not only allowed but even encouraged by the state. But activists continued to stick to a repertoire that came directly from Salafis, with their quest for formal religious knowledge and their aura of religious respectability and seriousness.

Husam sat me in a corner of the tent. The sunset prayer was still going on, and as it came to a close voters slowly started to fill the space. When Sheikh Nasir al-ʿOmar arrived, a crowd materialized around him, hugging and kissing him in an almost familial atmosphere of intense joy. Husam had vanished into the crowd and came back with the candidate in tow. Al-Turki locked eyes with me, giving me a steely gaze as he crushed my hand in his. He then walked to the podium and sat down near his guest. At this point, people were streaming into the tent, arriving in small groups and hailing each other with large smiles. Everybody casually sat down on the carpeted floor. The lecture was about to begin.

Nasir al-ʿOmar was in his late thirties when Iraq invaded Kuwait in 1990. He became famous for his participation in the Islamic Awakening's protests of 1990–1993. Imprisoned in 1994, he was released in 1999 and arrested again in 2018. When the municipal elections were announced in 2003, he made his support public and urged Islamic activists to register and vote. "The benefits of voting are, it seems to me, more important than the potential drawbacks," he wrote at the time. "That is why I recommend that you participate in the elections. . . . Cut the road in front of those who would exploit these positions of power for their own personal goals or toward other aims."[3]

Al-ʿOmar remained a staunch critic of U.S. policies around the region, which he interpreted as "a new colonialism."[4] Tonight, without renouncing his anti-Western sentiments, he publicly embraced the notion of civil society. Civil society, he said, was composed of "free and independent organizations" and of "everything the state cannot deal with, even if it touches upon politics," thus pointing to a space that would be both political and void of state control, a space of popular mobilization and collective action. He explained that, far from being a Western import, civil society had existed in Islam since the revelation and was a site of resistance to the state. But "all circles of society are under Western occupation; it is the West that created class divisions," in particular the distinction between citizens and the ruling class. Elections were thus a "new opportunity" to combat class divisions, to "participate in the country's reform against international pressures," and to strengthen "Islamic civil society institutions."[5]

"Here, religion is power," al-ʿOmar said. "And even municipalities have something to do with religion. . . . Hypocrites and secularists push religion into a corner, whereas it is God who governs all things."

For Nasir al-ʿOmar, God's sovereignty was not an authoritarian construct but a notion that enabled strong popular resistance to the power of the state. "Religion is power" meant that religious activities were possibly the only form of activism that could warrant its authors some measure of success. As he saw it, "Islamic civil society" was composed of Quran memorization circles in mosques, Islamic charities, proselytizing associations, wedding associations, and medical associations, all institutions that were urban and suburban in nature. The municipal, which had been overlooked by the state, could provide the means for a political renewal. He showed us a few PowerPoint slides: between 1990 and 2004, the number of Quran memorization circles in Riyadh had quadrupled (from 750 to 3,147) and their enrollment had more than tripled (from 28,260 students to 105,493). Islamic activist circles grew at a much faster rate than the Saudi population, which during the same period had only grown by 50%, from 16.21 million to 23.84 million.

Al-ʿOmar compared this spectacular growth with the parallel development of what he called corruption. He explained that coffee shops and hookah bars encouraged laziness and inaction; that drugs had penetrated the country on the heels of hookahs and cigarettes; that coffee shops had introduced pernicious Western habits and undermined family and social belonging; that internet cafés "allowed anybody and their dog to talk to our youth, whereas in the past only Sheikh ʿAbd al-ʿAziz bin Baz had some measure of influence."

"We do not want to ban these places, but to regulate them," he added, pointing out that this was "the municipality's responsibility." He explained that coffee shops were open all the time thanks to cheap, flexible migrant labor. "Work hours are unregulated because foreigners are working," he said, linking the exploitation of foreign labor to the alienation of Saudi youth, who he believed had become a leisure class and were the victims, not the heroes, of a fast-paced consumer society. In his vision, municipalities should regulate what the state had been unable (or unwilling) to organize, in particular labor policies. Municipalities could become Islamic institutions and compensate for an unjust and corrupt state administration. To those who wondered about his adoption of a Western vocabulary, al-ʿOmar responded with an anecdote.

"I went to Grand Mufti ʿAbd al-ʿAziz bin Baz once and asked him what we ought to do about television. He told me: 'Do not say that television and radio are religiously prohibited, but get in there, infiltrate them, create a consensus and get to work. Make the road narrower for *them*.' "[6]

The same applied to elections: al-ʿOmar urged his audience not to boycott them but rather to use them to "make the road narrower" for other political forces, in particular those secularists who, from the point of view of Islamic activists, were Al Saʿud's and the West's best allies. Al-ʿOmar concluded his lecture by explaining that elections in Iraq or Palestine barely made sense, for "how can you vote under the threat of an American gun?" Saudi voters, in that sense, were freer, even if the municipal councils had very limited powers.[7]

Al-ʿOmar left immediately after the lecture. ʿAbd al-ʿAziz al-Turki came to me and, along with Husam and several other youths, invited me to convert to Islam. The campaign site was almost deserted now. A small group of followers was watching a video featuring a biography of the candidate. One of the candidate's followers, a thin youth with a wiry beard, drove me back to my apartment after the session. In the car, he told me that, on the same evening, three times as many people had gathered around another Islamic candidate, ʿAbd Allah al-Suwaylim.

ʿAbd Allah al-Suwaylim attracted a grassroots mobilization so massive that the Islamic movement in Riyadh eventually lent him its support and dropped al-Turki. ʿAdel told me that al-Suwaylim, who was as grassroots and working-class as al-Turki was elitist and established, never sought to become a council member and had only yielded to popular pressure.

Al-Suwaylim "knows what society wants," ʿAdel said. "He invited his colleagues to come give lectures. There were people sitting everywhere around his small tent, maybe five or six times more than people inside the tent. The street was totally clogged. Nobody could pass through. He had literally made the way narrower for people."

He laughed.

"One of his supporters came and said, 'See the wedding hall, there? It is mine, and I will lend it to you for free until the elections.' And then one of the Quranic circles showed up and they organized a whole summer camp program, from mid-afternoon until late evening. And a restaurant man came and said, 'I will feed all this crowd.' And the Quranic circles also donated food. So it became . . . a people's movement. . . . They had fifty thousand visitors during the campaign. . . . I visited his site; there were three halls: the men's hall, the dining hall, and the women's hall. . . . The lecturer spoke in the women's hall, because it was the last room, inside. It was totally packed. The dining hall was packed. You could only find some places to stand in the men's hall. And outside, people were working like in a beehive."

Al-Suwaylim used all the resources of the Islamic Awakening networks, from Quranic circles in local mosques to Islamic awareness groups in schools and to the summer camps. But 'Adel's father still wanted to vote for al-Turki.

"My dad said, 'I want to vote for al-Turki,' because he knows him personally, and he does not know al-Suwaylim. He told me, 'Al-Turki helped me out in the past, and I know him well, he is a good man. . . . I will help him out too, with my ballot.' But my maternal uncle arrived and he convinced him. He said, 'We have made an agreement, and we expect al-Suwaylim to win, vote for him.'"

As 'Adel had hoped, senior Islamic activists in Riyadh, Dammam, Khobar, Jeddah, and other cities decided, in violation of the law, to create a coalition of candidates in order to help voters make their minds. This coalition material- ized into an electoral list, which was sometimes called the "Golden List" and was broadcast to voters through text messages before Election Day.

"They made a personal agreement before the elections," 'Adel said. "When the government first announced the elections and the electoral rules, a num- ber of them met. . . . They have had regular meetings for a long time; they are friends. They met and decided that they would participate in the elections. Al-Suwaylim did not want to participate until people came to him and asked him to be a candidate, in the name of the principle, 'make the way narrower for them.'"

"They agreed on a certain number" of candidates, 'Adel continued. "There were debates among them, which I think is natural. . . . In order not to violate the law, the decision was made by a number of people who did not run for council member but registered as voters. They considered this a form of charitable action: 'Me, as a citizen, I registered to vote, I am working for the good of society, and I believe that the best candidates are these ones.' Then they broadcast the list. That is what I think happened. This is how the list emerged."

The activist committee made a first selection of candidates, but the list remained open-ended. The final selection took place during the electoral campaign itself, which worked like a primary of sorts. Even though al-Turki was better known nationally, al-Suwaylim was more popular locally, and his network had started organizing from the very beginning of the campaign. Al-Suwaylim was both a local notable and a political entrepreneur. The rumor of his modesty added to his legend: many voters told me that al-Suwaylim first refused to run for office and only reluctantly accepted when local youths begged him to do so. In the end, al-Suwaylim attracted the most votes in the capital.

The electoral agreement bound activists who constantly hung out and were friends. It was borne of intimate interpersonal relationships, thus making it hard to gather information on the electoral coalition—or to repress it. According to 'Adel, the coalition members "hired seven lawyers to prepare for a legal battle," one lawyer for each electoral ward.

"I do not think these lawyers want money," he said. "It is a people's war."

The dense networks created around the Quranic circles, the Islamic awareness groups, and the neighborhood summer camps gave Islamic candidates the support of a structure that predated the electoral mobilization. For the candidates, an important benefit of the agreement was economic: Awakening activists offered the free labor of their followers.

"For instance," 'Adel said, "the guy who won in the fourth ward, al-'Omari, had a Quranic circle working for him for free. But if you go to bin Sa'idan, those who work with him do it for money. Why do they do this? That is quite something: they come every day to work with al-'Omari and pay from their own pocket. He does not ask them to do it. And he could pay; he is quite wealthy, too."

Badr bin Sa'idan, one of the main real estate investors and developers in Riyadh, was running in the fourth ward against 'Abd al-'-Aziz al-'Omari, who was an academic and a real estate developer, too, albeit on a much smaller scale. Bin Sa'idan had planted a luxurious tent on an empty lot surrounded by shiny new developments, directly in the central business district, along King

Fahd Road. He offered lavish feasts every night and displayed palatial luxury in plain sight of commuters rushing up and down the highway. Hasan Al Mahdi, a younger developer, also ran for office. Bin Saʿidan and Al Mahdi were each said to have invested several million riyals in their campaigns.

"And then you have al-Suwaylim, how much did the campaign cost him?" ʿAdel said. "It cost him sixty thousand riyals, as if he was saying, I am running, but I put my trust in God, that is all."

Sheikh Nasir al-ʿOmar was not the only prominent Islamic activist who called for electoral participation. He had garnered support from such clerics as Salman al-ʿOuda, who had also been jailed in the 1990s for his opposition to the Gulf War. But since al-ʿOuda was also under police surveillance, he was forced to cancel two lectures in support of ʿAbd al-ʿAziz al-ʿOmari. The second time he had to cancel, al-ʿOuda spoke to the crowd from his cell phone and apologized, explaining that "forceful circumstances" had prevented him from traveling to Riyadh.

During a campaign meeting in Jeddah, in the campaign tent of Husein al-Bar, a university professor who was running for the Islamic coalition, another prominent Awakening figure, Sheikh ʿAwad al-Garni (not to be confused with Sheikh ʿAʾid al-Garni), explained that elections were a way to implement the religious imperative of consultation.[8] He reminded his audience that religious jurisprudence obliged leaders to consult their fellow citizens and citizens to advise their rulers. Public consultation and advising the ruler were not activities you could choose to do only when circumstances were favorable, even though you had to do so gently, not forcefully. They were neither rights nor privileges, but something you *had to* engage in, even and especially when it was hard to do so.[9]

"In public affairs," al-Garni said, "consultation is compulsory: nobody can claim they can do without it. And through elections, we consult each other. This is what is also called opinion, and it is a fundamental principle of Islamic legality. . . . One can also implement the principle of consultation through elections, to give all force to Islamic legality. . . . By following the principle of commanding virtue and combatting vice, the community of believers will entrust its elected officials with the realization of its ambitions and hopes. . . . Through the vote, society exercises its right to command virtue and combat vice."

Like Sheikh ʿAbd al-Muhsin al-ʿObeikan in 1989, ʿAwad al-Garni did not think that the Quranic project to command virtue and combat vice should be a state monopoly or the mission of an intimidating police force. Unlike al-ʿObeikan, however, he thought that commanding virtue was the concern of all citizens, not of a small vanguard of activists. In his view, decentralized consultation was preferable to either state or Awakening centralism. ʿAwad al-Garni reinterpreted the idea of commanding virtue and combatting vice into an argument on the centrality of elections in Islam.

"In Islam's two first battles, at Badr in 624 CE and ʾUhud in 625 CE, the Prophet did not impose his choice on Muslims, but had them vote," he said. "Even at the heart of the battle, the prophet preferred voting over authority.... Religion allows for resistance against whoever wants to make decisions on our behalf. Religion allows us to keep our values alive."

"I am confused," somebody said in a loud voice after the lecture ended. "Why is it that elections, which not so long ago were considered an abomination, became all of a sudden a way to engage in consultation?"[10]

"You have to ask those who criminalized the elections, not those who for years now have advocated for reforms," the sheikh responded, nonplussed.

"Are municipal elections the outcome of U.S. pressures?" the man asked.

"The sheikhs are with you against U.S. pressures," al-Garni immediately replied, "because nothing good can come from over there. Our reform must be endogenous."

"The sheikhs should remain in mosques and not get involved in elections," the man continued.

"Render unto Caesar the things that are Caesar's, and unto God the things that are God's? This is the very principle of secularism," the sheikh replied, hoping to close the debate. He had amply demonstrated that religion should enhance public freedoms, not limit them.

"This lecture should be published somewhere," somebody else said. The candidate then suspended the session and ʿAwad al-Garni left the tent behind him.

The candidates of the Islamic Awakening were slowly garnering support, and their growing influence did not remain unnoticed. On February 4, 2005, halfway through the electoral campaign, the capital's daily newspaper announced that "some candidates had made secret agreements to support those who were closer to victory."[11] On the same day, the mayor of Riyadh, Prince 'Abd al-'Aziz al-Migrin, declared that any electoral promises that went beyond the advisory powers of the municipal councils would be punished. He instructed "candidates to respect the law" and threatened those who promised the moon by saying, "punishment could go as far as revoking candidacies."[12] The gloves were off.

On February 8, 2005 at 8:16 am, 'Adel received the following text message:

The sheikhs recommend the election in the following wards of:

1. 'Abd Allah al-Suwaylim;
2. Sulayman al-Rushudi;
3. Tariq al-Qasabi;
4. 'Abd al-'Aziz al-'Omari;
5. 'Omar Ba Sudan;
6. Ibrahim al-Qu'ayyid;
7. Misfir al-Bawardi

(so votes do not scatter). Forwarding is a good deed.

The seven candidates of the Awakening won the election by a large margin: the victors gathered on average 11,200 more votes than the candidates who came in second (the Islamic candidates winning an average 27.7% of the votes while the runners-up averaged 7.8%). This was an Islamic Awakening landslide.[13] The electoral list had played its role. Votes had not scattered.

A few hours after he received the list, 'Adel got another list from a certain Abu Hudhayfa. 'Adel knew of only one Abu Hudhayfa: the prophet's companion who had died in 633 CE in the battle of Yamama, northwest of present-day Riyadh. Abu Hudhayfa's list was identical to the Islamic list except for one name: Badr bin Sa'idan had replaced 'Abd al-'Aziz al-'Omari in the fourth ward. The real estate mogul, not particularly known for his religious inclinations, had probably thought he might be able to try and mystify voters into electing him.

During the Dammam and Jeddah elections, in March and April 2005, a variety of electoral lists were also "recommended by the sheikhs." In Jeddah, for instance, one candidate counted six different lists a few days before the vote: a list published by the daily *al-Watan*; a list published on the online forum *al-Sahat* under the title "Who do we vote for in Jeddah"; a list published by the website saudielections.com; the actual Islamic list; and two lists that were also published on *al-Sahat* and attacked the Islamic list. Lists had become popular, and Islamic activists had to find some way of authenticating their list, distinguishing it from the countless others that were also "recommended by the sheikhs." They dubbed their list "the Golden List" (as mentioned above) and published the names of "their" sheikhs to show that these were indeed Islamic Awakening leaders, some of whom had become famous in the 1980s and had been imprisoned in the 1990s.

Jeddah's Golden List provoked the ire of the defeated candidates. Pundits wrote about it as if it were a smoking gun: here was proof that Islamic activists had violated the electoral code.[14] Jeddah Golden List candidate ʿAbd al-Rahman Yamani responded to the accusations. He explained that recommendations were not evidence of an electoral coalition and that sheikhs were free to give advice to their fellow citizens. He also pointed out that pundits had singled out the Golden List for attack while leaving the other lists alone. This to him was evidence of collusion *against* the elected council members and a clear violation of the electoral code.[15]

On April 24, 2005, after the victory of the Golden List in Jeddah, a hundred defeated candidates lodged a complaint with the National Electoral Committee against the sheikhs who had recommended the list. The same candidates also complained to the Electoral Grievance Committee that the voting rolls had been sold to the Islamic coalition. They claimed that a disc containing the names and phone numbers of Jeddah's fifty-two thousand voters had been sold for sixty thousand riyals (fifteen thousand dollars).[16]

What the Jeddah plaintiffs seemed to find intolerable was that Islamic activists had not only organized but also politicized information flows. Text messages had created certainty about whom to elect in a political market that was crowded, tight, and above all confusing. Islamic activists were giving better and more reliable political advice than government officials. They repoliticized an election that had been depoliticized by state institutions.

"I wanted to do like one of my friends," ʿAdel said. "He would go from tent to tent, find the campaign manager, and tell him, 'Do you want to buy my vote? Do you know somebody who would buy it? I want to sell my ballot.' So before the list came out, I was thinking, by God, what is the matter with me selling my vote? At least let the votes scatter; a Bedouin will buy my ballot; I know some of them and they do not have any problem with that. By selling my ballot, I make some profit, and so does the Bedouin. But after the list came out, things changed. You no longer worked for money. . . . The list was more valuable than money."

The Islamic activists had politicized the vote by making it ideological, thus providing an alternative to the commodification of votes. Individual choices could be sold and bought; collective action could not. By giving clear indications for each of the seven electoral wards, the list also responded to the complexity of the system and solved the voters' potential confusion.

Voters had had a hard time locating the right candidates, these "good men" who were "men of religion." By drastically limiting the political offering, from 645 candidates in Riyadh down to 7, the Islamic list made voting easier: it was the Islamic Awakening against everybody else—liberals, businessmen, real estate investors, Bedouins, and princes—society against the state; religion against secularism; principles against opportunism.

The electoral activism of the Muslim Brothers, who won the elections in Riyadh, was communicated to the Salafis, who had initially been opposed to the idea of electoral participation. Then, in Dammam and the rest of the Eastern Province, a month after the Riyadh elections, Salafi candidates imitated the tactics of the Muslim Brothers. Other groups followed suit. Even the most secularist and conservative groups were compelled to organize voters and violate the code in order to find their place in an electoral market whose functioning had been redefined by the Islamic activists. Salafi candidates won the elections in Dammam and Khobar,[17] while Shi'a activists won a majority of seats in Qatif and Hofuf. The Salafi victory near the oil fields was all the more striking because the Eastern Province was seen as a bastion of the Muslim Brothers. Riyadh, which was supposed to be a Salafi stronghold, meanwhile, had seen a victory by the Muslim Brothers. What was at stake was not popular representation and indirect action; it was direct, illegal, subterranean action. A month after the Eastern Province elections, meanwhile, the Salafis and Muslim Brothers reached a compromise in Jeddah, where the municipal elections were won by a common list.

A few days after the results of the election were proclaimed in Riyadh, the interior minister, Prince Nayef, declared that "we are all Islamists and Muslims in this country."[18] This remark was ambiguous. Did the interior minister mean to undermine the Islamic mobilization? Or did he mean to send a positive signal to the Islamic coalition by telling them that he would continue to act as their interlocutor in government circles? Prince Nayef had both repressed Islamic activists after the Gulf War and negotiated their liberation in the late 1990s; in the process, he had built widespread networks in the Muslim Brotherhood and the Salafi movement. Some of my interlocutors in the Muslim Brotherhood thought that the royal family had instituted the "one man, seven votes" rule precisely in order to favor the Islamic Awakening and to better co-opt activists into government circles.

But the royal family seemed wary of the Islamic victory, and Prince Nayef's enthusiasm was either an exception or, more probably, a way to undermine the Islamic Awakening. The first public meeting of the Riyadh municipal council took place in June, 2006, a full year and a half after the vote. The meeting was organized at Prince Sultan University, a private institution owned by the royal family, rather than at the municipality. A few students were lingering in the hallways, near a buffet offering finger food and fruit juices, under the surveillance of private security guards. I walked into the main amphitheater, which was lined with wreaths, making the space look like a funeral parlor. Behind and above the flowers, the fourteen council members were already seated when I entered.

The contrast between appointed and elected council members was striking. The appointed members were mid-level bureaucrats who spoke slowly, sternly, and officially. The elected councilors were more incisive and political. One of them analyzed the municipal budget, explaining that measured per capita, it had dwindled over the previous ten years. He proposed to split the municipal budget from the budget of the Ministry of Municipal and Rural Affairs, an idea that broke with several decades of centralization. Another elected member talked about reforming the municipal administration.

After the council members' introductions, people in the audience asked about municipal services, from road maintenance through business licenses to pollution, sewers, and taxes. The appointed members pointed to the limited prerogatives of the council; the elected councilors tried to push back, but the appointed president shut them down. He explained that taxes, sewers, and pollution were not public matters: these were state decisions. A journalist from "a lousy area in the east of Riyadh" complained about poverty and crumbling infrastructure and contrasted the needs of the residents with the appearance of the council members, who wore official cloaks, were surrounded by luxury, and would not touch their fellow citizens with a ten-foot pole.

"What an insolent guy," two religious activists grumbled next to me.

The conversation took a sharp turn: since municipal services were apparently off-limits, the people in attendance, all male and mostly middle-aged, started asking about how to better control public places and young people. Some demanded the creation of more gated communities and asked that cafés be closed or tightly regulated. 'Abd Allah al-Suwaylim, the elected council member from the first ward, blamed boys who harassed girls and girls who "offered themselves to boys," pointing to the dangers of gender mixing in public spaces. He asked people to seek fatwas against gender mixing in public and to ask the municipal council to implement them. Municipal politics was out; moral repression was in.

This may also be what Prince Nayef had meant by saying "We are all Islamists in this country." By blocking public decision-making about such crucial matters as urban infrastructure, the state elites wished to lock the Islamic Awakening into a more generally conservative mood that favored gender segregation, youth control, and suburban isolationism. Suburbia, with its suspicious fathers and its moral surveillance, was not an easy place to organize, and young Islamic activists mobilizing in suburban mosques and schools were up against powerful adversaries.

PART III

AWARENESS GROUPS AND SUMMER CAMPS

■ ■ ■ ■ ■

Chapter 11 **THE HARRY POTTER DISSENT**

"ONE DAY, A GUY BROUGHT A CARTLOAD OF BOOKS AND GAVE them to the students, including two volumes of *Harry Potter*."

Talal, a good-looking twelfth grader with an air of confidence about him, was speaking in a clear, fast voice.

"Salman was next to me. I gave them to him. He started reading. He read thirty pages during class; he could not put the book down. The boy just loved it. He continued reading, went to the bookstore, bought volumes 1, 2, 3 . . . everything. And he started lending them to others. Everybody was reading *Harry Potter* and talking about it. People started using coded language to talk about it. Harry Potter had become famous."

Thamir, the religion teacher to whom Sheikh 'Abd al-Ilah had introduced me, had created a successful Islamic awareness group in his high school. Talal was one of his students and helped him manage the group. Talal was the head of a family within the group, a "pioneer"[1] in the Muslim Brother lingo. Husein and Sa'ud ran the group's other families. Salman, another twelfth grader, was the head of the group's cultural committee. He was also their organic intellectual and wrote for the small magazine that the Islamic awareness group published. The six of us were chatting and sipping Vimto in the men's sitting room of Thamir's parents' house, my tape recorder on.

When I started conducting fieldwork with this Islamic group, Talal had functioned as my ally and intermediary. Well-spoken and fast-thinking, he was the only student in the group who had traveled abroad, in particular to Syria and Jordan. He played with his multiple identities: Bedouin while talking to his peers; intellectual while talking to Thamir; wily, seasoned traveler with me. His versatility seemed to irritate the other students, who tended to be defensive during our recorded interviews. When the Harry Potter story came up, Talal took the lead, as usual.

"Some students, a small group, thought that, since there was magic in the book, and they were not too comfortable with novels in general—they thought novels were a waste of time, that they were tackling corrupt subjects—so some students asked religious sheikhs: are we allowed to read *Harry Potter* or any other novels? And the sheikhs—there were two or three of them—said: 'No.' So students started talking about it, saying that it was a sin, that the sheikhs had said so. . . . So we had students who were distributing the book, and others who were saying that it was a sin to read it."

The students who reached out to the religious sheikhs belonged both to the high school Islamic awareness group and to the local mosque's Quran memorization circle. The response they obtained from the sheikhs was a clear condemnation of the act of reading *Harry Potter* as un-Islamic, because the novel proclaimed a belief in magic.[2] The split, which students soon dubbed the "Harry Potter Dissent,"[3] was evidence of the rift between Thamir's Islamic awareness group, which was affiliated with the Muslim Brotherhood, and the mosque's circle, which was more Salafi.

"We started debating the topic in front of the youth," Talal said. "The younger students read [*Harry Potter*], and we debated with those older students who are against it and say it is a sin. And we were in shock because of their state of mind, those who are against reading. So we decided to have a meeting and we decided that people should be able to read, that it was normal, that we did not have anything to say about it, that reading [*Harry Potter*] was simply controversial and not a sin. And that, if the youth brought up a controversial topic, it fell upon those leading the awareness group to debate said topic. But for everybody to debate it like that would put an end to the dignity of the organization."

For Talal, some issues were not legal, then, but simply controversial. Reading *Harry Potter*, even though magic was religiously prohibited, was therefore not a sin, because reading the book was distinct from believing in magic or practicing it. A sin had to be prevented or stopped by fellow believers; a controversial topic, in contrast, was open for discussion and left to personal appreciation. But Talal also recognized that, in a centralized organization, some debates should not be public but had to be held in private, among the leadership. The rank and file would have to abide by any decision the leaders made, however debatable it might still seem to them. In Talal's words, nothing less than "the dignity of the organization" was at stake.

"Among the ambiguities of the story," Thamir said, "was that the Quranic circles to which some of our youth belonged got the impression that we read novels, *Harry Potter* and Agatha Christie. And they were surprised: it was something new to them, something not natural. And some of them started to tell others not to read."

"Of course, there is also a very strong repression at home," said Husein, the shiest member of the group. " 'Do not read non-Arabs.'[4] That was very strong in our family."

"Dogs," Talal shouted.

"That is, 'Do not read the dogs'," Husein said.

"Unfortunately, they say that kind of stuff at home," Thamir said.

"Yes," Husein said. "Even today, they still come to me very often and tell me, 'Those books written by non-Arabs, out of the house.' But I refuse, and I manage."

"The Quranic circles started a controversy," Thamir said. "And the problem is that it set in motion our members, and also the circles to which they belonged, all these others, whole groups. . . . So we examined the case and we said: those who are training themselves to read more can read [anything they want], but there should not be any public debate about their readings."

No debate with the enemies of debate: core members decided that some conversations should happen only between authorized individuals. By banning public debate, the Islamic awareness group risked appearing as authoritarian as the mosque's Quranic circle or the nationalist fathers who had banned non-Arab books from their houses. But its leaders did not want their projects to be hijacked by the Salafis. Self-improvement had to be protected, even through top-down means: reading was a form of training, something as important for young activists as religious expertise or physical fitness.

"In general, novels with no depravity or pornography teach us something," Talal said. "For instance, you will read two pages of a biography or of an academic book, and find it boring. As for a novel, the plot takes you in and, after a while, you realize you have just read four hundred pages. Reading becomes a sort of addiction. And once you have gotten used to reading, you can read books that are not novels. Anyway, we talked to other sheikhs, and most of them did not see any objection."

"Actually, *before we went to the sheikhs*, we met to discuss and decided that we would keep reading, not ban reading," their professor said. "And we agreed to say that we would heed the sheikhs' advice, but not consider it mandatory, if one of them said that reading novels was a sin. Of course, just to be sure, we talked to several sheikhs, and they said there was no problem. For novels in general, and for *Harry Potter* or Agatha Christie in particular."

"Sheikh Salman al-'Ouda usually says in his Friday program, 'This week, I read a number of novels,' " Talal said. "Because he believes that most novels are products of a civilization, of a wisdom, of the Indian or Chinese civilization for instance. He says that most novels are products of a culture, and that, by reading, you learn to know this culture.[5] And I am really surprised that so many people are afraid to read. . . . Everything can be read."

Consulting sheikhs who approved of novels was a way to respond to the mosque circle. The school's awareness group showed that this was indeed a controversial topic, which religious interpretation could not settle but could only help to explore further. Thamir and his students wanted to extract the reading of novels (and of *Harry Potter*) from the religious sphere.

"Some youths started participating in the *Harry Potter* forum in Arabic," Thamir said. He pointed to the head of the cultural committee, a thin youth with large eyes and a scruffy goatee. "There are four or five of them, and Salman is their leader. . . . He is their wizard; he taught them magic . . . and the phenomenon grew. Our awareness group is big, we have about sixty students, and one third of them started to read, even though their reading habits were initially weak."

The professor pointed to Talal: "This is the leader of the Agatha Christie clan. We have two schools of thought here, you see."

"Yeah, but my public relations are weak," Talal said.

The professor then pointed to Sa'ud, a lanky teenager who had been grumbling audible "what-the-fuck"s in the back as we were discussing the group's activities. It was not clear whether his anger was directed at me, at Talal, or at the interview situation as a whole.

"And Saʿud is the leader of the Hitler clan. We have a group of five or six who love to read about dictators. They read about Hitler, Stalin, Saddam Husein, all the bloody types. We have not found a book on Napoleon yet. . . . But *Mein Kampf*, most of them read it because it is the book you find everywhere. We have some youths who, even though they believe in democracy and everything, have that odd liking for dictators. . . . It is really bizarre. Even the most democratic students, I do not know why they like them."

"Our Islamic history lacks powerful figures," Saʿud said, "and these are people who succeeded."

"Maybe because somebody like Saddam Husein challenged America," Talal said. "It is because of the state of weakness that we experience in the Arab world. . . . This gives us a way out. Maybe the grass is greener on the other side. . . . If we had lived under him, we would hate him with a passion. . . . Even those who watch anime always hope that the villain will not be caught. . . . By God, villains are more impressive, and we always support them. Yes, we support evil with all our forces."

Everybody laughed. Talal was playing on the very categories (good and evil) that the United States and Al Saʿud had overused since the beginning of the War on Terror—categories that were foundational to the idea of cities on a hill that both the U.S. and the Saudi elites had claimed to establish. By embracing the stigma, he and Saʿud were poking fun at Western dichotomies and symbolic and military violence.

Saʿud had remained silent during most of the interview. When he did open his mouth, he tended to overplay his role as a "radical," as Salman called him another day. He himself admitted to being a "very strange" type for his classmates: this former joyrider came from a less privileged social class, one in which parents were either disinterested in their children or too busy to keep an eye on them.

At the end of our conversation, I tried to understand the amount of symbolic violence that the most vulnerable Riyadh youth were subjected to. The celebration of dictators among members of a movement that had been crushed by dictatorships in Egypt, Syria, and Iraq could only be understood by looking at overall political and social violence. These young Muslim Brothers were led to glorify individual success in a world where leadership positions seemed reserved to those who were strong, cruel, and virile.

"Anybody who distinguishes himself" and breaks rank "will be excluded, crushed," the professor said. "The creation of al-Qaʻeda is evidence of this."

To him the militant group had been formed by people who could not express their excellence anywhere but underground. Dictators, in a way, were successful rebels—hence the activists' interest in their biographies. To be crushed, or to crush others: this was the painful alternative that young activists faced at all stages of their mobilization. This political battle started in school and continued in the neighborhood.

Chapter 12 **ALL STREETS ARE JOYRIDING STREETS**

THAMIR WAS RUNNING HIS WELL-ATTENDED ISLAMIC AWARENESS group in the Tumiya neighborhood, on the outskirts of Riyadh. He commuted by car every day from an upper-middle-class suburb, where he lived in his parents' home. Tumiya had the reputation of being difficult. Recently settled by rural migrants—it was "95% Bedouin," Thamir told me—the neighborhood was seen by members of the sedentary middle class as a "drug den" and a "dangerous suburb." Not all suburbs were middle class.

Over the years I often roamed Tumiya onboard more or less decrepit U.S. gas guzzlers, drinking soda and chatting with a few friends I had met there. In Tumiya, "all the streets are joyriding streets," 'Ali, a small-time joyrider and drug addict told me. If most streetlamps seemed dead at night, it was because "too many cars hit them" while drifting, he added. The neighborhood was a shantytown until the 1980s. In some areas, wooden shacks and dismantled trucks were still used as makeshift stores. Elsewhere, small villas and low apartment buildings were set along a grid of perpendicular streets and avenues. Puddles of raw sewage rotted in the streets, garbage was strewn along the avenues, many houses were in disrepair, and screeching tires could be heard at all hours of the night.

Employed residents of Tumiya tended to work for the National Guard, the police, or private security companies, earning salaries ranging from the equivalent of around US$500 (in the private sector) to US$1,500 (in the public sector). Many youths embraced a military or police career right after high school, with the National Guard and the police being the most desirable choices. After four months of training, my joyrider friend told me, recruits were admitted, without an entry exam, into an easy job with a fixed income and a civil servant status. They could buy a car on credit and get married; they would often continue living in a room of the family home and only buy an apartment much later. Young women got married earlier; they lived secluded lives, first in their parents' home and then with their in-laws.

Unemployment and marriage kept Tumiya youth close to home. Marriage cost less than elsewhere in Riyadh: a typical dowry in the late 2000s was around the equivalent of ten thousand dollars, with the celebration costing half that sum. The groom would receive five thousand dollars from the state to cover marriage expenses and his extended family and friends would lend him the rest. Guests would bring somewhere between fifty and a hundred and fifty dollars each on the wedding day; the sums would be carefully registered in a notebook and the groom would have to reimburse his guests, either on their own wedding day or at the wedding of one of their close relatives. Not doing so would mean exposing oneself to a slow but certain social death.

Regular wages had allowed Saudi residents of Tumiya to build cement-and-concrete villas, buy apartments, and invest in small businesses. Yet many of Tumiya's residents, including Talal's family, were stateless persons, or *bidun*, an Arabic word meaning "deprived of" and used as shorthand for the expression "deprived of nationality." Even though the *bidun* were often Bedouin, the two terms are distinct: the word for Bedouin in Arabic is *badu*, meaning "nomads" (and the origin of the English word "Bedouin"). The stateless spoke Arabic with a Saudi accent and dressed like Saudis. They were given a specific "Arab migrant" ID that placed them slightly above the rest of the country's labor migrants. They could not buy property or invest in businesses, but they did not need a visa or a sponsor to work. These stateless persons had been overlooked by the state when it started granting Saudi citizenship, often because they lived far from administrative centers or were not aware of the citizenship-granting process. Although acquiring Saudi citizenship was theoretically possible, it proved more and more difficult.[1]

To obtain a Saudi passport, stateless people often claimed to be the son or daughter of a citizen. Until recently, they had needed only two witnesses to establish filiation; now the state required an official birth certificate. In addition, the applicant had to obtain a "declaration of recognition" from their *mu'arrif*, a civil servant on the state payroll who represented the tribe at the central administration. Corruption was endemic in these processes. The *mu'arrif* could be bought off, as could civil servants. People I spoke to in Tumiya estimated that it cost the equivalent of around ten thousand dollars for a *bidun* to acquire Saudi citizenship, bribes included.

Statelessness forced many Tumiya residents into precarious existences. The stateless often worked menial, ill-paid jobs and had to seek aid from their extended families. Citizens were significantly better off, but the lack of economic opportunities outside of the security forces was an issue. The cultural gap separating Tumiya from middle-class neighborhoods showed the structural violence its residents faced. One day, I introduced 'Ali the joyrider to a friend who was also Bedouin but who belonged to the middle class and went to college. 'Ali exhibited distinctly effeminate behavior while casually talking about his amorous prowess, including conquests of other young men. 'Ali was attractive, but the blackened stumps in his mouth shouted his lack of access to healthcare and his inadequate diet. After we left Tumiya, my middle-class friend turned to me in anger.

"I have rarely met anybody that gross in my whole life," he said. "Be really careful: he can be dangerous. If he carries drugs and if the police stop you . . . this guy is finished."

The youth of Tumiya responded to structural oppression in various ways. Even though the area was inhabited by cops and National Guards, it was known among middle-class residents for its unruliness.

"Look there," 'Ali said one day as we drove by, "that is the police station. By God, after they installed it, the day before the inauguration by the governor of Riyadh, kids broke in to steal A/C units and computers. Can you imagine? The governor comes, the station is empty."

Local youth also wrote graffiti on the walls of the police station, proclaiming in large letters: "We are the sons of Tumiya, nobody governs us."[2] Thamir's students told me how police patrols driving through the neighborhood were often pelted with stones or eggs.

When local youths were arrested, their mates would try all possible tricks to free them from the back of the police cruiser. When the police knocked on a door looking for a youth, the elder of the household would often come out and talk down to the police, sometimes hurling insults at them. Bedouin etiquette demanded that elders be respected, especially when they had a big mouth and were defending the honor of their house. Sometimes the police had to require tribal authorities to convince an elder to let them search a house.

A bank shut down after joyriders crashed into it; cafés were often invaded by droves of kids who would watch TV there without buying anything and break tables and chairs; many businesses went bankrupt. On the nearby freeway, water trucks often zoomed by at breakneck speed, bringing water to the neighborhood (there was no running water) or taking sewage away (there was no sewer system). Five of Salman's friends had died in car accidents on this stretch of highway. Truckers driving too fast were sometimes chased by local youths who would force them to stop and, sometimes, beat them up.

The walls of schools and public buildings were covered in graffiti spelling out lust, local pride, and a passion for joyriding. "I love you, Stinky"; "Falluja hood"; "I fuck Abu Muhammad"; "You crazy, throw this iron, your love will grow."[3] (Iron was a metonym for a car, and "throwing the iron," in joyriding lingo, meant joyriding or drifting.) "*Bidun*" was written on many walls. School walls became a site of competition among various graffiti artists as well as between them and the state. After one of the schools had had all the graffiti washed off and had been repainted, somebody wrote "Congratulations on the new paint" in large, colorful letters.[4]

Young Islamic activists also added their voice to the chorus, writing graffiti that said, for instance, "Pray before they pray at your funerals" or "Say good things and persevere."[5] Some graffiti showed elaborate designs and an attention to classical Arabic calligraphy. Salman told me that reform-school inmates had to learn a craft during detention and often chose calligraphy. To him there was a direct link between youth incarceration and street art: the more former inmates there were in a given area, the more graffiti one found on its walls.

Tumiya residents described their neighborhood as a microcosm of Riyadh, with a commercial street; primary, middle, and high schools; and even a small compound nearby that was inhabited by U.S. employees and defense contractors.

"But these are good Americans," 'Ali said. "When we joyride, they crowd up on the sidewalk, here, to cheer us on, and nobody ever says anything against them. It is probably the only compound in Riyadh that has not been bombed."

"Because you guys scare the shit out of al-Qaʻeda," said one of his friends.

Further away, between villas and apartment blocks, there were rest houses. Some were said to be owned by princes; one of them was rented by the fire brigade.

"You see these two lights outside?" 'Ali said, pointing to a rest house. "If they are on, it means the firemen are there, no joyriding tonight. If they are off, you can go."

Tumiya was a village. Like many of Riyadh's neighborhoods, it had a distinct identity, and its residents divided the world into two spheres: inside of Tumiya, and outside of Tumiya.

"I am outside of Tumiya," 'Ali would say on the phone to escape family duties, even when he was still roaming its streets. Being "outside of Tumiya" meant being untouchable, having set off for the wider world, away from the neighborhood's issues.

Many interlocutors told me how, in this deteriorated environment, their fathers had either abdicated their authority or become domestic tyrants who tried to keep their children away from the streets.

"My dad was a controller," Talal said. "He wanted us to walk straight. . . . One day, I started showing that I had had enough; I started getting angry. . . . Because the one who gets angry, they see him as a pain in the ass, and they start negotiating with him. . . . I was a real pain in the ass."

Everybody laughed.

"I started a crisis at home. I started to whack everybody, even the young ones."

Talal's predicament was light compared to that of children who were slapped, bitten, pinched, beaten, and kicked, terrorized by fathers or brothers armed with sticks, metal bars, knives, and guns.[6] "Kids need to be tamed" and "women deserve the red eye," the eye of anger: these were some fathers' mottos, and neither of those boded well for either children or wives.[7] No wonder boys wanted to flee into the street to escape domestic violence. (Girls did not have this option.)

"Your life is compartmentalized," Salman said. "There are very few outings. In most houses—I mean, I speak about our house here, really—your elder brother has full authority over you and controls you; you cannot do anything. That is, if the father is not there. . . . Before I turned six, I was home most of the time. We would never go out, except to visit relatives."

"Wait," Thamir said. "But there are always kids in the streets around here."

"Not in our family. . . . I told you, I am just talking about our family. We never go out. And even if the youngest one gets out and stays by the door, just like that, he gets slapped and yelled at. And he gets back inside. . . . They do not want to mingle with people from outside. Because in our neighborhood, there are . . . "

He hesitated to finish his sentence.

" . . . Bad things . . . ," Thamir whispered.

"Because in our neighborhood," Salman said, "there are people who smoke and I do not know what else."

When "people from outside" the house dealt alcohol and drugs or became embroiled in street fights and joyriding, no wonder fathers locked up their kids at home. Salman's siblings were expected to remain home and quietly work toward their social advancement.

"They encourage us to study," Salman said. "For instance, my dad comes with three books in hand and gives money to whoever will read them."

Keeping kids at home could be a sign of social prestige, or morality, or a simple precaution; it could also be undergirded by patriarchal violence. But other families in Tumiya were less strict when it came to the mobility of their (male) children, whether because the father was absent or because he did not see the street as a problem.

"In my family," Saʿud said, "it is considered normal: kids can go outside, it is not a problem. My elder brother knows the neighborhood, the streets, the stores. And the little ones could come and go; it was normal. . . . But I was not with them. I would stay home. I did not like the streets, honestly. . . . My parents allowed me to go out, but I did not like it. . . . Do you see the fights, the scraps that happen outside?"

The other students laughed.

"Me, I loved cats."

He sniggered.

"Yeah, even that one time, he slaughtered one," Salman said.

"Its mother, I do not know why, was yelling at me, somehow."

They all laughed.

"She had children. So, one time, when she was away, I grabbed one and I cut it into pieces."

"That is weird," Salman said. "Saʿud is not normal."

Tumiya youth lived in a violent environment. They were the victims of social and symbolic violence and the authors of some forms of violence, too. They suffered and inflicted suffering in turn. This multifaceted violence, toward children and animals, people and things, was precisely one of the issues that Thamir was trying to tackle through his local activism in the high school awareness group.

Chapter 13 **MUSLIM BROTHERS AND SALAFIS**

I FELT STRANGELY CONNECTED TO THAMIR, AND NOT ONLY because we were roughly the same age. I had taught philosophy in a few high schools north of Paris and we bonded over our experiences, mulling over what went wrong in the Saudi outer suburbs and the French banlieues. Thamir had joined an Islamic awareness group in the early 1990s, when he was fifteen. His high school group had about forty students and was linked to the Saudi Muslim Brothers.

"I joined because, in my first year of high school, a teacher came to class and said, 'We have activities, we do theater, and every other week we go out to play soccer.' I worshipped soccer and I did not know where to play, so I talked to others and we joined."

"Ideas do not play a role" in the decisions made by the young people joining Islamic groups, he said: leisure, fun, and sports were more important. Yet it was because of their diverging ideas that various Islamic movements held different positions toward fun and sports. The Muslim Brothers considered them great ways to attract students so that they could then preach to them. Until the Gulf War, they were the group that the most students joined, because their excursions "were all about hymns, night games, they were super fun." The Salafis proposed fewer activities. They banned theater, songs, and soccer, and only taught religion; it was more important to them to keep to their stricter ideals than to try to win over new recruits with nonreligious activities.

Thamir enjoyed the cultural competitions and training in public speaking that his awareness group offered. Islamic activists trained students to give seemingly improvised speeches after prayers.[1] After the communal prayer, one student would stand and admonish his fellow believers to behave more modestly, to care for social and religious causes, or to be better informed about domestic and international politics. Speeches after prayers were used by activists in a context of censorship and repression.

After the Iraqi army invaded Kuwait in 1990, tens of thousands of Kuwaitis took refuge in Riyadh and were housed in schools, including Thamir's high school. His awareness group organized housing, food, daycare, schooling, and even psychological support for the refugees. Thamir experienced Islamic solidarity firsthand. The Gulf War also changed the balance of power between the Salafis and the Muslim Brothers. The Salafis were at once more political and more rigorously religious. Their postwar fame, acquired through sparring with the government on topics pertaining to national reform, made the Muslim Brothers appear sheepish in comparison, as if they had made too many compromises with the revealed text and with their social and political context.

One sign of this change was that Thamir, along with dozens of others, moved away from the Muslim Brotherhood and closer to Salafism after the war. Thamir told me that a whole faction "originated in the Muslim Brothers but split in the early 1990s, and their ideas became distinct from the Brothers' projects."

The scission happened during the protest movement of the early 1990s, as Muslim Brothers witnessed the success of the more Salafi-identified activists Safar al-Hawali, Salman al-'Ouda, and Nasir al-'Omar. Prominent Muslim Brothers "thought the Brotherhood was outdated, that its thoughts were no longer suited to our present reality, to the dynamism of Saudi society and the kind of activism you found in the early 1990s," Thamir said. They "saw that Salafi sheikhs, people they were close to, like Safar al-Hawali, Nasir al-'Omar, and Salman al-'Ouda, played a role of guidance and attracted young people, while they themselves were in the basement of society, played no role, had no plan or strategic ideas.... They wanted to get out, to get away from that direction."

The scission from the Muslim Brotherhood produced what Thamir called "an activist group with Salafi ideas." The new group's members were interested in "organizing legal science circles and reading books about faith ... " and were "uninterested in the Muslim Brothers, whom they sometimes criticized. . . .

After the Gulf War, there was fear of the Brothers" in government circles, "fear of the Islamic movement, of Hassan al-Turabi, Rashed Ghannouchi, even of the Egyptian Muslim Brothers. The royals were not happy, and we heard that they convened the elite of the Muslim Brotherhood and posed certain conditions, including: no revolt against the line of the state and the Wahhabi spiritual leadership. As if a deal had been made between the political elite and the Brotherhoods."

Embracing Salafism was thus a way to avoid repression. Leaving the Muslim Brotherhood behind meant avoiding being taken for a political activist, showing formal respect for the state's brand of religiosity, which was closer to Salafism than to the Muslim Brotherhood. Yet embracing Salafism, with its overtones of quietism and silent self-improvement, also meant, paradoxically, being more politically active and moving closer to a protest movement that, led by such activists as the sheikhs Safar al-Hawali and Salman al-'Ouda, was making international headlines.[2] Wittingly or not, the Salafis capitalized on the recent protests and through them were able to attract more young people.

This Salafization of the Muslim Brotherhood also happened at a local level.[3] In the suburbs of Riyadh, schools and mosques often competed against one another, and different groups took advantage of the distinct opportunities presented by each of the institutions. Before the war, Thamir's high school, for instance, saw a profusion of groups. In 1990, "there were ten activist groups of all persuasions at the school: Salafis, the Najdi Muslim Brothers, the Hijazi Muslim Brothers, the Brothers of Zubayr.... The activities were super powerful and well-funded. Every teacher could start a group and do whatever he wanted.... There was a competition between the teachers to attract students."

This state of affairs changed when Islamic activists supported reform initiatives in 1991–1992. "It was no longer permitted to take students out for excursions, except if you had the authorization of the Supervision Center," an administrative tool controlling activities within the Ministry of Education. Funding was cut, and school principals started fighting Islamic activities. School activities "had become a shadow of themselves."

As a result, student activities migrated toward the mosques. Not only did the mosques favor the Salafis because of their more literal bent, but the Salafi activists were also already familiar with the mosques, where they had organized Quranic groups and protests. The change was spectacular: before the move, "the mosque was not important to us," Thamir said. "We would go there only two days a week, for the sundown prayer. After that, group activities were at the mosque every day, around the afternoon prayer."

The institution of the mosque library, which had been popularized by Ju-hayman al-ʿOtaybi's followers, was strengthened by repression.

"In the period leading to the split from the Muslim Brotherhood, most of our activities were lessons with sheikhs," Thamir said. "Sheikhs would come to our mosque, where we had a place we called the 'mosque library.' These were local sheikhs, not people who were well-known. They . . . were just average Salafis. After that, we would attend Sheikh Nasir al-ʿOmar's Sunday lessons."

Yet with his lectures against "Westernization, the cultural assault, and satellite TV . . . Nasir al-ʿOmar did not quench my thirst," Thamir added. "There was a lesson by Sheikh bin Baz at the same time. That is where I was going, alone. And I remember a dispute with my supervisor, who asked me, 'Why do you not come with us?' And I told him, 'Bin Baz is better.' And he said, 'Yes, but Sheikh al-ʿOmar has a better analysis, he has a vision of social reality.' But I was not convinced. . . . Bin Baz's audience was a small fraction of al-ʿOmar's audience. The Awakening youth were a majority of those going to al-ʿOmar's lectures, because there were direct instructions from the circles. Whole circles, twenty or so people at once, would go listen to him. But only those interested in religious science would attend bin Baz's lessons."

Bin Baz was appointed Grand Mufti by the king in 1993, replacing the previous Grand Mufti, Muhammad bin Ibrahim Al al-Shaykh, who had died in 1969. From 1969 to 1993, Al Saʿud had been content not to have a national religious leader who could challenge them. But after the protests of the early 1990s they needed a pliable yet influential figurehead to respond to the activists' challenge. Bin Baz, who according to Thamir was "widely aware of the notions of the Islamic world and Islamic action" and whose experience at the Islamic University of Medina had put him in touch with many of the country's—and the world's—Islamic movements, was a perfect candidate.

His interest in the legal sciences took Thamir away from social and political issues at a time when reform proposals, petitions, public lectures, and, sometimes, demonstrations, were drawing large crowds of young Islamists. He soon became the head of a "family" in his Salafi group. As a high school student, he was responsible for a small group of middle school students. He made sure they were reading useful books and understanding the world as it is. He would spend time with them, open them up to new political and social perspectives, offer them gifts, try to be a role model, and avoid letting his relationships with students become hierarchical or tainted with abuse and authoritarianism.

Thamir graduated from high school a few years after the Gulf War and enrolled in college, where he "studied medicine . . . for one month. I do not remember why I chose it, except that my parents pushed me toward it."

He then transferred to the school of sharia of the Islamic University of Riyadh.

"I had been interested in the quest of the religious sciences . . . since high school, because of the activities we did in the mosque circles. . . . I did not want to continue studying this in college, but after I experienced being lost in medicine, and after one of the people came to me . . . "

He paused.

"You can call them the 'educators,' or the 'preachers,' those who belong to a group that is quasi-Salafi. . . . One of those men came to me and advised me to study at the school of sharia."

"Educators" or "preachers": unlike the Muslim Brothers, Salafis did not like titles and labels, which they thought were a way to divide the community of believers. There were no "associations," "parties," "leaders," "pioneers," or "members" among them, but "youth," "educators," and "preachers." Salafis defined themselves by their actions and qualities, not by an abstract rank in a hierarchical structure.

"My dad was angry for a period of time. And I felt that I had challenged him [by moving to the school of sharia], because I had entered the college of medicine thanks to his connections."

Thamir joined the school of sharia not only to become a teacher but also to become a more efficient activist. The Islamic University of Riyadh had not always been an activist stronghold. Thamir told me that the university "had had powerful student activities" up until 1979, but that this situation had changed in the 1980s, before he joined the school.

"There was a regulation saying that there should not be any student activism at the Islamic University, so students in religious science, who are the future sheikhs and judges, would not belong to Islamic groups. . . . We felt that it was better not to be public about being an Awakening activist.... We would hear that So-and-So had not been hired by the state because he had been involved in some activities with the Islamic Awakening."

But despite this situation, after 1990 "there was a strong movement, among the Awakening youth, to join the school of sharia and the school of theology,[4] very strong. A lot of youth around my age, after high school, went straight to the school of sharia.... There was some awareness, inside the movement, that you do not want to provoke the state at the Islamic University. They did not want to create any activities there, but there was a general direction toward religious sciences and teaching as a career.... The Islamic groups wanted more teachers within their ranks. And joining the school of sharia or the school of theology was directly qualifying: you could become a teacher of religion, somebody who could create activities in schools."

Salafi activism in the early 1990s contributed to the prestige of the school of sharia. And state repression in the mid-1990s compounded this phenomenon: it was safer to be a student in a school that had been more immune to organized movements than the more secular colleges.

After he graduated from college, Thamir started teaching religion, first in a rural town and then in Tumiya. He could have aspired to a more prestigious high school in a wealthier neighborhood, but he preferred not to teach bored and arrogant middle-class kids. In Riyadh's Bedouin belt, in these neighborhoods that, from Nasim to Tumiya and from al-Dakhl al-Mahdud to Nazim, hosted a population of rural migrants, there were many problem students; the schools could be anarchic and noisy, and provocations, insults, and fights were an everyday reality. He thought that he would be more useful there than in more middle class areas.

In the early 2000s, the political balance tipped once again, this time in favor of the Muslim Brothers. After 9/11, journalists and pundits saw Salafism as a slippery slope leading to armed militancy, and the Salafis were more often targeted by security forces. So Thamir reintegrated the Muslim Brothers and opened an awareness group in his high school. If "ideas did not play a role" in the mobilization of everyday activists, who often did not know whether the group they belonged to was more of a Muslim Brotherhood group or more of a Salafi group, they were nevertheless important to the state and to the elite of the Islamic Awakening. The same individual could move from Salafism to the Brotherhood and back, depending on the political circumstances. He could also be a member of a more Salafi mosque group while at the same time being active in a high school movement that leaned more toward the Muslim Brotherhood. And in the end, while the Brotherhood had been Salafized, the Salafis, too, had been Brotherized. Ideological lines were fuzzy.

Chapter 14 **THE BEST AMONG YOU**

WHEN THEY WERE IN MIDDLE SCHOOL, THAMIR'S STUDENTS ALL joined the same Quran memorization circle at the local mosque. Becoming religious activists meant more freedom for them. The family house, with a controlling father and multiple restrictions, tended to be more regulated than the Islamic movement. And the Islamic group was respectable enough for fathers to relax their surveillance of their sons there. Nobody asked young Islamic activists about their whereabouts. Their fathers left them alone, which is what Thamir's students wanted.

"I could stay out until late at night because I had joined a religious group, which guaranteed that," Husein said. "Other groups do not give you the same freedom.... For instance, my older brother can never leave the house, because he did not join a religious group. I can stay out until 1 am; it is fine; there is a guarantee. One day, he came back at 10 pm, and it was very awkward. I, on the other hand, stay out until dawn sometimes, and sometimes I disappear for a couple of days."

Most students I interviewed shared this feeling of liberation. Salman confessed he was "a mosque man"[1] in middle school. Husein said, "becoming cultured is something that happens at the mosque.... Nobody reads outside of the mosque or other religious institutions: Islamic universities, schools of sharia and of theology." Even neighborhood atheists were often defrocked Islamic activists. "Here in Tumiya, we have somebody who became an atheist," Husein said. "He used to be very religious. He is forty now, and I know his brother; he has been writing books for a long time, but they did not pass censorship.... He went to Europe for two months and did not come back because he published an article insulting Al Sa'ud."

Joining a Quranic circle meant proclaiming one's "independence from the house," Talal said, and doing so in a manner that was hard to object to. It is only after this step was taken that students would discover how Islamic groups would change them and affect their behaviors and ideas.

"One of the things that changed my life is joining a circle," Talal said in front of Thamir and the other students. "There was a before and an after, this was a crucial coming-of-age experience.... Joining a circle makes you successful, your interests become more refined, you become somebody who serves the community, you contribute to civilization, you come back to the hours of glory, it is an important coming of age.... I started to feel that I could no longer cope with my father shaping my life. I had to be the hero of my own life.[2] The hero of this series, there. Seriously. From this point on, I became very enthusiastic."

Young activists often said that discovering the wider world was a positive effect of joining the Islamic Awakening. Joining an Islamic group also taught them that they were not powerless, even if they often did not know what to do or where to begin.

"The most obvious thing, on which all youths will agree," Talal said, "is that as soon as you join a circle, the initial germ they plant in you is getting you interested in the Islamic community. I mean that our reality is pathetic, and when you look into the past and read that our civilization was glorious, you become obsessed, you want to go back to this. But the actual issue, after your interest has been sparked and you become obsessed, is how to do it. How can you possibly do something? If you are not associated with someone who can explain it to you, guide you or something, you may spend your whole life being lost and not knowing how to make yourself worthy of the Islamic community and bring it back to glory. What I am saying here is that the circle and this obsession were a turning point for me."

This was a common narrative among the activists I met: the discovery of a shared responsibility for fellow Muslims and the rage at being unable to do much, to organize in the open, to act. This conflict could lead young activists to deep disappointment. But when I met them in private, no longer in front of their comrades, Thamir's other students tended to have more nuanced views than Talal. Husein, for instance, told me how the circle leader was cultivating this "obsession" in his students.

"The circle was very, very traditional, not inspired by the Muslim Brothers. It was just about memorizing the Quran, nothing more.... The guy in charge was maybe 28, and underneath him were supervisors who were high school students.... The circle was traditional until my third year of middle school, around 2003, when we started talking about the just war."[3]

2003 was the year of the invasion of Iraq by a U.S.-led international coalition, an event that many Arab intellectuals and activists saw as continuing a recolonization of the region that had started with the 1990 Gulf War.[4] Husein continued.

" 'You see, the government is looking for us,' the sheikh would say when we were at the mosque library. 'Hey youth, be really careful, do not leave videos praising the just war on the library's computers, somebody from the secret police might come and see them.' "

Husein, Salman, and a few others soon became bored with videos, the sheikh's paranoia, the ban on reading novels, and the way the circle was run.

"I saw one of the supervisors as a role model," Salman told me. "When he would text me, it would be as if the angel Gabriel himself had sent me a message.... He would read a lot and assign us stuff to read, and he had an answer to everything.... Now, after a few years, I can tell he was average, and less than average: less than less than average. But since I was less than less than less than less than average at the time, I thought he was something big.... Once he told me, 'Salman, if you see me do something, just do it too, do not worry about anybody else.' As if to say, I am the inspiration, everything I do is right.... But when I met Thamir, I knew that my previous supervisor was nothing. Despite everything that Thamir represents, he never speaks with all that self-importance, even though he would have the right to say: 'I have studied, I have read.' "

In private, Salman's judgment of the Quranic circle was scathing. This is how he reflected on the activists "from his generation" who were now "all supervisors" in Quranic circles:

"They are like the other youth, they go out, they have dinner outside, they go to bookstores, they go to the desert, they spend time in rest houses . . . they fight the void of their life a little bit, okay? They do not have important ideas. They do not think about how circles might be the most important project they work on. The hadith says, 'The best among you are those who learned the Quran and teach it.'⁵ The Prophet said, 'Teach it,' not: 'Make others memorize it.'"

When they were in middle school, Salman and a small group of renegades asked Husein to spy on the Quranic circle leaders.

"There were issues between us and them," Husein said. "We were revolutionaries, a group of five, we had issues with the . . . circle leadership. There was no justice. . . . The leader had a special group, he would take them with him, drive them around. He gave them responsibilities: '*You* get the cultural committee . . . *you* get this and that . . . ' and there would be a lot of problems between us."

He laughed.

"I would spy on them, act as if I was with them and collect information. . . . Talal was the closest to the leadership, and we were against Talal in a big way. I would be with him all the time to get information, stories, like that. So we would know how to revolt against them."

In the end Salman and Husein left the circle. As soon as he started high school, Talal joined the awareness group and got to hang out with Thamir, the charismatic high school religion teacher. Sa'ud soon followed him, then Salman and Husein. Things happened quite naturally: despite the differences among them, the group of friends was in a Quran memorization circle, and circle members in middle school usually joined awareness groups in high school.

"Talal and Sa'ud joined the awareness group before me," Salman said. "They were talking about Thamir, Thamir, Thamir, and I was awestruck by those around me, the man sounded so mystical. . . . Thamir was organizing an awareness rest house; they went there; I went with them. . . . The teachers who get close to students are usually the religion teachers, because they are real educators, not simple instructors who transmit information: they are people who educate you, who give you ideas. Of course, things are open, and you can end up with somebody like Thamir, a positive model, or with an extremist, somebody who will transmit his negativity to students and give them complexes."

Students were eager to contrast the Quranic circle with the high school awareness group. Even Talal seemed to have changed his mind about the circles after he joined Thamir's group.

"The awareness group is totally different from the Quranic circle," he said. "It is calmer. You feel that you belong, that you participate in decision-making, and hardly any decision comes from above. There must be consultation in our decisions, even if it is at a basic level. . . . We constantly consult each other about most things. At least that is what I do with the students in my 'family.' "

The conversation was going well, but my questions about the differences between school and mosque activities seemed to make Sa'ud nervous. He fidgeted and grumbled in the background. Salman and Husein were pouring large glasses of Vimto, gulping them down, and pouring again. The tension in the group became palpable when Talal started boasting about the strength of his own relationships with students and deprecating the leadership style of other family heads. He also criticized the local Quranic circle, in which Sa'ud, unlike Salman and Husein, had remained active.

"At the Quranic circle," Talal said, "the only goal is that you attend all sessions, and you will not find that in an awareness group. . . . I have the feeling that the awareness group gives a chance to good students: there are programs, you can develop yourself, participate in more activities, communicate with older students. At the Quranic circle, you will not find this interest in students; there you are seen as a generic being. Whether the students be brilliant or not, they are not interested in them."

"But the circle takes more time than the awareness group," Sa'ud replied.

The others turned to him. He had barely spoken thus far, except to mention joyriding or reminiscing about torturing stray cats.

"The awareness group meets half an hour every day," he continued. "We have meetings and a trip every other week. The Quranic circle creates much more powerful relationships than the awareness group. We constantly have trips and activities. In the awareness group, the contact and the programs are basic. Relations with the outside are very weak."

"Do you speak from the point of view of principles, or of reality?" Thamir asked Sa'ud.

This was a question he asked students a lot. He wanted them to acknowledge that many religious discourses were about principles, and that reality required other discourses and other practices. That Islamic action was the translation of these principles into the social and political reality that surrounded the students, not the idealization of reality or its obliteration for the sake of principles.

"From the point of view of reality," Sa'ud said.

"From the point of view of reality, I disagree with you," Talal said. "My relations with most students are very good; I meet them a lot, sometimes for hours; we go out together. . . . I think relationships are very important in general."

He let out a quick, proud laugh.

"How many relationships do you have with students?" Sa'ud asked him. "Three? Four?"

Talal was undisturbed.

"Maybe more than twenty," he said.

"Outside of the awareness group? And you see them?"

Sa'ud seemed more agitated now, almost jealous.

"I see them all the time," Talal said.

He laughed again.

"Let me tell you something," he said. "Most students who belong to a Quranic circle love to hang out with circle members only. I am not like that. Instead, I create relationships with students. And I feel that having a relationship with somebody younger and more faithful, and spending time with him, is better than hanging out with people my age. I have strong connections inside and outside the school."

The popularity contest became more strident.

"You have relationships with younger students?" Sa'ud asked Talal. There was a slight insinuation in his tone, as if he was implying that Talal had amorous or sexual relations with kids. "Outside of school? More than ten? You see them constantly? Not just from time to time?"

"What do you mean?" Talal sounded worried now.

"I mean every day, you see them, or you talk to them on the phone . . . "

"No, this is not what I mean. When I am outside of the Quranic circle . . . "

"These are different situations, you had different experiences," Thamir said, putting an end to the conversation. There was a silence. Relationships between younger and older students were key to the smooth functioning of Islamic groups, but they were also the occasion for all kinds of potentially problematic behaviors, including the rivalry between Talal and Sa'ud.

"What do you think of Vimto?" Salman asked me to break the awkwardness.

The bumpy relationship between Talal and the other youths had not evened out after they joined high school. Coming from a stateless family, Talal knew that, no matter how hard he worked, he would have a harder time going to college than Salman and Saʿud, who were Saudi citizens. He loved to throw his own excellence at them and would often speak to them in a curious mix of smugness and cajolery. Tall, handsome, and well-spoken, he gathered many younger students around himself. Other family heads, including Saʿud, were not as forthcoming or alluring. Talal thought their impact outside the group was minimal, and was not embarrassed to let them know that.

Both Talal and Saʿud were right of course, but different institutions had shaped their behaviors and expectations. Talal was always looking out toward potential recruits—he was an exoteric activist, so to speak. He was putting his social versatility and overall attractiveness to the service of the awareness group. Saʿud, by contrast, was trying to strengthen the group's cohesiveness without paying too much attention to the outside world—he was more of an esoteric activist. Each of the two students embodied a different way of growing the Islamic movement: one from the outside in, by adding more members and creating larger groups, but at the risk of diluting the message; the other from the inside out, by focusing the group's mission and creating a strong counter-society.

"In general, students are first attracted through the awareness group, and then they join a Quranic circle," Thamir said. "And sometimes the opposite: somebody who belongs to a circle goes to high school, follows those youth who are his friends and are at the awareness group."

The awareness group would officially gather its members for thirty minutes every day. Islamic activists were in charge of the half-hour break between morning and afternoon classes: the time they were officially granted was the smallest share of the time students spent at school. Yet in reality, successful activists would spend more time with the students.

"After half an hour," Talal said, "instead of letting the students go, we keep some of them working on a particular project, or for a meeting. We hang out with four or five students, and then they leave."

Activists were both with and against the school: the break between classes was an interstice in academic time, a breach that was at once inside and outside school time. Islamic activists presented their group as a part of what was going on at school; they could obtain funding—10% of the school budget, according to Thamir—use classrooms, and benefit from the institution. Yet at the same time, forced to convene their activities during the break, they could also cash in on students' endemic rebellion against class time and school repression. Islamic activism was both inside and outside the academic institution, both in favor of and against it.

During this half hour, young activists would organize a different program each day. They would launch a "cultural competition" (the religious equivalent of a Trivial Pursuit game), play sports, comment on their latest readings, or organize a "social program." "Social programs" were either informal conversations, held over tea and coffee, or a bake sale at the school. The group's three families would compete against each other and be evaluated according to their participation in the programs.

"There are rankings," Talal said. "Because everything is evaluated: attendance, time, focus, discipline . . . all these keep your enthusiasm going. And every other week, a family wins and you get prizes."

"The word 'program' is generic," Thamir added. "It can be a complex activity with different steps, or simply somebody choosing a book and reading it to others. It is as generic a word as 'activity,' which can name everything, from collecting stamps to political action aiming at the heart of government."

What was at stake in this awareness group, as in most awareness groups that were linked to a larger organization, was political. The awareness group was not only waging an undeclared war against the local Quranic circle; it was also engaged in a protracted dispute with the high school administration.

Chapter 15　　**THE TALAL AFFAIR**

ONE DAY SOMEBODY DENOUNCED THAMIR TO THE MINISTRY OF Islamic Affairs for spreading the ideas of the Muslim Brotherhood. He had given a series of talks and thought the accusation was linked to them. The blow was weak, however. The Ministry of Islamic Affairs could not dismiss him since he was working at the Ministry of Education. Yet the episode still revealed the widespread surveillance Islamic activists were subjected to.

Thamir thought the tip might have come from the Jamis. In Tumiya, as in the rest of Riyadh, the Jamis practiced close surveillance of all other Islamic movements. Their opponents called them Jamis in reference to the Ethiopian sheikh Muhammad al-Jami, whose quietist Salafi voice had spread through Saudi Islamic universities during the 1980s, starting from the Islamic University of Medina, where he was a professor. Other Islamic activists thought that the Jamis were supported by the state to compete with them from within the Islamic movement. Jamis attracted students under the pretense of studying religious sciences and becoming true Salafis.

Tumiya's Jamis gathered around a hundred members, and were busy opposing the Muslim Brothers and more politicized Salafis. For instance, they had blackmailed local mosque imams into closing down a Quranic circle whose orientation they deemed too radical. The circle members were forced to move from mosque to mosque around Tumiya until the day when, facing hostile imams everywhere, they simply could no longer exist as a group and had to dissolve.

"The Jamis are those who think that those in power . . . cannot be touched," Salman said. "To them everything the government says is right; the state simply never errs."

The Jamis were not very popular, even if they were active in several suburbs of Riyadh.

"The Jami library was burned to the ground, but I do not know if it really happened," he said. "They say of themselves that they are Salafis and they attack the sheikhs; they attack all those who bring anything new. They even attack people who to us are Salafi, for bringing new things. They attack anything that smacks of novelty, of anti-government activism, of revolt. 'Revolt against those in power is forbidden,' they say."

When he spoke of the Jamis, 'Adel was even more cutting.

"The Jamis are the flip side of secularism, you see?" he said to me once. "Secularists call for the separation of religion and state and want to take over politics. The Jamis reply to them, 'Take politics, we just want religion.'"

Jami surveillance did not penetrate only those Islamic groups they accused of political activism: it also extended to families.

"I went to Kuwait to visit relatives," Salman said. "I went to a bookstore Thamir had recommended, which sells lots of books by Muslim Brother authors. . . . I bought a nice collection that I left at home while my cousin and I drove around. My other cousin, a girl—I think they are Jamis—when I came back, the books were shredded up, as if a pack of rats had eaten them. . . . They have a problem with books. . . . That a girl becomes so intense. . . . She was wearing three veils, one on top of the other, from here to here, like bedsheets."

The high school principal was also Jami and had vowed to make Thamir's life impossible.

"The school principal usually plays an important role in Islamic activities," Thamir said. "For any awareness group to be successful, the principal has to cooperate, because he gives financial support, he authorizes the activities, he irons out controversies on the utilization of the school space . . . or he forbids it all. In principle, there is administrative control from above, from the Ministry of Education all the way down to the activities. But here, in Tumiya, this surveillance is weak. . . . And to be honest, the principal has an intellectual orientation that is different from ours. He is closer to the Jami movement. They do not like the Muslim Brothers' activities, youth movements, excursions, outings, hymns, competitions, sports . . .

"Administration here is very weak. They are not clear. They are temperamental. The relationship between administrators and teachers is bad; they do not know how to communicate with us. And it is not only we who suffer: it is the whole school. Schedules, classes: it is total anarchy. . . . The administration is not serious; it is temperamental. They make a decision and change their minds without a reason. They give something and then take it back; everything is in a state of permanent instability."

Activists had devised several ways to deal with the situation.

"We negotiate with the administration to manipulate it as much as possible . . . to try to satisfy it, to benefit from the opportunities they offer, and to find alternatives when they refuse something, even if we are not convinced by their reasons."

When negotiation and manipulation did not work, the activists tried to satisfy the administrators and submitted to their decisions in order to benefit from every opportunity, work the system, occupy any space left vacant. In case of a refusal to help, they created alternatives, took matters into their own hands, and organized despite the administration. The school's disorder meant that students had some leeway, especially those who managed the awareness group. Disorder from the top down was met with resistance from the bottom up.

"I am short-fused," Thamir said. "It is in my nature and in my roots; when I am in the principal's office and he refuses something, or wants to meddle in our affairs, I clash with him. . . . And the group's members do the same, Talal, Salman . . . " He turned to Salman: "You remember the face the principal made? Salman was extremely patient, but on the day the principal kicked him out, Salman did not let him do it: he just shouted at him."

"That day will go down in history," Talal said.

"But in general, we negotiate and benefit from opportunities," Thamir said. "In the end, precisely because of administrative anarchy, large avenues for action open in front of us. Sometimes we stay on the second floor from 11 am to 1 pm, we work together, whereas if the administration were effective, we would be forced to go back to the classroom. And we put ourselves at ease, we come and go with the students, we organize outings, and administrators are not there to bother us. Anarchy is as positive as it is negative.

"In Egypt, the Muslim Brotherhood spread in popular places because it took over the role of the government: it started helping the sick and the poor. It is the same here: the weakness of the administration in some domains allowed us to occupy this free space. . . . Organized action always tends to fill a vacuum, no more, no less. And we found vacuums to fill in students' activities. Take soccer, for example: in principle, the school must organize soccer tournaments. We took advantage of the fact that they were not interested in this activity, and we organized activities, tournaments, conferences. We were the only ones to do it, because the administration is incompetent."

Islamic action was a function of the growth of the administration *and* of its concomitant disorder. Activism flourished in the shadow of the state, within the many cracks and voids created by a sprawling, poorly organized administration. Activists had become experts at derailing even the simplest attempts by the administration to control them.

"In theory, an inspector is supposed to come from the regional administration once or twice a semester to inspect the high school's awareness group, to look at our work, our activities, our methods, etc. But when he came to visit us, I pushed back," Thamir said. The students laughed. "I told him, 'We need to get more funding.' And he said, 'Yes, we will see about that,' and he proposed—to evade the topic—that we join other groups, like the boy scouts, to set up a summer camp in a stadium that depends on the Ministry of Education. So I told him, 'Good, go ask the principal for his permission.' Of course, nothing happened in the end. He came back another day and talked to another teacher. I had told that teacher to say the same: 'Go talk to the principal.' I told him to ask for more funding, to tell him about our problems. Not that we need his help: but we want the administration to stop putting a spoke in our wheel. And he did nothing. From then on, he lost interest. The next time, he asked to meet me and I did not even show up. He was extremely angry; he was really surprised. Hmm. . . . I had understood how useless he was."

Skillfully maneuvering around the administration prepared activists for confrontations outside of the school.

"We see that as an experience for life," Thamir said. "What will you do if somebody treats you badly or puts a spoke in your wheel? If you get angry, if you overreact, if you lose it, you will fail. . . . But if, from the beginning, you keep your calm, you will see the stupidity of it all: these are simple maneuvers. You can develop. I personally benefited a lot from our troubles with the principal. Because they enormously developed my ability to know how to treat my opponents."

Thamir had talked for a long time, and Talal was burning to get some attention, too. He had a story to tell about repression within the school and the inordinate role of the Jamis in the neighborhood. He had written an article for the magazine of the Islamic awareness group, and the piece had triggered what students called the "Talal Affair."

"You remember the Dreyfus Affair?" Thamir said. "The same thing happened to Talal."

"We heard there was an extra tutorial," Talal explained. "The physics teacher was angry, because only a few of us had registered for it. So he gave us a harder exam than usual. . . . After that, he had the principal come to class, and they played their little comedy. The principal shut the door and said, 'Students, we tried everything to help. . . . We asked this professor to organize a tutorial. . . . So do not embarrass us, we hope he can teach you something useful.'

"All the students registered for a collective tutorial, and everyone had to pay four hundred riyals [around a hundred dollars]. And those who signed up for an extra individual tutorial paid eight hundred riyals. And there were three classes. That is ninety students. They all registered in one day for the physics tutorial. This is newsworthy. In the section of our magazine called 'School News' we wrote, 'Ninety students join extra physics tutorial.' A majority of students, you see. And you had to guess the whole amount they paid.

"The principal read it and said, 'Wow, you criticize the administration and the teachers? Your dad needs to come in and you have to apologize to the teacher.' I refused. I said, 'My father, where? That is not his writing; it is mine, and in any case, my father is not coming.' He told me, 'Get out.' So I waited outside. Then he kicked me out of school until my dad came. And I did not want my dad to come, out of stubbornness and for other reasons, so that he would not bother me later, forbid me to join activities, etc. And also, he would have met the principal alone and the principal could have said what he wanted, nobody would have known what had been said. So I was kicked out for two weeks."

Early in my field research, I had witnessed how college students protested against their university's administration for not paying them their monthly allowances on time. College students received a small stipend from the state, and they suspected that administrators had invested their stipend money in the fast-growing stock market.[1] The situation here was similar: the administration and the teacher were trying to milk at least nine thousand dollars from the student body—around six times an average teacher's monthly wage. Extra tutorials were a common practice in Riyadh; it was tacitly understood that they were a requirement for passing a class. But Thamir's students had decided to use the Islamic awareness group to push back against the school.

They printed the story in their monthly magazine, which usually published news about the awareness group or general items about education, self-help, or the meanings of success. The principal responded by shutting down the magazine and the Islamic awareness group. To the activists it was clear that the principal had used this as an opportunity to put an end to Muslim Brotherhood activism in his school.

"Note that we had not yet distributed the magazine," Talal said. "We had just brought the proofs to the principal, and he treated us as if we had distributed it. So I told him, 'We came to get your advice, to see that there is no mistake; and you punished me.' That made me even angrier. I seek his advice, and he kicks me out for two weeks? What a mess."

Since he did not want to tell his father that he had been expelled, Talal kept going to school, but could not enter the building.

"I would come to school every morning without my books. And I stayed by the main gate. After a while, they even gave me the school keys. I was the one who was ushering teachers, students, who would let them leave. . . . But administrators had decided that I would never come back to the awareness group. They banned the group. They banned the magazine."

"For one semester," Thamir said.

"And when they reopened the magazine, one of the conditions was that I not write in it, that my name be erased from it, completely. [But even before that, the Talal] affair had become famous, and we started joking about it with other teachers. And we spoke to students who have the principal's ear, and after a while . . . the principal himself came to me and said, 'Do not forget: bring your dad tomorrow.' And when I would go home, 'Say hello to your dad.'

'Bring your dad.' I would come back the next day, and he would tell me: 'Get out. Stay by the gate.' It became everybody's joke."

The pariah had become the school's gatekeeper. Talal would spend his days with the Indian doorman, "somebody so important that if he was not there, the whole school would be paralyzed." The doorman was "the school's most important employee," he said. Talal wrote an article about him once his detention ended and after the principal reauthorized the magazine. (The article was censored.) At the beginning of his expulsion, Talal would hide his face with his headdress when the principal walked by the gate. But after a few days, his story had become the talk of the school, and he understood that publicity was his best ally. After two weeks by the gate, Talal was reintegrated into school.

The group reopened, but its activities, and in particular the magazine, were subjected to increased censorship. This control provoked "dizziness," said Talal: out of sheer precaution, and to avoid being banned again, students now acted as if everything was off-limits—the school administration had won. The principal banned all educational topics, and students would sometimes erase half the content of the magazine, which forced Talal, who was still editing it, to "enlarge the font in order to fill the page." At the end of the academic year, the Islamic awareness group moved its publications online, but students were still weary of engaging in political topics. The administration had restricted their activities; going online would not change much about the new power relationship. Despite his messiness and unpredictability, the principal had not acted in a vacuum: he had implemented, at the scale of his high school, the policies that the Ministry of Education had devised in its war against Islamic activists and activities.

Chapter 16 — A STATE WITHIN THE STATE

THE NEIGHBORHOOD SAT ON BOTH SIDES OF THE OLD MECCA road, in the south of Riyadh. Built in the 1930s as a service area for travelers, it had expanded in the 1980s, after the oil boom. Behind the low-lying store-fronts lining the main avenues there were rows of identical concrete villas surrounded by barren courtyards. The summer camp I would visit that day was in the local high school, in the middle of a superblock, far from the main road and the noise of traffic.

The summer camp director had sent a young supervisor to wait for me on the avenue, several blocks away. I drove behind him to the high school, whose entrance was framed with large boards advertising the summer camp. We walked in, and there was bedlam all around. Students ran everywhere. There was a fetid stench in the air, a mix of cooking odors and poorly ventilated classrooms. Above all, the place was in a fantastic uproar, as both students and teachers seemed to be continuously shouting. The high school was a new building but looked as though it had been ravaged by generations of angry students. The floor was covered with empty bottles and greasy paper. There was trash everywhere. Graffiti covered most walls. Names, phone numbers, and email addresses were carved on tables. Even the sports field, outside the main building, was dilapidated and its equipment damaged.

Older students had escaped any manner of control. The director, a man in his late thirties with a furtive gaze, told me that he focused his whole attention on younger students, "because they are the future of this country." There were around five hundred summer campers there.

Two hundred primary school students were housed on the second floor, which was separated from the first floor by a series of gates and fences. Around three hundred middle and high school students shared the first floor, by far the dirtiest, noisiest place in the school. To avoid bullying and sexual harassment, the administration made a point of separating younger students from older students. This summer camp felt like a prison riot.

The director seemed overwhelmed by his role. His attention was being constantly snatched by teachers or students bursting into his office—a place he seemed to rarely leave. He had to make all decisions. His high school reminded me of Thamir's school, even if the neighborhood hosted a different population. Tumiya was mostly Bedouin, and the majority of its residents came from central Najd. Here, the director told me, the residents were mostly sedentary and came from rural, southern Najd, the plateau between Riyadh and the mountains of Yemen. Income levels were modest, and inner-city families had started to move to the area, where they could access private property and forget about downtown Riyadh's overpopulated dwellings and greedy slumlords.

The director took me on a tour of the school. We first went to the second floor, where a classroom had been assigned to each "family." But the rooms were so dirty and unwelcoming that students had deserted them, congregating instead in a game room at the end of a dusty hallway. There a supervisor with a broken voice painstakingly explained to us that he was about to rearrange tables; that he had organized access to Ping-Pong and foosball tables; that he had printed out numbers that students would draw out of a bag to take turns for the games. As he spoke, he waved a bunch of laminated cards in my face, while students pushed one another around the Ping-Pong tables, apparently trying to cut the line.

The director then took me to the sports field, where several soccer matches were unfolding. There were dozens of students around the fields, some playing while others waited in line, their hands on the shoulders of the student in front of them, sad expressions painted on their faces. The director pointed them out to me and said that he was proud to know how to organize youth. I turned my gaze away in embarrassment. The sun was setting behind a row of houses. The fine powder of the Riyadh dust was going up in columns around us.

We walked back in as supervisors were distributing snacks. Standing on a second-floor balcony, they were throwing bags of candies to the students massed in the covered courtyard below. Students were jumping around, trying to catch some food, landing on one another's feet. The deafening noise was barely interrupted by the call to the sunset prayer. One of the supervisors came down and stood in front of the crowd in the courtyard, ready to lead the collective prayer. Other teachers surrounded the students and tried to have them form the ranks required for the ritual. Slaps were distributed, shouts were exchanged, and the whole place descended into chaos again.

After the prayer, the director led me to his office, where the procession of solicitors resumed. I savored the relative calm of the moment, far from the sound and the fury of the courtyard. I asked if I could see the summer camp program, and the director looked at his feet. He said that one of the supervisors, who was a muezzin in a nearby mosque, had taken it away with him to carry out his religious duty; he would only be back tomorrow. The director's powerlessness—and his inability to tell a good lie—made him almost likable. Other directors I met during my fieldwork in summer camps served me a polished script while clicking away at their PowerPoints. Here, the institution offered itself up in its raw state.

During our conversation, a student who could not have been older than twelve, very fair-skinned, with an oval face and almost feminine features, entered the office and complained that "somebody" kept calling his cellphone. The director gently took the cellphone from the boy's hand, looked up the number, and tried to call back—no answer. The boy left the office to continue his inquiry and came back a few minutes later: "It is So-and-so" (another summer camper). The director asked the boy to fetch him. The complainant came back with the other boy: he was older, probably fifteen or sixteen, dark-skinned, and overweight. He stood in front of the director's desk in obvious embarrassment.

"Why do you keep calling him?"

"Just because, because I did not know where he was."

"How do you know him?"

"From here, from camp. I just know him."

"From now on, I forbid you to come near him or to call him again."

The director sounded determined for the first time since the beginning of my visit. The anger in his voice was palpable. The older boy was mortified and visibly shaken. I could not help but remember the stories of rape my inter-viewees and friends had told me. Most involved educators, religious preachers, family friends, or older students. Many had started with unwanted attention at school before developing into something else. One of my friends told me about a religious preacher who was lecturing at his middle school. After class one day, the preacher, who had regularly showered him with attention, drove him to the Wadi Laban, on the outskirts of town, and raped him in his car. My friend had not complained for fear of retaliation and punishment.

Yet at the same time I could not but sympathize with the older student, who might have been doing nothing more than expressing his feelings toward his classmate. Love between boys, which people pejoratively called *wir'anjiyya*, was widespread in gender-segregated schools, and a few phone calls were hardly a crime. In addition, being dark-skinned and overweight probably meant that the older student was more likely to be accused of all sorts of offenses. Both the younger student and the director were fair-skinned, in a context where skin color mattered yet remained unspoken and former slaves and Afro-Saudis were relegated to a subordinate status.

The main issue faced by this summer camp, however, was economic rather than moral. A student and a supervisor walked into the office. The student wanted to rent a projector for an activity; there was none in the school. His supervisor parleyed with the director, who refused at first and then, inexplicably, surrendered, asking in a faint voice how much this would cost—very little, as it turned out. I asked about budget. The director told me that the Ministry of Education ministry allocated thirty thousand riyals (eight thousand dollars) to each camp for the whole summer: not in cash, but in equipment distributed by a regional commission. The equipment was often inadequate, and the camp had to rely on registration fees for its day-to-day functioning.

Some summer camps were free. In wealthier suburbs, the fees sometimes amounted to two hundred riyals (about fifty dollars). In private camps, outside the purview of the Ministry of Education, registration fees could climb to two thousand riyals (about five hundred dollars). Here, the hundred-riyal fee (twenty-five dollars) was optional. If all students paid, the camp would be able to count on fifty thousand riyals (about thirteen thousand dollars)—but not all students paid. The al-Rajhi and al-Subay'i banks also made hefty donations to the summer camps through the local education administration. Elsewhere, businessmen often donated to their neighborhood's summer camp, but in this impoverished area, few donations came directly to the camp.

At least the air conditioning and plumbing were working. In one summer camp I visited, the A/C was off, with average daytime high temperatures above forty degrees Celsius. In another, teachers and students had to pay directly for the computers and video players that the Ministry of Education could not dispatch. In poorer areas, running a summer camp required a good dose of forbearance. A summer camp administrator summed up the situation by saying: "When one enters the summer camps, one no longer belongs to oneself."

Extreme centralization meant that the director took on more responsibilities, potentially made more mistakes, and faced constant nudging and nagging from students and teachers alike. Three local teenagers walked in and asked to join the camp. The director sent them to the supervisor in charge of registrations. But the latter was not around, and things started to go awry. A father walked in with his son in tow. The director knew the father and registered the boy on the spot. But the boy had not filled out his registration form, and they had to wait for a form to be brought by one of the supervisors. While he was waiting, throwing anxious looks right and left, the father made sure to ask how well the younger students were segregated from the older boys.

Behind him, the three teenagers were still waiting. The director refused to register them, saying that it was not his job, but everybody in the room knew that he had just helped a boy sign up. Outraged by this obvious injustice, one of the teenagers insisted. He stayed by the desk and adopted an attitude of silent supplication, his face and hands turned toward the director. He asked again and the director eventually changed his mind. He agreed to register the three teenagers and loaned them his pen, "the pen of the director himself," because no other pen could be found in his office. There was no stapler either, and everybody had to wait again until somebody brought one from somewhere far inside the school.

The main goal of the summer camps, according to the director, was to create among students a feeling of citizenship, which he defined as "the love of king and country." The camps also aimed to build healthy bodies, ward off idleness, develop students' talents, and organize their leisure. Such lingo was common among summer camp personnel and congruent with the descriptions given in the literature of the Ministry of Education. The language about citizenship was a direct application of the Saudi government's campaign to create a stronger sense of nationalism, away from both tribalism and Pan-Islamism. The concept of love was central to Saudi nationalism, which Al Saʿud had rebranded as "humanitarianism" in contrast to both Al-Qaʿeda's terror campaigns and Saudi-bashing in North America. Around Riyadh, huge billboards celebrating the "Kingdom of Humanity"[1] showed a grinning King ʿAbd Allah hovering over a crowd of Siamese twins, recently separated at the National Guard Health Program.[2]

Summer campers seemed less interested in citizenship than in negotiating, resisting, or provoking the educators, who responded cautiously and sometimes brutally. This summer camp looked and felt like a disciplinary space, where children and adolescents were parked several hours a day by their families and were subjected to the violence of either other students or the teachers. This sorry state certainly had to do partly with the personality of the teachers and the fact that this director was in charge of a summer camp for the first time in his life. But it also had a lot to do with state repression of the summer camps, from poor funding to finicky control over the activities.

I had wanted to study the summer camps since my first interviews with young activists—including ʿAdel—who had mentioned how important these structures had been in their politicization. The camps were open for six weeks every year, in June and July. They usually welcomed members of local Quranic circles and Islamic awareness groups. They were "like extended Quranic circles," ʿAdel told me.

"Students arrive around the mid-afternoon prayer. They have afternoon activities, then activities after sunset and after the evening prayer. Summer camps are an official thing, a state thing. But Islamic activists organize them and do theater, sing, play soccer, play sports, have social activities, cultural programs."

In Riyadh, 57 summer camps gathered around twenty-two thousand students in the mid-2000s, roughly one third of the number of summer campers across the country at that time.[3] I thought I could benefit from my budding Islamic activist network to get a foot in the door and study summer camps from up close. But Thamir gently refused to help.

"Our position—the position of the Muslim Brothers—is too fragile in Riyadh, we cannot help you," he said. "Go all the way to the top of the bureaucracy and trickle down from there."

The Muslim Brothers had contributed to the emergence of summer camps in schools and colleges and were once powerful in the organization. Many old-timers told me that summer camps had started in the early 1980s, when they were mere excursions to the southern mountain of 'Asir, near the border with Yemen. The idea was to seek cooler temperature in the highlands during the sweltering summer months. Camps often lasted two weeks and were individual endeavors, with little institutional support. Soon, though, the camps spread to four, then eight weeks, and most students would remain in Riyadh for most of that period. Summer was a good time to escape state control and experiment with more liberated student activities.

In the mid-1990s, the Saudi press accused the summer camps of spreading extremism. Some camps were denounced as training facilities for the armed militants who, in 1995 and 1996, had bombed U.S. military facilities in Riyadh and Khobar. The camps were suspended in 1995 by royal fiat and reopened two years later, after students and supervisors begged for clemency. A few pilot camps first operated under the control of the Ministry of Education. And when the camps fully reopened they were forced into an administrative straitjacket. The Muslim Brothers had lost their monopoly. A coordination committee was created, with two dozen inspectors regularly touring the camps. The Interior Ministry and the emirate of Riyadh (the provincial administration) also sent inspectors to make sure that the teachers' ideas were appropriately nonpolitical. Supervisors and teachers had to get ministry clearance every spring, and many seasoned activists were pushed aside. Camp activities were blueprinted and vetted months before the summer. They had become "a matter of implementation," a supervisor told me.

The debate over the summer camps raged again ten years later, after the 2003 Riyadh bombings against U.S. military contractors. Every summer, journalists and pundits wrote that the summer camps produced terrorists and Islamic activists responded, saying that they were organizing idle, potentially dangerous youths and that the summer camps, instead of fostering extremism, were actually preventing it. Both sides pointed an indignant finger at the specter of political violence. Both sides believed that youth, Saudi Arabia's dangerous class, was in need of supervision. 'Adel had witnessed the first crackdown on the camps when he was a teenager.

"When I was in middle school," he said, "the camps stopped for a year, because they feared their influence on society. It was after the 1995 'Olaya bombing. They got scared and they shut down the camps. Of course, right after that, statistics almost immediately showed a spike in crime . . . because the youth did not know what to do. And even those they call 'committed,'[4] they became committed because they went with somebody who controlled them. Whereas if nobody controlled them, they would go out with their cousins and say, 'Let's do some joyriding.' And joyriding is viewed as leading to crime, drugs, weapons, etc."

Our activities versus joyriding and violence: this was a common trope among Islamic activists. A camp director told me that, according to a study carried out by the Interior Ministry in the mid-2000s, youth delinquency dropped by sixty percent when the summer camps were in operation. If idle hands were the devil's workshop, one had to invest in leisure to keep young Saudis off the asphalt and away from cars. Islamic activists therefore did not think leisure was ungodly.[5] They actively invested in fun as a way to reach youth, to prove their own social usefulness, to organize in a domain that had often been crushed by state policies. When there were no movie theaters in the country, Islamic activists invested in theater. When there were no liquor stores, Islamic investors opened amusement parks. They had created family-friendly environments that fostered leisure and fun and allowed members of the middle class to meet their peers in semi-public spaces. (In that sense, Crown Prince Muhammad bin Salman, with his interest in leisure and entertainment in the late 2010s, was an heir to the very Islamic activists he so forcefully fought against.)

After Thamir said that he could not help me gain access to the summer camps, I asked the King Faysal Center for a formal letter of introduction. One of the center's administrators, who in a former life had played a role in the camps, recommended that I write a one-page research proposal. He then put me in touch with the head of research at the Ministry of Education.

In early June, I drove to the Ministry of Edutation's Directorate of Planning and Development, located in what looked like a former school in the middle-class suburb of Rabwa. Four decrepit buildings hugged a barren courtyard.

Inside, portraits of King Fahd, of King 'Abd Allah, and of the crown prince were hung in most offices. The head of research, a man in his early thirties, had written a master's thesis on the Saudi education system and was expecting me to carry out quantitative research. He was surprised when I explained my qualitative methodology and said that I did not have a survey questionnaire. He feared that some of my questions about family and economic background, which I had included in the list of topics I was interested in, would offend parents. He said that Saudi society was "conservative" and "exceptional" and urged me to seek help from the King Faysal Center if anything happened. To appease his fears, I said that I had conducted similar research among high school students in Tumiya, where things had gone very well.

"How did you meet them?" he asked, immediately suspicious.

"Through their teacher, who is also a friend."

He paused.

"You know, the Ministry of Education does not control everything in the summer camps," he said. "Summer camp administrators have strong personalities and do not like others to meddle in their business."

Yet he stamped my research project with the seal of the Ministry and attached it to an official authorization letter. He then ushered me into the vast, dusty office of the director of planning and development. Throned on an antiquated metal chair, the director, a debonair man with ample girth, kept on smiling as he signed the letter. He said a few words of approval and showed us out. The head of research walked me to my car, saying that he hoped my work would contribute to improving the summer camps' image. He then sent me off to the headquarters of the education department for the Riyadh province to have my documents signed and stamped there, too.

I drove there on a hot June day. My letter in hand, I first headed to the fourth floor of a modernist slab, where I met the chief of staff of the local director of education. The man was seated behind a desk in a long antechamber. Behind him, a closed door led to the director's office. In front of him, a dozen solicitors were handing him paperwork that he quickly organized into different piles. When it came to my turn he grabbed my letter, listened to my quick explanation, and told me to come back after the noon prayer.

I came back an hour later and found my letter signed. The chief of staff told me to take it to the first floor, where it was dated and given an administrative number, and then to go to the sixth floor to meet the religious activists who were managing the summer camps.

The sixth floor housed the department of student activities. As I exited the elevator, I noticed a change of scenery. Exit the secular-looking administrators, with their shaved chins and double black ropes holding their headdresses. Employees here cultivated a pious appearance: beards, shortened robes, and free-flowing headdresses were the norm. Unlike in other parts of the building, the walls, newly painted in pastel colors, were spotless. Mediocre seascapes replaced the portraits of the king and the crown prince in each office.

The head of student activities had a dour air about him. He read the letter and asked me to present my project. I spoke about the municipal elections and the link between student activities and mobilization. When I spoke about my fieldwork in Tumiya, the director loosened up a bit. He was probably pleased to see that I was not trying to link the camps to terrorism. He asked his assistant to bring coffee and tea, and asked me how many camps I wanted to visit. I said that I wanted to see four or five centers before choosing one for the summer. He called in Abu Ahmad, who was in charge of public relations at the summer camps' coordination center. Abu Ahmad, a bearded man in his early thirties, was a fast-talking journalist with an automatic smile who published a weekly page about the summer camps in the local *Al-Jazira* newspaper.

"Is that not the newspaper that launched a campaign against the camps in 2003?" I asked.

"Bravo," he said, before telling me that this campaign was the reason why his position had been created. He told me that he would call me in a couple of days to plan out my field research. Walking to my car, I kept thinking about the relative oasis of calm, neatness, and outward religiosity constituted by the department of student affairs in this messy, rather dirty, and secularist looking ministry building. It was precisely the existence of this distinct space, which could escape the control of the Ministry of Education, that journalists and pundits had criticized.

The summer camps' coordination center was another example of what some of my interlocutors called "a state within a state." Located near the Ministry of Education's sports stadium, the coordination center also seemed off-limits to secularists. It housed several committees that reported on activities, dealt with funding and equipment, organized competitions between camps and trips to the country, and coordinated inspections.

Abu Ahmad introduced me to the summer camp inspectors, these envoys of the central administration who toured the camps all summer long and made sure that activities stayed within the ministry's guidelines. The inspectors were amphibious beings. In between the administration and the schools, they shared features with both worlds. Religion teachers for the most part, often in their mid-forties, they were committed to the autonomy of student activities while also relaying Ministry of Education policies, thus apparently undermining the independence of the summer camps. These conservative types did not want to create trouble; their guidance was gentle and they exerted continuous surveillance over the activities, which they wanted, ultimately, to maintain.

Abu Ahmad said that my visits to the camps would take place during inspections. This made me uncomfortable. How could I work properly under the gaze of the central administration? How would camp directors and supervisors react to my presence? Yet as a former high school teacher myself, I also felt comfortable in the company of the inspectors. These idealists on a stipend felt a lot like my ex-colleagues in the French education system, and it was relatively easy to talk to them. There would be some benefits to their presence, too: they could act as middlemen, give me some background on the various neighborhoods, or explain what I was doing. In a word, they would help me pass. But things did not go as expected.

Chapter 17   **THE DOOR WHENCE THE WIND COMES**

A WEEK BEFORE SUMMER CAMPS STARTED, TEACHERS AND supervisors toured the neighborhood and tried to reach as many youths as possible. They put out posters, distributed flyers, and organized soccer tournaments. Then, during the next four weeks, from mid-June to mid-July, the local camp would be its own advertisement, and more students would join as activities became stronger. During the fourth week, the campers, now well-trained in the various activities, would hold competitions to determine the camp's best family, and Riyadh's best camp. The fifth week would be "dead," as administrators would be busy preparing the camp's annual trip, which took place during the sixth week. In August, in a bid to retain summer campers before the start of the school year, teachers and preachers would organize religious classes and Quran memorization circles in local mosques.

Despite its best efforts to attract more recruits, the institution tended to draw from a limited pool of already religious students. 'Adel's favorite preacher, Sheikh Muhammad al-Duwish, believed that summer camps had actually failed to mobilize youth.

"There are several trends among the young," he said in a public lecture. "There are the religious types. They need our care lest they fall into exaggeration and extremism, and they need to invest their energy in something useful. And there are the womanizers and the deviants. We need to deal with all types of youths. But summer camps are limited, because they target only certain types and not all young people. We should focus instead on troublemakers and nonreligious youth, because their energy is not utilized, and because religion encompasses the whole Islamic community, not some to the exclusion of others. We should attract those who do not behave the way we want. We should offer them activities that are suitable to them, without forgetting why we are preaching to them."

This was a widespread opinion among Islamic activists. The anonymous author of an online evaluation of the summer camps, published on a prominent Salafi website, certainly agreed with al-Duwish. "My problem with many summer camps is that they only target already religious students," he wrote. "This begs the question: if you and I only draw students from Quranic circles, who will take care of the lost, misguided youths? Do not blame the young only if you see them drinking, joyriding, sinning, or misbehaving. The young bear only a fragment of the responsibility; you and I bear the rest of it."[1]

Supervisors and students often said that summer camps were the climax of their high school, college, and mosque activities. They treated them as closed structures, whose members had to prove the exclusive nature of their commitment. But several voices had spoken against this exclusiveness, which not only undermined the religious message of the centers but was also detrimental to their political vocation. There was a debate within Islamic networks about the summer camps, and it seemed that the Ministry of Education had adopted al-Duwish's perspective.

Education administrators renamed the camps "summer clubs"[2] to dull their militant edge and make them more welcoming to "all those young people who do not have the means to travel or join luxurious clubs, which are too expensive for them."[3] A high-ranking education bureaucrat had explained that the new name would "include sports, leisure, social, and societal issues. We want students and supervisors to welcome the whole of society."[4] The most cooperative activists would implement the reform. They were those who had climbed up the official hierarchy of student activities and manned the positions from which the more political activists had been dismissed.

But political control was not a one-way process. It was a messy business, full of patches and holes and weaknesses. State surveillance could only exist as long as some activists benefited from it and continued to organize in the shadow of the state. Some activists thought that the reform would shield them from what Sheikh Salman al-ʿOuda had called "a new McCarthyism": constant attacks from those liberal intellectuals who wanted to "eradicate" Islamic groups.[5] "To believe that summer camps are the source of extremism . . . is accusing our schools, our religious institutions, and our charities," a journalist wrote in *Al-Jazira*. "Some journalists repeat the following saying about the summer camps: 'Shut the door whence the wind comes and take a break.'[6] But this does not make religious or rational sense. Religious law requires reform, which is the way of prophets, clerics, and preachers. And reason tells us that by shutting the door, you might block the wind, but you will also cut the airflow. If you want proper aeration, change the orientation of the door."[7]

Reforming and coopting the summer camps was not putting them to death, however, and the camps were still there, although their functioning had evolved over time. The summer camps' splendid isolation was indeed a myth: these structures were part of their social and political environment. On the one hand, the reform protected the quasi-monopoly of Islamic activists on student activities. On the other hand, it severely limited the opportunities for political mobilization, especially when teachers or directors were dismissed or replaced by inexperienced administrators, as in the chaotic summer camp I had visited near the old Mecca road.

Chaos was one visible sign of reform. Excessive order was another. Visiting a summer camp in an upper-middle-class suburb, I realized that calm could be as alarming as turmoil.

I had gotten lost in the sprawling landscape and I was late. Spotless streets were lined with trees and large sidewalks on which nobody walked. The inspector who was waiting for me at the camp had told me that this was the second-wealthiest area in the city, "after the north." It had been designed as a model suburb in the 1980s by a government agency and sold on credit to civil servants. Since then, its beautiful homes, impeccable street design, and convenient location had attracted more businessmen and high-ranking bureaucrats, and prices had gone up.

The primary school housing the summer camp was flawless. Inside the building, brand-new signage showed the different rooms and activities, giving the school the air of a trade fair. As if to confirm this first impression, the director, a thin, pale man with bulging eyes and slow speech, explained that the camp's main theme, this year, was "the stock market," and its motto, repeated on signs and banners across the school, was "invest with us." (The previous year's theme had been "real estate.") This camp targeted the scions of the wealthy, who were destined to one day become investors and businessmen, what everyday Saudis called "big fish."[8]

The video game room was called "Technoshop" (in Arabic and English), and a sign by the door read: "Whoever does not know this language—the language of knowledge—is illiterate." In three other rooms, named, in English and Arabic again, "Optics," "Quranic School," and "Smarts," a few numbed students were watching Egyptian TV, reading books, or playing board games. The director showed me an oral expression class. The teacher called on a student, who walked to the blackboard and launched into an exalted post-prayer sermon. His sophisticated classical Arabic, serious tone, and air of absolute conviction contrasted starkly with the banality of his message: fear God and think about Judgment Day. The director and the inspector listened intently, their wide-open eyes riveted on the student's face, but they decided to leave the classroom right in the middle of his speech. The student dropped his jaw as we walked out the door. We then force-marched through a leadership class, a computer science class, a knitting class, a karate class, a self-help class, and a dialogue class (which turned out to have closed the day before because of low enrollment).

The silence and order were overwhelming. The students did not behave like children or young men. They looked like elaborate puppets mimicking adults, speaking in starched tones, striving for productivity and profit. The rooms were quasi-empty and a thick air of boredom exuded from everything: most of the sons of the wealthy were obviously summering elsewhere, far from Riyadh and its sweltering heat. The director made me watch a pompous video about his camp, edited like a TV report. He then gave me a box of local perfumes, a Swiss watch, a Quran, and two brochures about Islam in French. His good deed completed, he showed me out.

The summer camps could become a springboard for ambitious educators who wanted to climb the hierarchy of the Ministry of Education. After leaving the upper-middle-class suburb, I drove off to another camp, located in a majority-Bedouin, working-class suburb. Here the scene was again totally different. A procession of teachers and students was waiting for me in the hallway behind the director. One of the students sang a welcome hymn, and I was ushered to a room where refreshments were served. The director confessed that he had thought I would be coming with Ministry of Education officials and a translator. He had obviously tried to make his camp look good.

In the previous camp, I had been in close contact with the director only; here, everybody wanted to steal a glance at what was going on. Students, teachers, and supervisors surrounded us at all times. As usual, I used the time of the evening prayer to record my field notes in the director's office. Two posters made by students hung above his desk. One read: "Falling does not always mean failure, the proof being that rain falls," and the other: "The hardest thing is to know oneself."

This director was a doctor of theology who had worked for several years at the Islamic University of Riyadh before transferring to the Ministry of Education, where he became a primary school principal, then a middle school principal, then a high school principal. He had chosen to spend his whole career in this Bedouin suburb and drew some pride from that. The area, like Tumiya, had a reputation for unruliness and disorder among the capital's sedentary population. The director, who hailed from a prominent sedentary family from Central Arabia and lived in a lush middle-class area, saw himself as a missionary, somebody who could make a difference in this derelict social environment. "I prefer to be eighty percent useful here, rather than ten percent useful in another neighborhood," he told me. He sounded like an older version of Thamir, and I instinctively warmed to him.

He explained the summer camps' funding model to me and expressed his trust in the Ministry of Education, while adding that he hoped that administrators would trust the summer camps in return. His engagement in a "difficult" neighborhood and allegiance to the hierarchy did indeed get him appointed, a few years later, director of one of the administrative sections of the Ministry of Education. This charismatic educator had proven his worth on the front line of the camps and was rewarded. He was among those activists who embraced reform and benefited from it. Other directors, while also committed to their careers and to the success of the new summer clubs, were more critical of the context in which they operated. Unlike the last two camps I visited, their camps not only socialized students but also actively politicized them.

Socialization and politicization were two conflicting operations. Socializing students meant, for religious educators, helping them adapt to an environment where one was expected to show respect for mainstream opinions and abide by strict hierarchies. Politicizing them, by contrast, meant educating them to international causes, prompting them to look beyond the Kingdom's borders, and giving them the desire and the means to change society and politics. Many activists strove to bridge this gap: like Thamir, they wanted to help students both adapt to the wider world and acquire the theoretical and practical tools to transform it.

A group interview with ministry inspectors allowed me to better understand how the summer camp cadre thought about socialization. Abu Ahmad organized the meeting for me during a party offered by the coordination center, halfway through the summer camps. I interviewed three inspectors from two different generations in one of the dining rooms of the Riyadh Palace Hotel, whose slightly decrepit high modernist slab dominated the low-lying landscape of al-Murabbaʿ, north of the old city.

Seated at one end of the table, the older inspector seemed to take a keen interest in the few half-naked adolescents wading in the swimming pool outside the window. He put his glasses on to take a better look, then turned toward us, an air of sharp contempt on his face. He had joined the summer camps in the early 1980s and never left. He sported a religious look—longer beard, shortened robe, no double rope around his headdress. He was indulgent toward me, and seemed to pardon my incoherences and hesitations. I had spent the night roaming around Riyadh with joyriders, and was barely awake when I showed up at the Palace Hotel.

The two younger inspectors, appointed to replace dismissed activists, had joined the summer camps only the previous year. More mainstream in appearance and tone than their senior colleague, they were also more prone to speak on behalf of the Ministry of Education, and treated me like a slight nuisance. They defended the idea, key to state propaganda, that "decision-makers" and "those in charge" knew better than anybody else what society needed. Their memories zeroed in on the 1995 ban on summer camps, which they had experienced as either teachers or students. There was a before and an after, a golden age followed by decadence. Yet when I asked why they thought the summer camps had been shut down, the responses were elusive.

"At that time, I did not work in the summer camps," a younger inspector said. "I believe you can obtain this information from the decision-makers. Those in charge will explain the causes of the ban in detail and clearly."

"But they might not convey the experience of those on the ground," I said. He cut me off.

"In general, the ideas you will find on the ground are not correct, and you will end up collecting rumors. Those in charge will give you the right answer."

The inspectors promoted a very official narrative, based on the notion that some ideas were "correct" while others were not. According to the same inspector, summer camps were meant to "exploit students' free time with activities that benefit them."

"The goal is to fight holiday idleness," he said. "So, to avoid having students on the street, where nobody can control them, we gather them in one place, and then we release their energies through sports and leisure. Fighting idleness is fighting deviance."

"For sure," said the other young inspector. "The education policy strives to prepare students totally, completely, and at all times. This effort must be continuous. And the summer holidays are part of . . . "

He paused.

"You do not want to lose students from sight, even during holidays."

These inspectors promoted the idea that young men are intrinsically deviant and need to be kept in check at all times. They saw youth as a source of energy that could be harnessed through various activities. To them youthful energy was a zero-sum game: if you did not allow it to be released at school, it would wreak havoc in the streets. The older inspector shared their outlook. According to him, summer camps were a "safety valve,"[9] to empty out the pent-up energies of the youth. In a repressive system, youthful energy was either with Al Saud or against them.[10]

"Before, there was no tourism culture. Tourism appeared only recently," he said, keeping an esthete's eye on the teenage swimmers. "Sons stayed at home, because they had nothing to do during the summer. And summer camps became an important safety valve, they were really successful at the time. They have declined in the last few years, because families travel more. The idleness there was in the beginning has diminished in wealthier families. That is why, in the north of Riyadh, where the economic situation is better, there are fewer students in summer camps: fathers and families travel. Families living downtown or in some other areas cannot go on holiday. They fill the free time of their sons by putting them in summer camps."

He paused.

"Where in Riyadh have you lived?" he asked me.

"In Nasim for a bit, then Sultana," I said.

Both were lower-middle-class districts with a reputation for petty crime, joy-riding, and unrest. Nasim was a majority-Bedouin neighborhood, while Sultana, in the south of the old city, was more sedentary. The inspector relaxed a bit.

"Then you've gotten an idea of the material situation," he said. "Many students, in some areas, cannot find a sports field or any organized activities. We offer these in the camps."

He linked idleness to socioeconomic conditions. Lower-income youth were more prone to it than middle- and upper-middle-class kids. Class differences were crucial to youth behavior and expressed themselves in the space of the city: the inspector opposed the north of Riyadh to the inner city and to "some other areas." These other areas, like Tumiya, were an anti-geography of sorts, made of places whose names he did not utter. Idleness had become an object of sociological study at least since the 1970s oil boom, and many religious activists and preachers had adopted this sociological discourse.[11]

The two younger inspectors relaxed, too, and their speech grew more informal as the interview unfolded. One of them described the social situation in popular neighborhoods before summer camps took off in the 1980s.

"I do not remember traveling much during the summer," he said. "In general, everybody stayed in Riyadh during the summer. And the summer break was long: four months. You get the picture: families at the time were really big, with six, seven, eight kids or more, thank God. So you imagine, all these people in one place, for four months. And kids were bothering parents, creating trouble. . . . Education started in the street and, unsurprisingly, kids adopted sinful behaviors, because there was neither control nor surveillance. They were governed by the system of kids, the system of small groups."[12]

"Do kids run more risks in the streets today?" I asked, thinking about what I had witnessed during joyriding parties: car accidents, police crackdowns, and other nighttime perils.

"There were problems before," he said, "but they were commensurate with what was going on in society. There was less alcohol than now, fewer drugs. Kids were sniffing Pattex or glue. . . . Society was poor and simple. We considered smoking cigarettes a grave offense. . . . There was some violence, some brawls, for sure. But there is a difference in style today. Imported behaviors are on the rise, sure, but the truth is, corruption starts in the street—violence, deviance, that type of behavioral deviance we call homosexuality."[13]

The inspector contrasted an idealized past, where fathers exercised a relative authority over sinful youths, to a corrupt present in which fathers had lowered their guard and caved in to globalization and its lures. In the past, kids would "sin," that is, violate religious tenets; they now "deviated" from social norms. There had been a shift from religion to normativity, from sacred injunctions to social standards. Summer camps had become more secularized with time.

As the institution transferred its focus from sin to deviance and from faith to values, it was the body of the student, more than his soul, that became the object of the educator's attentions. The summer camps were founded on a physics of the student's body, which had to be placed in a certain environment and whose energy had to be geared toward certain directions. The older inspector's fascination with half-naked adolescent bodies might after all have been a professional tic. The body was subjected to temptations. It had to be disciplined and shielded from too much freedom of movement.

"Of course, the main goal of the summer camps was to exploit students' time," the older inspector said. "And if this goal was not fulfilled, many negative consequences would enfold. But to be in a state building under the responsibility of educators prevents many evils. It allows students not to harm themselves or others. . . . I remember a colleague who was running a summer camp around Huraymala," an outer suburb of Riyadh. "He said that the local police chief cooperated with them. Cops would tell them, 'You guys prevent problems, crimes, delinquency.' Because young men are idle, there are all kinds of issues and crimes going on. And they do not sleep a lot, these young guys. They pull all-nighters all the time, which has a very negative influence."

Summer camps were competing with whatever the street, the internet, and peer groups had to offer. Riyadh's streets were a marketplace in which educators vied for youth's attention with far more seductive competitors. As a result, the summer camps used self-help as a solution to many of the issues that they thought youth faced, and their educators claimed to satisfy students' desires.

"Before, there were no self-help sessions," the older inspector said. "Now there are some. But students do not accept just any instructor. They want certain names, they want famous names. Before, we would just focus on sports."

Both younger inspectors nodded in agreement.

"Self-help is in fashion these days," said one.

"Yes, since it is available in the stores," said the other.

"Yes, since it came out in the Arab world, people started getting interested in it. Some American and Canadian names have become household names. People started thinking self-help could play a role. A market opened and institutions supported this. Now, at the coordination center, we are all attending self-help sessions."

"And, for instance, we have sessions to help students develop their ability to dialogue, this is a new addition this year."

Many activists I had met seemed to be holding the Quran in one hand and *The Seven Habits of Highly Effective People*[14] in the other. Translated into Arabic in the 1990s, Stephen Covey's book had been a revelation for Kuwaiti, Saudi, and Egyptian Islamic activists, especially those who, like the Kuwaiti Tariq al-Suwaydan, had been exposed to self-help during their studies in the United States. An Egyptian activist was even reputed to have said of the book, "After that, we no longer need the Quran."[15]

But self-help lacked the transformative impetus that guided many activists. In highly repressive contexts, it was tempting to take refuge in self-help. But in redirecting activist efforts toward the private sphere, self-help became a decentralized, individualized form of repression. With their neoliberal leanings, these inspectors were starkly different from Thamir. The summer camps, created by the Muslim Brothers, had had their contentious edge amputated by their administrators and been turned into training facilities: their politics had shifted from mass mobilization to self-help and individual change.

"A student's destiny is to join the job market and fulfill himself," the older inspector concluded. "This is the kind of profit he can draw from the camps. The son of the nation must come back to the nation."

Chapter 18 **FIERCE AND LOUD**

THIS SUMMER CAMP WAS HARD TO FIND. THE SCHOOL THAT ABU Ahmad sent me to first was closed for construction. He then directed me to another school, to which the camp had moved. I navigated the narrow streets of the inner city, between mud brick houses and small cement buildings. Unlike in the suburbs, the streets here were alive. Shaded by apartment blocks and lined with busy storefronts, the streets sustained constant foot traffic, even on this hot June afternoon. The school was a four-story concrete building forming an L. From the offices on the fourth floor, the view of old Riyadh was stunning. But inside, the heat was unbearable. The A/C, which had been cut off for a while, started humming again, as by a miracle, a few minutes after my arrival.

The director said that his camp was seven years old and kept moving from school to school, depending on their state of disrepair. Students were poor and there were no compulsory registration fees, though wealthier families were asked to contribute twenty to thirty riyals (five to eight dollars). But "even twenty or thirty riyals, for certain families, is something they cannot afford to pay," he added. The director told me that his camp offered eighteen different kinds of training sessions, including computer science, mechanics, and self-help. They had a boy scout group and a theater troupe. They were preparing their students, the majority of whom were Afro-Saudis, for a job market that was tough on racialized minorities. Abu Ahmad and the coordination center inspector had told me that most students here were from "Sudan, Chad, and black Africa." They were actually Saudi, probably descendants of slaves. Abu Ahmad and the inspector loved to sing their love of the Saudi nation; they were also prompt to exclude from it whoever did not fit their idea of what Saudis should look like.

The inspector and I followed the director to the "social activities" room, a classroom whose walls were covered with boxes of cookies and bottles of fruit juice. "Social activities are dedicated to bodily nourishment," the inspector whispered. We sat down among the camp's supervisors, who were having their weekly meeting. The supervisors managed social activities, culture, sports, science, boy scout activities, and student affairs. There was no religious supervisor, however: as in other camps, religion was euphemized as "cultural activities." Religion was both controversial and ubiquitous: it had to be available, but under another name, lest the summer camps be politicized again, like in the 1990s, when they had supported the Islamic Awakening in its nationwide campaign.

The director, the inspector, and I sat on the floor, facing the supervisors who, while talking to me, were looking at the inspector out of the corner of their eyes, as if to assess his reactions or make sure he recorded their complaints. They explained that their summer camp was a charitable institution that offered what the street could not provide: a sense of self-worth and self-respect. Their camp bore more responsibility than others yet had less financial means. They held sessions for girls in a separate building, with cooking, sewing, and child-rearing classes. Most parents in the area wanted the camps to remain open all summer; some wanted them year-round. The supervisors wanted yearly financial support from the Ministry of Education to organize activities; they also wanted a separate structure, outside of the schools. The inspector was taking notes.

One supervisor brought up the example of 1995, when summer camps closed "after the 1994 Burayda demonstration," he said. Camps had to be replaced by police stations and local jails because of the rise in crime.

"The camps were closed for political reasons; they reopened for security reasons," he said.

The conversation, which had grown noisier, was interrupted by the resounding call for prayer. Then, after the prayer, we joined a "picnic program." The camp's three families competed in the school yard to build the best Bedouin tent, make the best fire, and prepare the best green coffee. The director sat me among the supervisors and gave me a grading sheet. We were asked to assess each family's quality of dress, hymns, coffee and tea, and excellence of execution. The first and second prizes were two hundred riyals (about fifty dollars) each, and the third prize was a hundred riyals (about twenty-five dollars).

Each family marched in procession from the school building to the sports field. Students carried banners and chanted slogans, brandishing their fists in the air. The banners showed the name of each family, and the slogans spoke of their determination and courage. These processions looked like demonstrations and could easily have been replicated in the streets if Riyadh's main arteries had not been gigantic freeways. Then the families lined up on the starting line, in the middle of the sports field. The director gave a signal, and students rushed toward us, picked up the equipment at our feet, and ran toward the field. Each family pitched its tent, made a fire, prepared coffee and tea, and played out what were meant to be Bedouin hospitality scenes. But the costumes, the scenes, and the vocabulary they used had more to do with widespread sedentary stereotypes than with actual nomadic life.

"There are no Bedouin in this camp," the director told me, and the students appeared to be quoting freely from the TV series *Tash ma tash*, which had aired every Ramadan since the 1990s.

One of the families gathered around "Sheikh Fu'ad," a comical *Tash ma tash* character whose linguistic and sartorial quirks students perfectly imitated. *Tash ma Tash* was written from a Najdi sedentary perspective and the character of Sheikh Fu'ad, a big-city simpleton who became a tribal sheikh after the death of one of his relatives, was meant to mock nomadic customs and pre-Al Sa'ud society.[1]

Finally, each family sang its hymn, and the supervisors compared their grades. The family on our right won, and the students roared in unison.

"They need to shout, to spend their energy like this," said the director. "At home, they are constantly asked to shut up, to avoid noise. Our programs must be fierce and loud."[2]

He invited me to join him and the supervisors for dinner in a small restaurant near the Ring Road. I talked about my research and mentioned the municipal elections. A supervisor nodded in agreement. He had managed the electoral campaign of one of the elected Islamic candidates. Another supervisor said that he had participated in the campaign, too. The director was very active in several charities that had supported candidates.

In low-income areas, socialization was in itself politicization, and there was neither ambiguity nor tension between the two. Summer campers acquired a more legitimate form of social and cultural capital: they were introduced to religious thinking (significantly renamed "culture") or asked to mimic sedentary middle-class attitudes, along with their attendant stereotypes (in particular, about the Bedouin). Summer camps extracted the students from their local, neighborhood-based attitudes and gave them the means to speak *to*—and in certain cases *against*—the wider Saudi society.

I had told my hosts that I worked on politicization. But even those supervisors who had volunteered in the municipal campaign refused to use the term "politics." They preferred to talk about fighting extremism or educating students to be good citizens. They insisted on the formation of the student as an individual, made ready for life after school and outside of the camps. In the past, summer camps had featured "closed" programs that were meant to create a counter-society. The camps were now "open" and catered to students' choices. There had been a shift from exclusive commitment to freedom of choice, from camps to *clubs*. Those supervisors and teachers who were still activists were working within this new framework and showed students how to protest, express their opinions, and organize, even in ways that were not automatically recognizable as such. The summer camps were still political, even if their politics had become more neoliberal and consensual. But this situation did not please everybody at the Ministry of Education.

Chapter 19 **HOW WERE
YOU FUCKED?**

SEATED ON A LONG COUCH IN THE CAMP'S MAIN OFFICE, THE
deputy director of student affairs for the Riyadh province was holding court.
In front of him, a young fast-food worker was dancing from one foot to the
other. Walking into the office, I thought that the deputy director's presence
there was probably no coincidence. The man's impeccably ironed robes exuded
an authority that his shrill voice comically undermined. The camp director,
the coordination center inspector, and a supervisor were seated on the couch
next to him. Their deference seemed tainted with a hint of irony.

The fast-food worker explained that the chain he worked for had sixty-one
restaurants in Riyadh, and that there were fifty-eight summer camps; he asked
if they could help by giving free meals to the students. The deputy director asked
about his background and why he had chosen to come to this school in particular.

The worker said that he had attended the summer camps: that is where he
learned leadership, he added. And he had come here because he lived in the
area. He wanted to give his managers, who were Westerners, an idea of the
camps and of what they were about.

The deputy director raised an eyebrow at the mention of the foreigners.
He explained that this was an institution, that people had to go through appropriate channels, and that one could not do what one wanted. Solicitors
should go to the central administration and could not just walk into a school.

The young man stopped wiggling and looked at his feet. His enthusiasm quickly evaporated. The deputy director drew his mouth into a sadistic grin. He told the young man to tell his managers that they could offer free training sessions instead of meals—and that they had to reach out to the central administration anyway.

This was not a bad idea, but it sounded like vengeance. The deputy director turned away from the fast-food worker, who mumbled something before disappearing into the hallway. The deputy director then turned to me, his voice considerably softened but still carrying a tone of cutting superiority. He demanded to hear my first observations about the summer camps.

This was my fifth day conducting fieldwork in the camps, driving from neighborhood to neighborhood, being received here with pump and circumstance, there as somebody who could give a hand. In some camps I had been given a supervisor's badge. In others I had been dined and entertained. In yet others, I was swiftly shuttled around and then shown the exit door. I had seen a variety of neighborhoods, some poor and dilapidated; some middle-class, orderly and well-tended; and some obscenely rich. This particular school sat in an upper-middle-class suburb and seemed to cater to very wealthy students.

"It is a bit early for me to talk about my experience, since I just started visiting the camps," I said. "I can maybe sum up my impressions with two remarks. The first one is that summer camps seem to offer students a positive model and give them social skills and cultural competences. My second remark is that I have noticed huge disparities from school to school. In poorer neighborhoods, schools are sometimes in a state of disrepair, and the camps run on less money."

Behind the back of the deputy director, the inspector nodded and blinked in the direction of the principal and the teacher. I felt encouraged by his sign.

"I have seen broken air conditioners, and even a school with no electricity. Sometimes, teachers and supervisors have to contribute their own money to run the camps, or give extra time to the institution."

The deputy director was taking notes. Without commenting on the point I had just made, he questioned me about the camps' activities. He seemed particularly interested in the citizenship workshops, which were part of a nationwide program to reform the camps and purge them of their supposed extremism. A few days earlier, I had been hanging out with a twenty-six-year-old artist with disabilities who gave painting lessons to summer campers. He had shown me the students' projects and some of his own works: bold paintings of old Najdi cities and of men surrounding the Saudi flag. The winner of a drawing contest about "Loving Our Dear Homeland" had painted a map of Saudi Arabia on which the green Saudi flag sat on top of the Ka'ba. Around the map, the student had written "My homeland, my love," "I love my homeland," and a quotation from the Quran: "Their affairs are organized by consultation among themselves."[1] In the midst of a dry exercise in patriotic admiration, this student had had the spirit to quote a verse undermining tyranny and promoting popular participation.

"The notion of citizenship as it is taught, citizenship as the love of the homeland and of the leaders,[2] does not seem appropriate," I said, emboldened by the memory of this student and his artist mentor. I then inexplicably decided to speak totally out of turn. "Is not love reserved to family relations? Would it not be more efficient to teach citizenship as the awareness of one's rights and duties? And is the love of the homeland and of the leaders compatible with Islam, which is not limited to a single country and a single national elite?"

He cut me off and said that, when he was forced to migrate to Medina, the Prophet famously said to Mecca, his homeland, "What a nice city you are and how ardently I love you."[3] He added that the love of the homeland[4] was key to Islamic patriotism; when in a foreign land he saw an office of Saudi Airlines with the symbols of the country, the two swords and the palm tree, he was submerged by his love for the homeland.

"Tribal identity, regional identity: we seek to crush them," he concluded.

I thought that the Prophet Muhammad had loved Mecca all right, but he did not migrate to Medina out of "love for the leaders"; quite the opposite: the Prophet actually fought the aristocrats of Mecca for a number of years. But I bit my lip.

The deputy director then said that he had not been aware of my research, although he was the director of all the summer camps. He took a sheet of paper from the coffee table in front of us, and started drawing an administrative chart. I had somehow bypassed him while getting the permission of his superior.

"I am sorry for not introducing myself to you earlier," I said. "I got my authorization from the director of education. I did not try to hide anything."

He asked what had prompted me to study the summer camps. After a moment of hesitation, I decided to be honest. I had told all my interlocutors, from the office of research to the office of student activities, the coordination center, and the camp teams what my research goals were, and I thought it both futile and shameful to start lying now.

"Last year I studied the municipal elections and observed that the summer camps were very active during the electoral campaign. I interviewed members of an Islamic group, and they confirmed my hunches. So I came to the camps to verify my hypotheses."

He cocked his head and asked if I had ever set foot in a school before.

"No, I just met the supervisor of an Islamic group and the group's 'pioneers,' who were his students . . . "

"Pioneers are never students: these people did not give you a correct image of extracurricular religious activities in schools."

He told me that what I said about the elections revealed a very different outlook than his. He then said the camp director would take me on a tour of the school. As I had done in other summer camps, I turned to the director, pulled out my camera, and asked him if I could take photos.

The deputy director didn't let the principal respond. His tone of voice suddenly gentle, he explained that I would get a copy of the DVD presenting the summer camps, that I could get everything I wanted from them indeed, but that I could not take photos. He asked if I had taken photos elsewhere, and if I had had permission from the administration.

"Yes," I said. "I asked every camp director for their permission. They all allowed me to photograph during my visits."

The camp director and I walked out. During our quick tour of the classrooms, I asked if the deputy director was a frequent visitor. He told me that his visit was a surprise. After our tour we walked back to the main office. I had hoped that the deputy director would be gone, but he was still there, writing a letter at the director's desk.

"You committed a legal contravention by taking photos in the summer camps," he said, handing me a letter he wanted me to sign.

The letter said that, during our conversation, there had been a disagreement between us about my research; that he was putting an end to my fieldwork from this moment on and summoning me to the Ministry of Education to discuss what had happened; that I should surrender all my photos to the Ministry of Education, which would refer them to the Interior Ministry and the Ministry of Information; and that, if I wished to continue my fieldwork, I should submit a list of potential interviewees. The evening call to prayer resounded. The deputy director sent a student to type up the letter.

After the prayer, the deputy director handed me the typed-up letter and a pen. The letter had been signed by himself, the camp director, and the inspector.

"I do not agree with this letter," I said. "I have been honest about my research since the beginning, and I wrote a proposal that was stamped by the Ministry of Education. I have an authorization to conduct fieldwork, and I do not see why I should start all over again. I will not sign this."

The deputy director took the letter and the pen and wrote that I had refused to sign but would abide by the letter's injunctions (to go to the ministry, hand over my photos, and stop visiting the camps).

"I am sorry for having annoyed you," he said, defiantly. "I hope that you did not get too bad an impression from this visit."

"I feel very annoyed indeed," I responded in the same tone. "And I had a very positive impression of the camps, which you certainly ruined today."

He handed me the letter again, looking me in the eye, and said: "Here is the letter, feel free to tear it up."

I was astounded. He ripped up the letter himself. He then grabbed another sheet of paper and started taking frantic notes.

"What do you have against me?" I asked, adding: "This office looks more and more like a police station."

"You seem to have a wrong idea of the general situation in this country," he said, still scribbling away. "And you were dishonest by not revealing right away that your research was about the municipal elections."

"But everything I wrote about the municipal elections has been published," I replied, "including an article in Arabic, which came out with the authorization of Prince Turki al-Faysal, the director of the King Faysal Center."[5]

When I said the prince's name, the deputy director's hand immediately stopped writing and an inkblot formed under the tip of his pen. He looked up and asked me about the research center in a much softer tone. Then he stood, gathered his belongings, and walked toward the exit. The name of a prince was all it took.

"I leave you with the director," he said, waving at the deserted hallways outside the office. "You can continue your visit." It was now 10 pm, and all the students, teachers, and supervisors were gone. Our conversation had lasted five hours. I turned to the camp director and apologized for causing such a stir with his director.

"He is not our director," he said. "He has no authority over us."

"Do you think that the deputy director is hostile to the summer camps?" I asked as we walked toward the exit.

"Perhaps. He is one of those who are not happy with the summer camps."

I thanked him, bid him farewell, and drove to the rest house where Thamir and his friends were having tea and chatting about the day's event. Still shaken, I told them what had happened at the summer camp.

One of Thamir's friends said that the deputy director was a man of power, a government bureaucrat who had become alarmed when he heard me breaking political taboos. Since he was against the summer camps, he had tried to scare me away and to prevent me from conducting any more fieldwork.

Thamir nodded in agreement. I understood that I had been caught between government officials and more activist educators; that my visits to the southern suburbs, while showing me how contentious the camps could still be, had also given me a sense of false assurance, prompting me to be more open with the deputy director than I should have been.

The situation became clearer during the following weeks. The deputy director visited the King Faysal Center several times to ascertain whether I was in good standing with that institution. He also sent a formal complaint to the emirate of Riyadh, which dispatched to the King Faysal Center the secret police officer who had been following my activities in Riyadh.[6] I was not in when he arrived, but the explanations he heard convinced him to close the investigation. I was informed that I could resume my fieldwork. By that time, the summer camps were in their sixth week, and I had lost some precious time.

I drove again to the coordination center, where Abu Ahmad was waiting for me. He asked me—again—about my research interests, a hint of suspicion in his voice. I told him that I had arrived in Riyadh during the electoral campaign and quite naturally studied it, although the elections were not the main focus of my work. Abu Ahmad seemed relieved. He said that the government was not at all satisfied with the results of the elections, and that bringing up that topic in front of the deputy director had not been helpful. Without a word, he then showed me copies of the coordination center newsletter, which advertised a lecture by an elected municipal council member.

Abu Ahmad told me that one of the teachers had probably raised a complaint after meeting me and that the deputy director had been sent to investigate the matter. I had assumed that my honest, transparent communication style, which had worked with so many teachers and activists, would also gain me the favor of a high-ranking administrator. This was a mistake. The deputy director had been threatening: I had waved the name of Turki al-Faysal to protect myself. Alarmed in turn, he had sent a complaint to the emirate of Riyadh. I was glad the escalation had stopped.

Abu Ahmad, as formal as on the day we met, said he understood my work, because he was a journalist and knew what was going on outside of Arabia. As for the deputy director, he continued, he was not as open. At this point, the bespectacled inspector who had shown a keen interest in half-naked adolescents walked in.

"What did you do to that summer camp?" He asked me with a huge smile. "Or rather, *mazha fu'ila fik?*" In classical Arabic, this strictly meant: "What was done to you?" The same question also meant, in Saudi colloquial, "How were you fucked?" The inspector's large grin, as well as everybody's laughter, showed he meant to say exactly that.

The inspector gave me his analysis of what had happened. He told me that in addition to the department of student *activities*, I should also have visited the department of student *affairs*. I remembered the chart the deputy director had quickly drawn for me: he headed the student *affairs* department and not the student *activities* department, which was an Islamic stronghold. As Thamir and his friends had correctly grasped, I had been caught in an internal conflict about the meaning of the summer camps and the political exploitation of students' free time. Some wanted to turn summer camps into an electoral resource. Others, including the deputy director, wanted to use it to inculcate students with "the love of the homeland and of the leadership" and to promote a secularized form of leadership.

A few days later, I drove to the summer camp in the southern suburbs where I had witnessed mayhem and a powerless director. The director had invited me to their end-of-summer party, which took place on the sports field.

I sat between a father with his younger son and a boisterous family of six. The guest of honor, a stern-looking professor from the Islamic University, sat in front of me, in the first row. A student passed between the guests, handing out the last issue of the camp's magazine, which featured a large advertisement for the local Quranic circle. "When the camp bids us farewell . . . the Quranic circle calls us to join," the ad said. The head of the Quranic circle, an older man with a long beard tinted red with henna, walked in and sat near the Islamic University professor.

The director arrived and addressed the fathers about their sons. But the uproar was constant and the sound system was booming over everybody's shouts and calls. A group of youth behind me laughed about everything. Kids were running everywhere. The head of the Quranic circle took out his cellphone and showed a video to the university professor, who was captivated by whatever was playing on the tiny screen. The director courageously went on, explaining that summer camps taught kids to be good Muslims and good sons. A coffee boy was passing around trays of teacups and cakes.

A student recited a poem mourning the loss of the camps and the departure of the students. The Islamic University professor tore himself from the contemplation of his neighbor's cellphone, went on stage, and took the mic. He praised the summer camps. He regretted that they did not last longer and ultimately abandoned youth to themselves and to the void of Riyadh. He then distributed prizes to the families who had won Quranic, sports, and social competitions. The family pioneers stepped onto the stage to collect their prizes: plastic shields with the name of the camp and stacks of books. The party ended with a quick dinner. Leaving the school, I was presented with a gift: a beautiful imitation of a Parker pen inscribed with the name of the camp.

As I walked to my car, I could not but reflect on the gift: it was an instrument of power ("the pen of the director himself") and a sign of middle-class respectability, exactly the type of pen that civil servants and businessmen would stick into the chest pocket of their white robes. It was also an instrument of intellectual power and embodied one of the goals Islamic activists had set for themselves: reforming society through writing, publishing, petitioning, and organizing. The pen suggested the type of gentility that Islamic groups were calling upon their adherents to emulate. Yet in the context of crackdown, little remained of these ideals, and Islamic activism itself had become one of the tools government used to try and tame youth. Summer camps, once feared for their contentious activities, had become closer to neoliberal theme parks. No wonder some young activists were becoming more vocal and extreme and others, choosing to move on, had actually left Islamic activism behind.

PART IV

LEAVING ISLAMIC ACTIVISM BEHIND

■ ■ ■ ■ ■

Chapter 20 **THOSE DAMNED LIBERALS**

I WAS ATTENDING A ROUND TABLE AT THE RIYADH BOOK FAIR ON "Cultural Difference: Me and the Other." Several Saudi intellectuals and a German diplomat were sharing the stage and droning on about the importance of dialoguing with the West. In the audience, a group of religious activists grew visibly irritated. At some point, one of them stood up and interrupted the speaker, a renowned Saudi social scientist.

"You liar!" he shouted.[1]

All heads turned toward the interrupter, who launched into a harangue, lining up words with the confidence of a trained orator. Bristling with indignation, he said that it was preposterous to talk about dialogue with the West when the U.S. Army was occupying Afghanistan and Iraq and imprisoning, torturing, and killing Muslims there and elsewhere. What kind of dialogue was one supposed to hold with an armed invader?

A second activist, as indignant as the first one, asked the social scientist to respect academic boundaries and to leave questions of religious doctrine to specialists of that discipline. To him, relationships between Muslims and non-Muslims were not a matter of opinion, but of faith, and fell under specific religious tenets: it was for religious clerics to discuss them, not social scientists. Other activists erupted in shouts and accusations. People in the audience sat still and held their breaths, watching the stage where the speakers seemed petrified. A few people, visibly afraid, left the room as the crowd of indignant men became more vocal. The commotion grew louder. A voice rose above the hubbub, "Where is security?"

The conference speakers stepped down off the stage, one after the other, and walked toward the exit. But the activists spotted another target in the audience, a well-known member of the Shura Council who had advocated for women's driving. (The Shura Council, appointed by the king, was an advisory body with no legislative powers.) A group of activists swarmed him, large smiles on their faces. Several of them were holding cell phones and filming the encounter. I got up and inched closer. I recognized among them a famous Salafi sheikh who had called for a boycott of the United States after the invasion of Iraq in 2003. A large, carnivorous smile across his face, the sheikh engaged in a brisk dialogue with the Shura councilor who, trying to keep his cool, smiled back at him.

The sheikh asked the councilor why he had publicly supported women driving and demanded that he publicly retract his statements. The council member, looking distraught, let out a short laugh and tried to walk toward the exit. A friend of his, a young journalist wearing enormous glasses, tried to clear a way out for the councilor. Seeing this, someone pulled down the journalist's headdress from behind, stopping the journalist short as he raised his hands to grab his headdress and double rope. Young activists sniggered behind his back. The sheikh, still smiling, invited the Shura member to dinner. The council member invited him to dinner in return. Somebody said that the police were on their way, and everybody cleared out before the uniforms showed up.

Outside the conference hall, the council member and the journalist looked relieved. The Shura member pulled out his phone and told an invisible interlocutor that he had been cornered by "terrorists," even though the exchange had remained cordial until the end. The journalist also called somebody and told him: "Those sheikhs gathered their troops to stand up to *those damned liberals*."

I told the story later to a friend who said that the scene was typical of Salafis and of their tactics. The Salafis were specialists in hadith; they were particularly interested in the trustworthiness of their sources, and one of their main methods was called "criticizing and praising."[2] By examining the lives and reputations of those who had transmitted sayings of the Prophet, they decided whether to trust them or not. They would recuse some hadith narrators and restore the dignity of others, which could significantly change the geography of the doctrine.

Salafism was "the science of men,"[3] of their actions, and of their behaviors, my friend continued. Using this age-old method, Salafis often launched ad hominem attacks to discredit those they saw as false authorities. Sheikh Muqbil al-Wadi'i and his disciples, for instance, would say that their opponents were "trumpets" who made a lot of noise without bringing much light; "invertebrates" with no intellectual backbone; or "wet rags" with no shape or consistency.[4]

Salafis had become experts at breaking their adversaries during spectacular verbal jousts or from the safety of online forums and chatting rooms. They often subverted common labels. In Yemen, they had nicknamed the Muslim Brothers[5] the "bankrupt brothers"[6] and called their magazine, al-Sahwa (the Awakening) al-Ghafla (Ignorance).[7] There was an element of fun in these plays on words. This popular art aimed at summing up an opponent in one character trait. "You liar"—and everything was said.

The Salafis did not argue ad rem, but ad hominem. But their opponents also questioned the very credibility of "those sheikhs" and avoided engaging in public debate about the issue at hand: the power of the West, the subservience of Saudi elites, the lack of imagination of all parties. This was a massive political difference, and it seemed as though the frontier between "me and the other," instead of separating "Islam" from "the West," ran between irreconcilable ways of seeing the world among Saudi activists and intellectuals. Some were working with the Saudi state to restore its international credentials while others were trying to create a resistance movement against the United States's invasion of Afghanistan and Iraq. 'Adel brilliantly summed this up when he said one day: "Some Saudis are dying to meet a Westerner, while others would rather die than meet one."[8]

Islamic activists had lost ground since their heyday in the early 1990s. Back then, Sheikh Salman al-'Ouda was at the forefront of protest. Now, when the Riyadh Book Fair invited him to speak, he gave a lecture on "Society and the Horizons of Change" that could have been written by one of those intellectuals the Salafis had come out to rail against. Salman al-'Ouda spoke two days after the Shura member was swarmed by activists. He invited his audience to actively contribute to change, lest they be subjected to a change that would be violently imposed to them. Salman al-'Ouda asked his listeners to be self-crit-ical, to read widely, and to stop being yes-men. The Najdi Arabic equivalent of yessir was *sem, tal 'umrak*, and al-'Ouda used the neologism *semsema* to describe "those who keep saying *sem*, aye, affirmative." He said that "those who do not buy into *semsema* and keep asking questions are often seen as undesirables, even in our religious and Islamic circles." To contribute to social and political reform, one had to make oneself undesirable.

The bespectacled journalist who, two days before, had come to the coun-cilor's rescue was there too. He raised his hand and thanked Salman al-'Ouda for his contribution.

"You carry a formidable responsibility for the change that is happening now," he said. He was so emphatic that I thought for a moment that he was being ironic. But he seemed sincere and willing to find a common ground between secularists and Islamic activists. To him, al-'Ouda was a modernist sheikh, a "liberal Islamist,"[9] someone who was limiting the scope of the reli-gious doctrine, championing rational interpretations, and relativizing the power of those Salafis he saw as the enemies of change. As for al-'Ouda, he was obviously toeing the line drawn by Al Sa'ud and trying not to lose the slim margin of freedom he had gained since he had been liberated from prison.

Repression, then, was what made the difference between the Islamic ac-tivists' clout in the early 1990s and their relative powerlessness in a time of global War on Terror. But there was something else going on within the Islamic Awakening. Activists were growing dissatisfied not only with the general lack of political outlets, but also with the behavior of other activists. Those who "keep asking questions are often undesirables," and these undesirables either left Islamic activism behind or tried to reform it from within. Their stories intersect with the story of state repression—and of repression within Islamic organizations.

Chapter 21 **THE STOREHOUSES OF THE LAND**

I MET FAWWAZ ON TAHLIYA AVENUE, WHICH RIYADH YOUTH lovingly but also sardonically nicknamed "the Champs-Elysées of Riyadh" for its sidewalk life, large cafés, and Second Empire cast-iron streetlights. Fawwaz, aged twenty, was a friend of a friend and a student in history. Short and slim, he spoke volubly, throwing in hypotheses and fieldwork ideas. He had recently left the student activities of the Muslim Brotherhood and instead joined a club whose members met every week or so to discuss politics, society, and culture. Several such clubs had emerged in Riyadh and Jeddah in the mid-2000s, and Fawwaz had made the transition from the mainstream Muslim Brotherhood to an intellectual circle that openly debated individual rights, the relationship with the West, and political pluralism.[1]

Fawwaz was open to political experimentation, but he still considered himself socially conservative. He was against the opening of movie theaters and against female driving, too. "These are trivial questions," he would casually say, shifting the conversation back to what he thought were more pressing issues: democracy, human rights, and political reform.

Fawwaz was an instant fieldwork ally. He was enthusiastic about my research; he volunteered his help, brought me into his new circle of friends, proposed to drive me around his neighborhood, and spent hours with me walking around the city and chatting while holding hands as intimate friends do.

On the day we met, we bumped into two of his childhood friends. Prompted by Fawwaz, they talked about how they had joined Salafi groups (through family connections for one, school for the other) and how they imagined their own Salafism (as a move away from politics for one, in reaction to the Muslim Brotherhood for the other). The conversation was promising, and I asked if I could interview them. They agreed; I never saw them again. Most of my interlocutors, in fact, would meet up with me once, exhibit polite interest in my research, and disappear without leaving a trace.

But Fawwaz stuck around, and his zeal was sometimes excessive. "When I saw you, I felt myself opening to the Other," he said at the end of our first meeting, as if he had been one of the speakers on that stage at the Riyadh Book Fair. He wanted to call me *ustadh*, "professor." I declined the label. "Friend, then." I nodded, still puzzled at the speed with which he had embraced my research project. He was interested in the history of Islamic movements. He wanted to read my first book. He wanted to know the latest gossip about those academics who, trained in Paris like me, were working on Saudi Arabia.[2] He wanted to prove himself in his new circle and to buttress his reformism with a Western friendship. I wanted to understand what had gone wrong in his relationship with the Muslim Brotherhood. I hoped that he would help me conduct field research.

Fawwaz introduced me to his club a few days later. Around fifteen people were splayed about the living room of a suburban home. In their late twenties and early thirties for the most part, they hailed from Muslim Brother and Salafi circles and were students, professors, lawyers, civil servants, and businessmen.

The speaker that day was the very social scientist who had been called a liar by Salafi activists at the Book Fair. He spoke about the relationship between state and religion and explained that, contrary to widespread assumptions, the alliance of politics and religion in Islam had only been in effect during the rule of the first four caliphs (632–661 CE), after which state and religion had split in practice, if not always in theory. He said that the Saudi monarchy had never claimed it had a divine right to rule; instead, the princes managed public affairs and reserved a few sectors (female education, public morality, the courts) to the oversight of clerics who were tightly controlled by the princes.

He explained that, by subjecting religion to state control, Al Saʿud had embraced the very principles of absolute state sovereignty that characterized

European nations. The French state had banned headscarves from schools under the pretense of prohibiting conspicuous religious symbols; the Saudi state had banned other religious expressions under the pretense of protecting the sanctity of the holy land. Both the French and the Saudi states claimed to be the ultimate regulators of human activity. Religion had no real autonomy, he said, and was a tool in the hands of the state, which had acquired quasi-divine powers over its citizens.

The social scientist was bold; he was saying out loud what many Islamic activists were thinking: that Saudi Arabia was no religious paradise, but a graveyard of clerics, a secularist state. The difference was that he seemed rather satisfied with secularism, whereas his Salafi adversaries were not.

Fawwaz passed me a handwritten note saying, "This guy seems to have a problem with the French; why do you not say something?" I scribbled back, "Maybe because I have a bigger problem with the French?" After the talk, Fawwaz paraded the notes in front of the other club members and sent a long text to his high school friends to announce that we would visit his childhood neighborhood and interview them.

A few days later, Fawwaz picked me up and took me for a ride. He was driving his small Toyota with one finger while calling friends to set up interviews, carefully balancing susceptibilities in the process.

"Awesome, you can come, too. . . . No, wait, I am afraid Yusuf might take issue, I did not tell him yet you would come, you know? And maybe he does not know that other guy. . . . What?. . . . Good, no problem, but it is better to meet alone. Pascal usually prefers to meet one-on-one. He uses the direct-interview method with people. . . . So I am telling you, it is better to meet individually. . . . Okay? Good?"

Yusuf was Fawwaz's former supervisor in the Muslim Brotherhood, and Fawwaz was trying to manage his sensitivities, of which he apparently had many. Like Fawwaz, Yusuf had left the Muslim Brotherhood behind, but Fawwaz seemed to have a conflicted relationship to him, an odd mix of admiration, fear, and exasperation. Outside the car window, the urban landscape was fading in the setting sun. In the distance, the limestone cuesta of Khashm al-ʿAn gleamed in the day's last rays of sun. Inside the car, Fayruz was droning on the sound system, her languid voice covering the speed alarm's staccato beeps.

"Record, give it a try."

Fawwaz paused Fayruz and pointed to the voice recorder. The speed alarm was still beeping furiously.

"It is already recording."

"Is it now?"

He straightened up and started describing the Muslim Brotherhood in stilted classical Arabic, goggling at the recorder from the corner of his eye. The contrast between his hurried, colloquial voice and the expert tone he adopted now was almost comical. ("I adore speaking in classical Arabic," he said later. "In general, I do not like colloquial too much.")

"Our Islamic movement started preaching Islam and calling people to religion," he said. "With time, they created student activities in middle schools, high schools, and colleges. I do not know how many have closed down: every year they shut down groups, because there is no administrative team, no supervisors, and student enrollment is lower; there is more than one problem . . . "

The crisis in Islamic activism was a constant theme in conversations with Fawwaz and Thamir. While Thamir had eventually come back to the Muslim Brotherhood, Fawwaz had left for reasons that became clearer as we drove around. Yusuf had played a role in this story.

"Yusuf is twenty-eight. He climbed the group's ladder starting in high school. He studied engineering and worked with us middle school kids as a university student, until he became a supervisor."

Fawwaz's phone rang again. It was another potential interviewee.

"Hello? Peace be upon you. . . . No, what is wrong with you? We are driving around, having fun. . . . No, no, no: he is a PhD student at the Sorbonne, in France. . . . I met him through somebody, not at the university. . . . Talk to him; chat a little. Are you being shy? . . . Oh, are you a little afraid to meet him? . . . No problem. . . . No, my good man, what is the matter with you? It would be for a chat, not an official meeting. . . . All right, not a problem, but I would love to have dinner with you, walk around with you, it would be good to hear your perspective, brother. . . . No, you do not need to have a historical dimension or be a leader. . . . I do not know, you seem . . . No, on the contrary, I am excited, he is excited, I told him about you and he wants to meet you. . . . These social scientists try to meet as many people as possible, you see? Otherwise they would read books, my brother, and books are deeper than Yusuf or you or . . . What? . . . Okay, this weekend, God willing. Bye."

He hung up, paused, and turned to me:

"My brother, problem. That was 'Ali. He is a good guy, but he is underselling himself; he says, 'He is not going to learn anything from me.' But, brother, you do not need to be a leader to be interesting."

Fawwaz came back to his issue with the Brotherhood.

"Supervisors were trying to control the rank and file. There was individual supervision, collective supervision, and supervision of the wider group, of the activities as a whole, forty to fifty people. That is why the subdivision of Islamic groups into families and cars is very useful from an educational perspective. The supervisor controls the whole group. Every member of the mosque circle, within a family or outside a family, is subjected to the supervisor's surveillance. . . . The supervisor is usually the family leader; he is responsible for all the cars and all the members of a family. From time to time, the supervisor imparts a kind of education and behaves in a professorial manner. It is only rarely that you will find a form of fulfillment, of brotherhood, you see."

From Fawwaz's point of view, there was little brotherly love in the midst of the Muslim Brothers. The movement controlled its members through an elaborate hierarchy. Supervisors confused control and education, which allowed them to keep the upper hand over individuals.

"There is harshness, but also a kind of education," he said. "Supervisors behave arrogantly. 'I am in charge, you are just a student . . . ' They behave with pedagogical arrogance."

The Muslim Brotherhood was a teachers' movement with no clear boundaries between hierarchical authority, pedagogical authority, and symbolic violence. Yusuf, Fawwaz's former supervisor in the Brotherhood, seemed to embody the ambiguity at the heart of the Brotherhood: the movement strove to elevate its members above the fray while contributing to the violence of its environment. But he himself had become a target of the group's coercion.

"In the latter period," Fawwaz continued, "Yusuf ran into trouble because of his writings online. There was this new reformist wave that he was praising; he started reading, and . . . he says that he took his distance from the group; that he left the Muslim Brothers behind. He became undesirable among them. He started to criticize the group. The trouble with student activities is usually that people attempting to reform the activities are considered undesirable, and sometimes pushed aside. I do not think Yusuf was banished from the Brothers, but he limited his involvement with them. He may have seen that the Brothers were useless. Now he cares more about his own education, especially since he got married, and he works long hours. He also writes a weekly column in a local newspaper, so . . . I think he is all set. No doubt he holds open-minded opinions, but he maintains his allegiance toward the Muslim Brothers."

Fawwaz drove into Malaz, where we wanted to have dinner. The car was whizzing along a straight avenue lined with cafés and restaurants. The notion of allegiance to the Brothers was another issue he had with the movement.

"Allegiance to the group is instinctive, and I do not think there is a formal pledge of allegiance to the Brothers. But think about this. You live in a group for five, six years, if you joined during high school; ten years if you continue with them through college. The group shapes your outlook and your culture, and you do not rebel against it. In Egypt, even the rank-and-file pledge their allegiance to what they call 'the cells.' But not here. We only have social and cultural activities, and there is no pledge of allegiance. Or if there is any, it was in the past, or within some groups, or among the leaders. But the question also is the nature of students' allegiance to the activities, or to the Brothers, or to the Salafis. And the degree of allegiance is very, very high, to the point of fanaticism sometimes. You do not rebel, even if you see an obvious mistake."

He suddenly turned to me, visibly alarmed, and gestured toward the voice recorder:

"Careful, this is the political prison, hide this."

We were driving by a drab building. Two guards manned a checkpoint in front of the main gate. I hid the recorder. Fawwaz slowed down and rolled down his window.

"Peace be upon you, God give you life, guys," he said in their direction with a nod.

They waved him past and he rolled his window back up.

"Scary, huh? That is where they locked up so many people.

"Allegiance is still very high among the Brothers. I even asked to take my distances from the activities, precisely because of the very strong allegiance. At some point, we had daily activities. Every day, except Friday, the holiday of the Filipino [maids and servants]. Between an hour and a half and six hours daily. Sometimes I would see the Brothers more than my father. There was bread and salt, there was a life. You knew you lived with people. And you faced injustices. . . . Students were in a position of permanent inferiority."

The very name of "family," which was given to the second-smallest unit in Islamic groups (above the "car"), showed that allegiance had to be strong, even if, for reasons of secrecy and safety, it did not happen through a formal pledge. Allegiance stemmed from proximity and habit; according to Fawwaz, it ended up turning the "family" into a violent environment. When he said that group members had as tough a schedule as did the Filipino maids, meeting every day but Friday, he was hinting at the limits of the familial metaphor: families were exploitative units, too, and their members were not always rewarded for their dedication to the group.

"They thought I was wrong, in a way. They had a number of reservations about me. But the student they love, for instance, the accomplished student: they would see him as the good student. Think about this: I was with the high school activities for three years, and I was never given any leadership functions, even though students usually fulfill that role. For instance, we have a trip, once a month, outside of Riyadh, another one, once a year, to Abha, and two trips per year to Mecca. And usually, the guy in charge of the trip, the emir of the journey[3]—the *emir of the journey!*—everybody abides by his opinion, even supervisors. And that person is most often a student in his last year of activities, a twelfth grader. But they never gave me any leadership mission."

He smirked while repeating "emir of the journey," an inflated title that did not reflect the reality of preparing picnics and organizing hiking trips.

"My cousin, for instance, is my age and managed three summer camps. But *I* was undesirable, and personal questions played a more important role than they should have. True, I was undesirable to several supervisors: I caused trouble, I often criticized the activities, I criticized the Brothers; but this does not allow you to deprive me of my right. It is a student's right to be given leadership missions from time to time. And even in the Quran, Yusuf told Pharaoh: 'Appoint me over the storehouses of the land.'[4] So their leadership model, which subjects student activities to the whims of the leader, is a failure. We should better focus on educating students to become leaders or managers, to organize activities, to build the group."

The prophet Yusuf, who had divine dreams and visions, was thrown into a well by his jealous brothers. But Yusuf was rescued, sold as a slave to an

Egyptian and, thanks to his visionary gift, was appointed by Pharaoh "over the storehouses of the land" and became the superintendent of Egypt. The story ended well; but in the beginning, Yusuf's father had told his son, "Do not tell your vision to your brothers lest they plot against you."[5] After Fawwaz had told his visions to the Brothers, they marked him as a pariah, and he now compared himself to the prophet who had been saved by an infidel king.

The storehouses of the land, rather than being a matter of implementation, were the place where an accomplished prophet such as Yusuf could prove his value and the worth of his visions. Good management was a sign of strong faith and personal excellence, and Fawwaz too wanted to become a manager. The fact that he was let down and thrown into the well, so to speak, was evidence, to him, that the Muslim Brothers, with all of their family talk, had a management issue. They were unable to retain talent within their ranks. They let dedicated, independent spirits such as himself slip away. They did not properly tend to their own storehouses; how could they be trusted with the storehouses of the land? For Fawwaz, the Muslim Brotherhood, like Yusuf's brothers, had become a murderous bunch acting out of jealousy, unable to discern merit or to see his value as a potential leader.

Chapter 22 **PEOPLE DID NOT FALL FROM THE SKY**

THE NEXT WEEKEND, WE DROVE TO FAWWAZ'S CHILDHOOD SUB-urb. This was a middle-class area where streets were straight and wide, single-family homes were surrounded by high walls, and everybody moved around by car. We first met Yusuf, Fawwaz's former supervisor in the Muslim Brotherhood. The three of us sat in a café on one of the main avenues. The business had opened recently; everything in it, from the bar to the carpets, seemed new, and the place was almost empty. We found a nook where I could run the voice recorder without being disturbed and where our conversation would be out of the employees' earshot.

"I am not so famous that you can sell me for money," Yusuf told me right away. "You know, many others would sell themselves."

"You mean, you sell yourself but you are not *that* famous," Fawwaz said.

"May God curse you." Yusuf let out a laugh. "It is a good business, you know."

Many interviewees tended to assume—even if jokingly—that I was after money. In the fast-paced Saudi media landscape, it was not uncommon to see journalists become local stars by interviewing the main figures of the Awakening and publishing about them.[1]

Yusuf's tone was very professorial at first. He explained that the Muslim Brotherhood used to be more political; their first aim was to "reconstitute the Islamic Caliphate. That was their goal before, but then there were several revisions in their way of thinking, and they decided in 1994 that this goal was unrealistic."

In 1994, young Egyptian Muslim Brothers discussed a national charter that put forward constitutional and political reforms. The leadership's refusal to endorse it led to the split of the Wasat party from the Brotherhood.[2] This was in a way what marked the birth of the reformist, liberal branch of the Islamic movement—which both Yusuf and Fawwaz eventually embraced.

"In the beginning, the Muslim Brothers had a political way of thinking about things. They moved on to politics through the education of the soul, they educated individuals to have a sense of responsibility toward social reality and toward their own goals. That is why the Brothers paid attention to the political situation."

In the face of increased state repression, the Brotherhood had renounced its initial political project to focus on less dangerous goals. That is at least what Yusuf had observed when he was in charge of a small group of students, within a mosque circle.

"Yusuf was picking us up, he was a car person," Fawwaz said.

"Yes, I was in charge of a mosque circle, with that car, there . . . " Yusuf waved toward a worn Honda Accord parked outside the window. "But a circle supervisor carries out a purely educational mission, without any political dimension. We only help students shed what is bad in them. Moral issues, bad-mouthing, slander, lies, things like these, no relation to politics, you see. Circles are not linked to politics. It is all about reforming souls. My dad was a Muslim Brother, so I was born inside the Brotherhood, so to speak. . . . I never really joined the Awakening: I was born in it. And then I started participating in the summer camps. People would play soccer, create theater pieces, they would have *fun*. And they would try to raise your interest in prayer and in the reform of the soul. Then I continued in a mosque circle, first in middle school, then in high school, and finally in college."

" . . . Only because you were desirable," Fawwaz cut him off.

"What do you mean?"

"You continued with them only because you were desirable."

Fawwaz had been jumpy since the beginning of the conversation and wanted to weave his own critique of the Awakening into Yusuf's curated narrative. Like Salman al-'Ouda, Fawwaz was interested in the ways being desirable or undesirable played out in the Islamic movement. There was an element of desire and repulsion in the Awakening—between older mentors and younger members, between the more and the less righteous—that had contaminated Fawwaz's journey with Islamism and his relationship to Yusuf. The reform of the soul was planted in the bodily soil of desire and disgust, and Fawwaz was trying to turn the tables on his former mentor.

"Yes, only because I was desirable," Yusuf repeated. Then, in my direction: "Desirable and undesirable: these expressions characterize your discipline, your daily attendance, your interaction with the activities."

The interview slowly turned into a battle between the two men. I was silent, and it was Fawwaz who was asking questions and testing Yusuf's perspective on the Muslim Brotherhood. He rubbed his own recent expertise in Yusuf's face, telling him that, as a regular member of his club, he was now regularly meeting "people who had had leadership positions within the Brotherhood."

There was a toxic dynamic to our interview triangle. Fawwaz had decided that he could trust me, but Yusuf did not know me and was understandably reluctant to express political sentiments in front of a stranger. Fawwaz wanted to take revenge for what he thought was Yusuf's failed leadership and to show him that he, Fawwaz, had become important. Yusuf, in turn, was unsure how to behave, since this embarrassing conversation was being recorded by me, whom he did not know. The interview was turning into a setup, and I felt more and more uncomfortable. I was beginning to resent Fawwaz's intrusion into my field research. Not only was he making appointments in my stead; he was also using my project to wage what looked like a proxy war against his former fellow activists.

Their main disagreement revolved around the idea and reality of polit-ical organization.[3] Fawwaz wanted Yusuf to talk about the functioning of the Brotherhood and about its internal politics. But Yusuf was contesting the very idea that there was such a thing as an organization. Not only were organizations illegal and cracked down upon, he explained, but the Muslim Brotherhood was also very far from being organized in its everyday actions. He described the nitty-gritty of a movement that, according to him, suffered from disorganization. Fawwaz said that the Brotherhood was an organization even if it was disorganized. Yusuf tried to prove him wrong.

"What happens in reality," he said, "is that when somebody becomes the head of a circle or creates a circle, he gathers a group of individuals who, in the future, will become supervisors in the circle. The circle head or one of his supervisors may create another circle. Then you have two groups, and then three, four, five, etc., a thousand if you want. Do you really believe there will be no coordination between them, since all these people know each other? You want to call that an 'organization'? Do you know that in the circles, there is no method to train the supervisors, no tool to train them? The thing is that, if you see somebody perform well, you will tell him, 'Go, create a circle.' And the supervisors train themselves only through their mistakes. Do you really believe we have an organization?"

His tone of voice had become drier, and Fawwaz tried another tactic. Instead of asking about the Brotherhood, he praised his former supervisor for his contribution to his own politicization. It was thanks to Yusuf that he had become interested in politics, he said. He was trying to coddle him into acknowledging his own politicization.

"As an educator, I was avoiding political questions," Yusuf replied, sensing the trap.

"But I remember some members asking big questions about Palestine, for instance," Fawwaz insisted.

"Let me tell you something. The bottom line is the reform of the soul. And of course, sometimes, political causes come up, depending on people's interests. For instance, if a student is interested in music, I will adapt to his taste because, as an educator, I need to create a common ground with the student to transmit anything to him. I will ask about singers; I will want to know more about them. So, when a student wants to talk about intellectual issues, philosophical topics, the big questions, it is only natural that I also adapt to these questions, especially since I find them enjoyable in themselves."

Yusuf cunningly compared "the big questions" with music, an activity that Islamic activists abhorred, while carefully avoiding talking about "politics." Fawwaz cut him off again.

"No, you actually caused a revolution in my mind, when we talked about the Palestinian cause, about various conspiracies in the region . . . "

"This is your issue, not mine," Yusuf said.

"But these causes are political," Fawwaz replied, "and you triggered an explosion in my mind. I remember that, in high school, the debates between students and supervisors were political. This was around September 11th, and that is what prompted me to study history: it was like an obsession that had gripped society, we wanted to understand our relationships with the government."

Fawwaz's memory was precise, but Yusuf remained impassive. After he had left the Islamic Awakening behind, Yusuf focused on his studies and landed a well-paying position in the public sector. He no longer wanted to talk about politics and tended to downplay the contentious flavor of his previous activities. Fawwaz and Yusuf were very similar despite their bickering about pretty much everything, from the politics of the Muslim Brothers to their ideology—or lack thereof—and what it meant to be a post-Muslim Brother activist. During his time being involved with student activities, Fawwaz had clearly not played by the book; Yusuf had not either, but the two former Muslim Brothers had an intimate animosity toward one another.

Driving home that night, I remembered what Thamir and his students had told me about the Brotherhood's authoritarianism. In his high school, Thamir had been waging a war on two fronts: against the school principal, who did not want any activist groups in his school, and against the local mosque circle, whose members were more Salafi and accused him of corrupting youth with his liberal ideas. Earlier in life, Thamir had also been the target of repression within the Muslim Brotherhood, and had briefly left the movement before coming back to it. Since activists, according to him, were the products of the very situation they wished to reform, he thought that leaving was cowardly. One had to stay put and contribute to change.

"School is repressive," Thamir had told me, "and so are the Islamic circles. Family is repressive; it is like that everywhere. Repression rules supreme in universities, too. Wherever you go, you have to get used to this: the guy above imposes himself on the guy below; he tells him that *he* is the best one, that *he* is the best leader, and that nobody is better than him—by force. He lets no one follow their own paths; he consults nobody. That is how society works. And Islamic circles are just like that: people did not fall from the sky."

Talal had cut him off to explain how Islamic group leaders had revised their values to spread a culture of blind obedience to their rules, rewarding their weakest members.

"The guy who accepts their domination is, in their eyes, a remarkable individual," Talal had said. "As for the guy who opposes their order, who feels

that they harm his personal freedom or violates Islamic tenets, they say that
he is a cad, a lout, things like that. That is what they say to whoever resists
their authority. As for the guy who puts up with the situation, who behaves
just like they want or like society wants or like the guy above wants, he is the
best; he is a hero."

On our second day in his neighborhood, Fawwaz and I met a few of his
school friends and former fellow activists. Fawwaz had deprived me of the
anthropologist's best asset: the ability to navigate the field on one's own, to
choose—or be chosen by—interlocutors and allies, to make mistakes, to experience social reality without intermediaries. I had become his hostage, so to
speak, and I was condemned to witness his social and intellectual revenge. He
had been frustrated by the Muslim Brothers; now was his moment, the time
when he would rub in their faces his recent belonging to reformist circles and
new openness to the Other—myself.

Among Fawwaz's former comrades was 'Ali, the man he had talked to on
the phone from his car and who was "shy" and "underselling himself." After
mumbling a short prayer, 'Ali, visibly uncomfortable, explained that his experience of the Islamic Awakening had mostly consisted of "innocent leisure";
there had been nothing political, cultural, or even religious about it.

"In our religious awareness group, there were neither classes nor lectures;
we were being entertained in a conservative way, with soccer and swimming
classes."

The mosque circle was the only place he was allowed to go besides home
and school; religious activities were a sort of liberation. Why would he talk
about anything political, since he did not know me? I was increasingly resent-
ful of the fact that I had agreed to play along with Fawwaz and come visit his
neighborhood with him. Fawwaz had compelled his friends to extend their
hospitality, and the evening we spent eating delivery pizza and drinking tea
and soda felt immensely awkward. More than an hour into the party, one of
the young activists left without a word. Fawwaz finally got the hint, and we
also left an hour before the dawn prayer.

Chapter 23 **BRATS AND
BRAGGARTS**

THE NEXT DAY, 'ALI TOLD FAWWAZ THAT HE DID NOT UNDERSTAND what I was doing and that he thought I was a spy. This did not surprise me, but it seemed to shock Fawwaz. He told me that I should have convinced his friends of the soundness of my research; he almost lost his temper with me in the car.

As we were driving to yet another impossible interview, I stayed silent for a long time, confused and embarrassed. I had hoped that Fawwaz would become a strong ally, helping me to understand the daily experience of becoming a Muslim Brother and leaving the Brotherhood behind. The relationship seemed not to be working out the way either of us had expected. His eager enthusiasm; my own cautiousness; the many meetings he had organized; his desire to show his friends how much more sophisticated he was: none of this helped. He broke the silence and assured me that he would continue to assist me with my project, but something had soured, and we did not go on any more field expeditions together. This felt almost like a breakup.

I still attended the club's sessions, but Fawwaz and I slowly drifted apart. At the club I hung out with other former Muslim Brothers who, like their reformist counterparts in Egypt in the 1990s, had grown tired of authoritarianism and of the highly personalized patterns of loyalty within the movement. Some were lawyers who specialized in sharia law and commercial law and studied issues pertaining to real estate or stock options. Others were businessmen involved in charitable activities. Others still had managed the electoral campaign of elected Muslim Brother city councilors. They often spoke about Riyadh's Islamic landscape with an entomologist's eye for taxonomy, exploring the many differences among Muslim Brotherhood groups and between the Brothers and the Salafis.

Another favorite topic—at least in these rambling chats they would have after the day's lecture—was neuro-linguistic programming (NLP), a 1970s Californian self-help method based on the idea that one could modify one's psyche by changing one's behavior. "Frogs into princes" was the motto of NLP gurus, and the royal reference may not have been lost on Saudi aficionados.[1] Many activists believed that neuro-linguistic programming would help them achieve social and political success. The reform of society and of politics started with the individual, they often said; one had to gear oneself for success, and no self-help strategy was left unstudied. Some of them had obtained certificates in neuro-linguistic programming and trained others in turn, sometimes against a fee. NLP sounded like another way to reform one's soul.

A senior club member explained to me that he had left the Muslim Brotherhood behind because he had "faced incomprehension when he started critiquing intellectual references and asking for a renewal." He and others within the Brotherhood "wanted some opening to other ways of thinking, to others, to non-Islamists." They "started listening to al-Turabi, to Ghannouchi, to those activists who have a different way of thinking about intellectual issues." But their Islamic group "was against us reading about philosophy or Western literature, or even reading non-Islamic Arab thinkers." The gap grew wider, until a small group of members created this club. They started holding sessions within the Islamic movement, "inviting intellectuals, Islamic thinkers, and then others. This caused divergences within the Islamic group. [Group leaders] did not want this intellectual offer, and they feared younger members would absorb modern ideas. They warned us against that."

Reformists soon realized that other Muslim Brothers, in other groups, were following the same divergent pattern, revolting against the hierarchy of the movement and opening up to other ideas.

"So some Islamic activists, from different branches of the Brotherhood, and some independents started meeting every week and debating. For us, this was a new thing, something amazing going on; it prompted a progress of our awareness. This was the beginning of an organized critique of the Islamic Awakening."

Like many Islamic Awakening rallies, each session of the club centered on a guest and featured a lecture followed by a Q&A session. There was a small podium with a microphone and a sound system; club members took turn jotting down meeting notes for their archives, and one of them moderated the debate. Guests were often university professors and researchers who explored historical, sociological, and political topics: the making of the Saudi state, the relationship between religion and politics, questions of legal reform. Some guests were foreign academics and politicians, often reformist Islamic activists themselves. The sessions were always enlightening, either because of the quality of the guest's presentation or, even more regularly, because of the debate that followed. Session after session, the young reformists drafted the lineaments of an original political philosophy, which refused to contribute to the growth of the cold monster of the state and developed the idea of Islamic action as individual practice, social liberation, and legal experimentation.

After a few months of attending sessions, I noticed a grim evolution. The club meetings had become less frequent and not as well attended. The Q&A sessions were not as long and less exciting. And then, one day, the club was gone. The suburban home was deserted, probably turned over to new tenants. Some of the club members still met, but they no longer organized lectures or held long, impassioned debates. They rented a rest house on the outskirts of Riyadh and spent their time together watching soccer, playing cards, and talking about the latest game. The exciting intellectual club had withered into a very ordinary group of young professionals, one of many the capital counted. Some of them looked awfully depressed, and a few totally disappeared, not returning phone calls and messages for months. Fawwaz was one of these. When he finally resurfaced after a few months of silence, I pressed him with questions about what had happened to the club. I told him how sorry I felt to be deprived of everybody's energizing presence and how much I missed our regular sessions, but he remained elusive. He said that the group had dissolved as a result of aging and life obligations. A few college students had created it years earlier; they had now reached the age of marriage and professional responsibilities. They had children and had no time to dedicate to intellectual matters.

They were still meeting at the rest house, I argued: why did they not use this time to continue the important work they had started? Fawwaz said that many of them, himself included, had withdrawn into themselves and their personal projects, whether these be familial, professional, or political. The end of the club did not mean that its members were no longer interested in politics. One of them was writing full time, mostly about his experience with the Islamic movement. Another was active in a nationwide campaign to free political prisoners. Yet others were studying abroad.

One club member told me that the work they had done, while it was revolutionary a few years earlier, was much less original now that online spaces allowed all kinds of participation. Politics had moved online, and most Saudi intellectuals and activists had some kind of Internet presence; a few of them were now regularly invited to speak on television. Repression happened online, too, and it was only a matter of time before e-activism would be shut down by the authorities.

Also concerning was the criticism the group had received from the Muslim Brotherhood and from established Salafi intellectuals. Some Muslim Brothers reproached them for leaving the movement. The most obtuse cried treason; the most open regretted that the club members did not try to reform the Brotherhood from within. A Salafi writer told a member of the club that they were just a bunch of "brats and braggarts who loved the sound of their own voices."

Driving to the group's rest house one day, I got stuck in traffic on Khurays Road during a soccer game between Saudi Arabia and Kuwait. Young men were blocking the highway, dancing on car roofs and on the pavement while others honked or threw colored smoke bombs into traffic. At the rest house, my friends told me that Saudi Arabia had lost the game; I wondered what kind of ruckus the drivers would have raised if their team had won. Inside the tent, once again, the conversation was depressing. Some ex-activists had acquired a habit of correcting others and chasing down fragments of state discourse in what was being said. These censors were not only preoccupied with their own political correctness; they also spent time rectifying dates and historical facts. It was as if the group's rich historical and political consciousness had mysteriously evaporated. The victims of the senior club members' ire were either new additions to the group, who did not share the same ideological baggage, or simply less-committed individuals who had let their guard down and no longer really cared about historical or intellectual rigor.

What had happened? The group may have been threatened by the security services, perhaps in the kind of way that made it impossible for any of them to even talk about it, especially not to me. They might also have experienced the void of the political sphere and the impossibility of organizing within it. With a few exceptions, they had retreated to the private sphere and decided to cultivate their own garden. Most club members had transitioned from the Muslim Brotherhood to Islamic reformism and flirted with the ideas of democratization, institutionalization of rights, and Islamic social justice. They had received no reward for it, only the temporary thrill of connecting with more secular intellectuals and Islamic reformists abroad. In the end, the experiment would appear to have been a failure.

"From an experimental point of view," one of the members told me, "the club was wonderful, because for the first time we left the narrow framework of the Islamic groups, which were choking us. It was the first time we met people with the same interests, the same readings, the same culture. It opened a space to develop our awareness through disputes and debates, which were very open and did not take place in the Islamic groups. But we did not attract a lot of people. We launched projects, true, but they were temporary. Nothing big came out of it. And the club was interrupted for periods of time, because organizers would get busy doing something else and could not form a team guaranteeing any continuity."

The Salafi writer who had said that they were brats and braggarts was wrong. They did not love the sound of their own voices: they were actually sick of listening to themselves and would have loved to open their doors to larger crowds. They had perhaps grown more aware of something they knew all along: that the issue at hand was not as much intellectual as political and needed more than academic lectures and Q&A sessions. The bitterest outcome of the overall repression was the scattering of their group into a collection of individuals who met around soccer, the card game of belote, and passive-aggressive bickering. Age, children, and professional responsibilities were probably partly to blame. The oligarchic monarchy certainly was, too.

"The general idea was that the window of opportunity had closed, that the club had played a role for a certain period of time," the same member told me.

"This group, which in the beginning was very enthusiastic about reformism, which spread ideas and launched debates, dispersed itself in the end. There were no longer any projects to unite it."

I told Thamir this story and asked him what he thought. While he knew of the reformist club, he himself had adopted a very different approach vis-à-vis the Muslim Brotherhood. He was aware of the Islamic Awakening's weaknesses and had also broken from the movement at some point in his life, but he had come back into the fold and was now trying to change it from within. He thought that his own approach to the concerns that he shared with the re-formists was more sustainable and responsible. He defended Islamic activities tooth and nail; he thought that they were "the only means, for high school and college students, to find a space for action and organization."

"If we had trade unions, political parties, and associations, the Islamic Awakening would probably crumble," he said. "But this is not the case, and in the absence of other means of politicization, it is the only way to do and say anything."

The political situation was terrible and had to be changed; activists did not have the luxury of retreating into intellectual debates or waiting for others to act on their behalf. Something had to be done now, with the meager political resources at hand, and those resources consisted of the circles and groups of the Islamic Awakening.

But Thamir did not seem to know what could be done, and he sympathized with those who left Islamic activism behind: according to him, they did not have much of a choice. Individuals who were disappointed with their Islamic group would rarely try to join another movement. It was relatively uncommon for, say, a Muslim Brother to switch over to a Salafi group, or even to jump ship within the Muslim Brotherhood and try to find another branch of the movement to join. Islamic groups "evolved together," Thamir said. "Their mem-bers grew up together." People switching groups would be "seen as complete strangers, as intruders." Few activists, knowing the secrecy of Islamic activities, would likely want to cope with the lengthy process of once again proving their activist credentials. But there was another issue as well.

"People do not generally see huge intellectual differences between the Brothers and the Salafis," which further limited the options. Of course, "somebody who gets annoyed with his Islamic group will most certainly get annoyed with his new group: all activist groups have roughly the same issues. If this person is annoyed with organized action, then all groups will feel the same to him. So few people think about moving to another group because they would be intellectually closer to it. Few people weigh the various options in front of them. If they are annoyed, they will either leave or stay: there is no third way.

"If the Islamic Awakening was officially a political party, then in the end, the party would deal with them," Thamir said. "Here, no: social relationships are paramount. The activism of the Brothers and of the Salafis confuses individual preferences, social life, religious tenets, and activist challenges. . . . They form an inward-facing society, and it is hard for anybody to join such a group."

It was hard to leave, too. Group members were caught in daily community activities and it was nearly impossible to disentangle the many small ties that linked them to the movement. Many activists preferred to cut the knot rather than take the time to untie it and therefore left the movement abruptly. It was hard to distance oneself without becoming a renegade and an enemy. All of that said, Thamir wanted to stay.

"For those who want to create a movement, participate in activities, join a group, and engage in any kind of action, the Islamic Awakening is essentially the only place to go. It is where people care for the public interest, where the elite can learn how to manage a project. Society is closed to projects and actions. Cultural activity is limited. The public space is very narrow in general; it is wider in the Islamic groups, in my view. I was a firm believer—and I still am—in the fact that, no matter what the project of these groups is, you need to get closer to their members to create anything in the future, to influence them or change the way their elites do things because, in contrast to the rest of society, they are educated. They are politicized to a certain extent. And they are prepared. This was my strong motivation, and I did not want to move away from these groups and this milieu; I wanted to continue with them."

Thamir could understand the excitement of leaving Islamic activism behind and the exhilaration of intellectual independence. He had seen some of his friends step out of the Awakening and meet more people, read more, write more, become visible on the Internet and in the opinion pages of newspapers. But he felt that "it was all futile" and preferred to remain "in a place

I find comfortable, a place where there is no pressure." The main reason he had stayed in the Brotherhood was organizational. Unlike Yusuf, he believed that the movement was relatively well organized, given the circumstances in which it had emerged.

"Look," he said, "in Saudi society, there is a bigger issue with the idea of organization. One of the main advantages of the Islamic movement is that you can organize people there. Because in our society, the idea of organization is not well entrenched; organizations are not something you can emulate: there are none. Obedience, the ability to embrace a common vision: these dispositions are simply not present" outside of the Islamic Awakening.

"Those who passed through the Islamic Awakening are able to embrace organized action": this to Thamir was in the end the reason why he had stayed in the Brotherhood.

"In the end, your presence within an organized movement may have a real influence. That is the difference between the reformist club and us. The reformists were few in number; they were dispersed and limited; they did not engage in organized action. In the Muslim Brotherhood, those who work the most right now are the university students, who do direct educational action. This is not my thing right now, even if I do it too; because when you join the Brothers, you need to make a name for yourself among the students if you want to influence them. I am interested in intellectual reform more than in political reform, and that is why I do not want to distance myself from the human resources and the elites of the movement. When I am among the Brothers, I feel that this is a place where I can start projects. There are fewer personal quibbles among Islamic activists, which means that you can do more things. It is especially true of the Brotherhood, where there is a higher level of individual politeness. All the preaching we do ends up polishing individuals. Others are more individualistic. The Brothers are a reservoir of amazing human resource. And in Riyadh, we know that that is the most important thing."

The Salafis were more cutting, what with their love of public insults and ad hominem attacks. Yet in the end, Thamir looked at the Islamic Awakening as an academic enterprise, and that was a very Salafi idea, too.[2] Within the Awakening, one could cultivate one's analysis of the world, create a following, and engage in a long-term activist career, which was barely possible anywhere else. Political change was still the horizon of one's action, but everybody knew that repression was the context of their political situation and that organized action would have to be very gradual.

The Muslim Brothers had remained an informal structure and evolved in the shadow of state institutions; its members wanted to be good teachers and polite citizens and to move things forward in a slow, quiet manner. The Salafis, by contrast, were bent on disruption, as their mobilization during the Riyadh Book Fair had shown. After they were ejected from the fair, all public debates in the city were put under heavy police surveillance.

A few months later, other Salafi sheikhs and activists jumped onstage during a theater production at a private university north of Riyadh and shut down the event. The police intervened, shots were fired inside the theater, and the police arrested a large group of activists. I was also attending the play and saw university students vigorously fighting the Salafis. Fights erupted all around the theater and the uproar was deafening. A friend heard Salafi activists say that this university in particular, like all private, secular universities in the country, was a "time bomb,"[3] and that they were out to defuse it. The Salafis acted with more urgency than the Brothers. They thought that the end was near and that somebody had to say and do something about it.

The Salafis and the Muslim Brothers were involved in Islamic action at two different levels. The Muslim Brothers were patiently building their influence and their networks, organizing their own movement in the hope that, one day, they might encompass the whole society around them. The Salafis saw themselves as more academic, more rigorous, and more scientific than the Brothers, and that is precisely why they saw it as their duty to intervene when the wrong people, in their eyes, were becoming influential in society. They criticized those they thought were false elites, these liberals and secularists who opposed Islamic action. As heated as they were, however, their battles remained local and were lost in the vast space of suburbia. In the end, the state elites remained in control. They were protected by police repression, to be sure—and also by the massive sprawl they had patiently engineered. Saudi Arabia seemed as though it would remain a graveyard of clerics for many years to come.

Chapter 24   **DETAINED**

I WAS DETAINED ON VALENTINE'S DAY, 2016.

After several years of teaching and doing research in the United States and the United Arab Emirates, I had come back to Riyadh to research working-class driving habits. One of my interviewees was a sturdy thirty-something who had created a construction business. With the help of four Indian immigrants who lived in his workshop, he assembled construction elements that he then delivered as far away as Dumat al-Jandal, near the Jordanian border. He had a great deal of anger at the government; he was prone to road rage, too.

The former governor of Riyadh, Prince Salman, had become king in 2015 and had almost immediately waged war on Yemen, Saudi Arabia's impoverished southern neighbor. Between 2015 and 2019, the war killed more than two hundred and thirty thousand Yemeni civilians and forced several million out of their homes.[1] The war was also felt inside Saudi Arabia. The past two months had been the worst my interviewee had gone through.

"The war on Yemen destroyed everything," he said, "and the king gave thirty billion dollars to the Egyptian president, Sisi, instead of helping us get by."[2]

Another interviewee, Badr, was a Saudi day laborer who lived off his truck. He waited for customers near markets and department stores and delivered their purchases to their homes. Badr was also suffering from the slump. He had grown up in the poorest part of town, the inner city[3] of ill repute, and although he had studied at an Egyptian university for four years, his truck was now his daily bread. But there were fewer customers and less stuff to bring home. Riyadh had become "a vast jail," he said.

Badr and I spent Valentine's Day touring the markets—the wood market, the sheep market, and the Haraj bin Gasim, the city's sprawling wholesale market. The shops were empty. A Bedouin who came from Hafr al-Batin, near the Iraqi border, tried to sell us a magnificent sheep with a fluffy back and "flesh as tender as almond." He had been waiting for potential buyers all day.

By nightfall we had not met a single customer. We headed toward Ikea, whose glowing blue-and-yellow sign loomed over the capital's eastern sub-urbs.[4] Badr parked in the loading area, near the exit. Five or six other drivers waiting around the gate tried to sell me their services. When I declined, they shouted words that I couldn't understand. One of them, a man in his forties whose wide-open mouth revealed two rows of shiny, blackened stubs, apolo-gized for his colleagues' rowdy behavior.

"They have small brains," he said.

We exchanged a few words. I saw a counterfoil book in his hand and asked if he worked for Ikea.

"No, I am independent. I have workers who put together furniture at peo-ple's places."

He handed me his business card: "Abu Nayef, assembly."[5] I told him I was studying driving. A few customers trickled out of the store and Abu Nayef headed back to the gate. I took a few photos of Badr posing next to his truck, of the store, and of its lights.

Abu Nayef came back after a few minutes. Badr and he chatted about how slow the market was and how few clients there were. Above their heads, there was a no-parking sign showing a truck towing a pickup and the words: "PICK UP ZONE." My camera was still in my hand, and I pointed it up towards them and the sign together.

Abu Nayef turned to me in an instant and blocked my lens with his book. "No photo!"

But my finger was already on the trigger, and click! I took a photo that showed the gray cover of his counterfoil book. I said I would erase it on the spot, but Abu Nayef snatched my camera and, turning to Badr as if I did not exist, complained about my rudeness.

"I apologize to you," I said. "Please give me my camera."

He pulled out his cell and dialed 999, the emergency number.

"I am calling the police," he said.

The other deliverymen surrounded us. While waiting for an answer, he commented on the situation.

"Last time, one of those journalists came to this store and, next thing you know, my friend had his photo on the front page."

The pickup drivers worked informally and did not want to attract attention. I still found it puzzling that, instead of letting me delete a photo that did not even show him, Abu Nayef preferred to call the very cops whose curiosity he was weary of.

"We are sons of this fatherland!" he said. "We are patriots here!"

A few drivers cocked their heads in my direction and gave me such a hard look that I preferred to stay away from the group. I bumped into Badr, who was also worried about the crowd bulging around us. He told me to go inside the store and that he would drive away and meet me on the other side. He got behind the wheel and started his pickup. I walked toward the gate, asking for the bathroom. I heard sharp voices behind me, turned around, and saw six or seven pickup drivers pushing Badr's pickup back into its parking spot. We were stuck.

The police patrol arrived, a lone cop in a black uniform behind the wheel. He stayed inside the car and opened his window.

"You called us for *this*?" he said to Abu Nayef.

Abu Nayef launched into a diatribe, explaining how the situation was dangerous and how everybody needed to keep an eye out otherwise all of this would go from good to bad and from bad to worse.

The cop asked for everybody's IDs. Badr handed over his driver's license and I gave up my passport. Abu Nayef had left his residency card at home. This staunch patriot looked and sounded Saudi, but was a foreign migrant from a neighboring country—probably Jordan or Iraq. The cop shook his head, closed his window, and started making calls.

Another interviewee had told me he knew many cops and that, if I ever had a problem, he might help. I pulled out my notebook, retrieved his number, and started dialing. The cop called me over at that moment and I walked to his car, my phone and notebook in hand. He saw the notebook.

"What is this?"

"My notebook."

He asked to see it and I handed it to him. He started reading those rare pages where I had jotted down notes in Arabic—interview questions and technical car terms. He continued turning the pages until his face changed color. I cocked my head to read what he was looking at, and my heart jumped in my chest. I had totally forgotten that *that* was in there.

In the middle of a page written in English, there was one line in Arabic. "Fahd, you donkey, you sold Mecca for one dollar."[6]

"I can explain," I said. "I was at an academic conference, one of the participants said that to me, and I wrote it down."

The phrase was a slogan used in demonstrations held in 1990, after King Fahd had invited a Western military coalition to fight Iraq from the Saudi soil.[7] I had written it down to remind myself that I needed to find its source; then, like a rookie, I had taken that same notebook with me out to do more fieldwork.

The cop put my camera and my notebook on his dashboard as though they were evidence for a crime and took us all to the police station.

The police station was entrenched behind concrete blocks. Attacks on police stations were not rare in Riyadh, especially in such rough neighborhood as this one, infamous for its drug traffic and its knifings. Badr and I waited in a hallway as the cops took Abu Nayef to the holding cells. Badr was let go after his brother drove to the station to vouch for him. Abu Nayef was freed a few hours later. I alone remained in custody. The situation was threatening yet comfortable; I was in the lieutenant's office, my heart in my throat and my spirits down. The lieutenant was a young man and we spoke in the rural Central Arabian dialect I had learned among my Bedouin friends; he sounded very familiar but exuded a sharp power.

My reach was still considerable. The cops had left me my iPhone and I called friends and acquaintances, trying to find an easy way out. I called an adviser to Prince Turki al-Faysal, whose name had saved me when the deputy director of education was investigating my field research.

"The prince cannot do anything for you," the adviser said. "Be strong."

I called a friend who knew a friend who knew a general of the police. He told me his friend could call the general the next morning. I called a French diplomat I knew well; he woke up the French consul and they both came to the police station. I felt elated, but the arrival of the two diplomats did not clear the situation. The lieutenant said that my file had already been sent to the prosecutor's office, along with my notebook and my camera; it was now out of his hands. The consul said she would leave, since she had ascertained that I was being detained in humane conditions. I implored her to stay, explaining the political nature of the infraction and the potentially dire consequences. She finally agreed to spend the night at the police station.

A new shift arrived in the morning. The day lieutenant made a few calls, served us shawarma sandwiches and hot tea, gave me back my notebook and my camera, and let me go. The prosecutor's office had probably never been contacted; the night lieutenant may just have been waiting for more seasoned officers to weigh in. The situation had de-escalated as fast as it had escalated; all in all I had spent more than seventeen hours in police custody.

Living for several years in the comfortable bubble of academia had dulled my fieldwork senses, once sharp enough to help me navigate the complex Saudi environment. But times had changed, too, and conducting field research in Saudi Arabia had become harder. After the Tunisian, Egyptian, Syrian, and Yemeni revolutions of the early 2010s, the Saudi regime had once again embraced its counter-revolutionary ethos.[8] King Salman, whom my interlocutors had nicknamed "the Saddam Husein of Saudi Arabia" when he was still the governor of Riyadh, had appointed his son Muhammad crown prince and heir apparent in 2017. The two men had cracked down on dissent with renewed ferocity. Organizing was hard in the 2000s; it was even harder in the 2010s.

Abu Nayef's blaring patriotism was but a by-product of a new ultra-nationalism, whose early promotion in the summer camps I had witnessed. He tragically embraced a political passion that excluded him by definition, since he was a foreigner. Saudi nationalists exploited the audible, visible presence of foreigners to police the nationality line and "otherize" non-Saudis.[9] For all that Abu Nayef had Saudi-ized himself in dress, speech, and attitudes, this disguise went up in smoke when the cop that he himself called asked him for proof of his identity. He was unceremoniously thrown into jail while I, the alleged violator, was kept in the officers' quarters. The country's new ultra-nationalism was still a colonial construct, and Saudi cops still operated within the racial hierarchy that the U.S. oil company Aramco had imported in the 1940s.

Police crackdown on any dissent increased after 2015, and feminists, intellectuals, and Islamic activists were detained or disappeared.[10] The most
influential activists, including Salman al-'Ouda, 'Awad al-Garni, Muhammad
Musa al-Sharif, and Muhammad al-Hudayf, were arrested in September 2017,
summarily accused of spying, and imprisoned without due process.[11] Some
of them were threatened with a death sentence.[12] Thamir, who at the end of
my field research had planned to continue organizing within the Muslim
Brotherhood, has given up hope in recent years and has also left Islamic activism behind.

What prompted the state elites to intensify their repression is probably
the fact that a number of powerful social movements came out of the Islamic
Awakening in the 2000s and reinforced Al Sa'ud's fears of dissent. Islamic
Awakening activists and human rights advocates created the Association for
Political and Civil Rights, or HASM, in 2009.[13] *Hasm* in Arabic means determination, and it may not be a coincidence that Al Sa'ud dubbed its war on
Yemen Operation Determination Storm.[14] HASM demanded an end to repression, defended the rights of political prisoners, and called for the creation of
a constitutional monarchy.[15]

According to 'Abd Allah al-Hamid, Islamic activist and HASM member, the
"struggle by words"[16] or "non-violent struggle"[17] should be the primary means
of opposing state violence. HASM criticized both the tradition, encouraged by
the royal family, of giving private advice to the ruler, and the crackdown on
political activism, which state clerics condoned. For HASM police crackdown
and the ban on peaceful protest were the main causes of the emergence of
al-Qa'eda and the escalation of political violence in the late 1990s and early
2000s. Most HASM activists were arrested and tried in front of the Riyadh
Specialized Criminal Court, created in 2008 to adjudicate terrorism cases. The
HASM trials became occasions for collective action and advocacy; activists
used them a platforms to criticize repression and promote political reform.
The Specialized Criminal Court dissolved HASM in 2013.[18]

The demonstration that Sa'd al-Faqih organized in October 2003 marked
the beginning of a popular anti-repression movement composed of relatives
of political prisoners, in which mothers of prisoners were central. After 2003,
the relatives of political prisoners held regular demonstrations and sit-ins
in Riyadh's mosques, in front of the Interior Ministry, and in several cities,

especially in the central region, where "the Advocates,"[19] as the movement called itself, held dozens of protest actions and regularly confronted the police. Protests continued through the Arab revolutions and included women as well as men. In 2011, dozens of women marched to the Interior Ministry in Riyadh and demanded fair trials for their relatives. They chanted, among other slogans, "Release the innocents," and "Where are our children?"[20]

It is tempting to believe that Islamic activism—any form of activism, really—is over and done with in Saudi Arabia. In the bleak landscape of this graveyard of clerics, is there any reason to hope, or is one condemned to believe that Al Sa'ud will have all the answers?

During the Cold War, Al Sa'ud embraced suburbanization as a way to organize a pacified society and undermine popular politics. In the new suburban Arabia that urban planners and princes have created, the centers of power are far from the reach of crowds; people are scattered to far-flung peripheries and burdened with housing and consumer debt. Mass protest and street politics had been a central feature of Saudi popular politics from the 1930s to the 1960s. It was now much harder for everyday Saudis to have their say in local or national politics.

But Al Sa'ud and its allies did not manage to crack down on all protests during the Cold War. Suburbanization was in part the response of the elites to certain forms of protest, and in part the condition of possibility of new forms of protest, including Islamic activism.

It is not easy to organize in sprawling suburbs. Getting together is often challenging, and public spaces are harder to occupy: there is no longer a center toward which to converge, no longer a bottleneck to take possession of. Low-density planning dismantled the denser cities, where busy nodes and packed streets, squares, markets, and public monuments were easier to politicize. People were already there; the centers of power were close at hand. By contrast, the suburbs and the post-suburban sprawl are simply not dense enough to allow any crowd of people to assemble easily or, once there, to create a disturbance.

Saudi suburbia nevertheless became a fertile ground for religious activism. Salafi movements and the Muslim Brothers—the two main branches of the Islamic Awakening—reacted differently to suburbanization. The Salafis created powerful suburban counter-societies and tried to turn suburbs into a religious utopia. Like the eighteenth-century English Evangelicals, they promoted a "new ideal of conduct that emphasized the role of the family" and strove to separate themselves "from the profane metropolis."[21] Salafis either took refuge from society in the suburbs or used them as a base to change society.

Riyadh's southern suburb of Suwaydi has been a stronghold of Salafi activism since its creation in the 1970s. A dense network of mosque study circles, religious groups, and Islamic bookstores has created a more rigorist atmosphere. (This is where 'Adel became an activist, but once he was out of Suwaydi, he migrated toward other Islamic groups, including the Muslim Brotherhood.) The most extreme version of this isolationist trend can be found among the Burayda Brethren, a Salafi group that left mainstream society to recreate premodern living conditions in a suburb of Burayda, northwest of Riyadh.[22]

Other groups used suburban beachheads to prepare for confrontation with the state. After the 1990 Gulf War, armed militants targeted the symbols of U.S. and European presence in the country, in particular military training facilities and gated communities. In the 2000s, al-Qa'eda members bombed several Western-majority so-called "compounds," these gated suburbs that, inspired by European colonialism, were of crucial significance to the U.S. empire. Al-Qa'eda militants saw suburbia as both a resource and a target. They became thoroughly suburban themselves and cultivated a subculture to which cars, weapons, bodily fitness, self-organization, and DIY activism were central.[23]

The Muslim Brothers also had an ambiguous relationship to the suburbs. The Brotherhood emerged in Egyptian cities in the early twentieth century as a teachers' movement. The Saudi Muslim Brothers, a movement of educators and preachers that emerged after the 1950s, have been wary of the freedoms that suburbs afforded younger generations. They warned against the perils of suburbia, denouncing the atomization and individualization of society and organizing against the cultural onslaught of the suburbs. They considered leisure, free time, and deviance to be expressions of Westernization and a menace to the Saudi cultural and social fabric.

But the Muslim Brothers were also well equipped to tackle the challenges suburbs presented to political organization. They created loose networks of activists in each region of the country, keeping a low profile to dodge repression. They recruited in suburban schools and mosques. They used suburban resources to organize against what they thought were suburban menaces. To fight idleness, they politicized leisure and exploited free time. Their organization itself reflected their suburban orientation, with the car as the smallest unit and a range of cultural and social activities specially designed to fit commute time. Cars and suburban connectivity became crucial to the creation of strong activist networks.

The Muslim Brothers actively turned suburbia into a political resource and a springboard for intervening in the public sphere. They protested the U.S.-Saudi alliance and proposed political reforms during and after the 1990 Gulf War. Their suburban networks engineered the victory of Muslim Brother candidates in most cities of the kingdom during the 2005 municipal elections.

In the end, both Muslim Brother and Salafi networks have embraced the suburban landscape, with its decentralized institutions, its vast interstices, and its lack of density. They are hard to repress as a consequence. They may survive crackdowns thanks to their decentralized, bottom-up nature and the wide appeal of their critique of Al Sa'ud's power.

In the past, Saudi opposition movements have harnessed boredom and indifference and turned them into a political resource. *La mubala* is the suburban condition. It is indifference to one's surroundings, which have been flattened out by planners and experts to keep everyday people from entering the political realm. Saudi elites have striven to fill this vacuum since the 1970s. Al Sa'ud created the General Presidency for Youth Patronage in 1974; its mission was to mobilize young Saudis around collective sports, in particular soccer, and to keep them busy far from the mosques and the public squares. King Salman created the General Entertainment Authority in 2016 and renamed the General Presidency for Youth Patronage the General Sports Authority.

The General Entertainment Authority organizes festivals and licenses movie theaters and theme parks. In Nazi Germany, the *Kraft durch Freude* organization fought boredom and offered a substitute for the workers' organizations that the Third Reich had annihilated. Today the General Entertainment Authority aims to mobilize support for the regime among everyday Saudis while boosting the tourism sector. In so doing, it offers Saudis an alternative to the movements that have been repressed, in particular the Islamic Awakening.[24]

Saudi elites understood early on that boredom was not an inert emotion but a creative force and a source of energy.[25] By seeking to entertain the people, the Al Sa'ud elite wanted to spur everyday Saudis to forget themselves in leisure and sports. But these elites underestimated the weight of the heavy, deadly boredom that exudes from the new Saudi suburbs. *La mubala*, or the indifference to the consequences of one's actions, has been a more potent force in the recent history of Saudi Arabia than have Al Saʿud-sponsored soccer games and culture festivals.

Indifference is the overwhelming silence in which one could find one's political self, the great passion and the courage to act. The Islamic Awakening gave itself the mission of waking Saudis from the slumber into which Al Saʿud had plunged them. By organizing in the cracks of religious and educational institutions, the Islamic Awakening has managed to grow along with the state it criticizes and opposes. Islamic Awakening activists hold the state in suspicion and have the suburban dream of making do as if there were no state, yet at the same time they operate in spaces that the state has created: the suburbs, the mosques, and the schools.

Saudi state elites turned sprawling cities into a graveyard of clerics in the 1980s and 1990s. They repressed Islamic activism and any form of criticism or dissent. This cemetery was the landscape in which I conducted my field research in the 2000s and 2010s. Al Saʿud had created a state that—to quote Achille Mbembe—results in "the power to manufacture a crowd of people whose nature is to live on the edge of life, on the external edge of life: people for whom living is to constantly parley with death." Their state is "a permanent simulation of the state of exception." It "justifies the 'war on terror' as an indefinite and absolute war of eradication that claims the right to cruelty, to torture, and to unlimited detention." Saudi state sovereignty is "the often violent projection of a 'world without'—the 'world of the good riddance,' which got rid of the Muslims who crowd cities, of the Negroes and of the foreigners who must be deported, of the (presumed) terrorists whom one tortures directly or by proxy, of the Jews about whom one regrets that so many escaped the gas chambers, of the migrants who come running from everywhere, of the refugees and the castaways."[26] That "world without" produces the graveyard—of clerics, of preachers, of activists, of foreigners, of women, and of youth.

Saudi Islamic movements cannot be understood outside of the suburban indifference that fueled them. These movements are fragmented because they came together in a fragmented landscape, a landscape whose organizing principle was fragmentation itself. This fragmentation required a change of focus and an adapted methodology. Most studies of Islamic movements are written from the point of view of the capital city, of urban centers, and of the activist elite.[27] These studies tend to assume that Islamic activism is political by definition, that its practices are geared toward seizing state power or changing the way the state organizes society. The fact that, of all the Islamic movements of the twentieth century, the movement led by Ayatollah Khomeini was the only one to create a state in the name of religion[28] should be an indication of just how uninterested in state power Islamic movements generally are.

In contrast, Saudi Islamic movements organized under the radar of the state and grew in the anti-urban landscape of the Cold War. To understand how Islamic movements have turned boredom and indifference into a political resource, one needs to replace a top-down story, that of Islamic activists conquering the state, with a bottom-up one, of grassroots movements and local politics. But this is not enough. One also needs to shift the focus from the state to the everyday, from central areas to sprawling suburbs, from the elites to the rank and file, from politics to anti-politics, and from the results (will Islamic movements take over the state?) to the process (how and where does one become an Islamic activist?).

As a result of my field research I abandoned the notion of Islamism: this notion, which focuses on the ideology of protest movements, cannot describe or analyze the type of political action I encountered in Saudi Arabia. For many observers, including those who have decided to study "Islamism," the persistence of Islamic movements has shown that Middle Eastern politics are still mired in ideology and, therefore, "not yet fully modern."[29] In the same vein, generations of anthropologists saw ideologies as a useful guide for "adolescent" Asian, African, and Latin American nations transitioning from tradition to modernity and in need of a "new symbolic framework" to overcome their "loss of orientation."[30]

Islamic activism, in Saudi Arabia or elsewhere, cannot be seen as a temporary outfit halfway between tradition and modernity, or as a compromise that would dissolve at the advent of liberal rationality. My goal was to understand what my interlocutors and interviewees mean when they talk of "Islamic action." Instead of ideological genealogies I examined the landscapes of Islamic activism:[31] the political geography in which something like Islamic action becomes possible, the world of highways, suburbs, high schools, academic lectures, voting centers, universities, and mosques where activists mobilized.

Islamic movements are not remnants of ancient political traditions, about to be swallowed in a democratizing wave that would make them obsolete or undermined by an authoritarian state that detains, tortures, and buries. Islamic movements are not the last folkloric sigh of the oppressed creature, about to be liberated by the next U.S. war. Whenever Western powers have told Muslims to reform and adapt, this call "was at the same time an act of violence"[32]—and these acts of violence gave birth to the political prisons of Tora, al-Hayer, and Abu Ghraib, and to the CIA's dark sites. Saudi Islamic activists resisted the violent integration of their country into the U.S. empire, from the global oil trade to the global arms trade and from the Cold War to the War on Terror. In the face of this sheer violence, taking over the state was never an option. Organizing in its cracks was, which means that the Islamic Awakening is probably not dead, but in abeyance, and may resurface when the conditions are ripe.

Boston to Mexico City,
September 2015 to November 2019

Acknowledgments

A week before I turned in the final version of this book, I wrote Kate Wahl, the editor-in-chief of Stanford University Press, to ask her advice on a crucial matter. I had come to realize that the book's original structure—six chapters with a prologue and an epilogue—was too rigid and dry for the kind of ethnographic description I was working on. I asked her if she thought dividing the book into twenty-four chapters would be a good idea.

Many publishers would have recoiled and urged me to stick to the plan. But a day after I emailed Kate, she wrote back, "I think you wrote this manuscript from the start as twenty-some chapters. We had just not realized it yet!" She explained why she was writing on a Sunday—she had taken my manuscript home that weekend—and gave me two pages of incredibly useful comments, advising me on the best ways to move to a more fluid, more narrative book structure.

I hope that this vignette conveys the extent of my admiration for Kate Wahl and her editing style. She is the most generous, sensitive, and dedicated publisher one could dream of working with.

This book could not have seen the light of day without the help of two other editors: my colleague Omer Shah, who took time out from his exciting research on Mecca to read, edit, and comment on a still very rough version of the manuscript; and Stanford University Press's copy editor, Marie Deer, who lent her precise words to my unclear thoughts in more sentences than I can count.

I thank my interlocutors, friends, and colleagues in Saudi Arabia for having coped with my curiosity, my awkward questions, and my long recorded interviews for all these years. If I miss living in Riyadh immensely, I miss their company even more. Their courage and humor has been a constant source of inspiration and I hope that this book, despite its overall pessimistic tone, does them justice. My thoughts go out to those of my interlocutors and friends who are in prison as I write these lines. La lutte continue.

I thank all the friends and colleagues who, in one way or another, have helped with this project, including Farah al-Nakib, François Burgat, Steve Caton, Anne Clément, Gareth Doherty, Samuel Dolby, Youssef El Chazli, Sarah El-Kazaz, Yasser Elsheshtawy, Muriam Haleh Davis, Serra Hakyemez, Toby C. Jones, Jeffrey Karam, Laleh Khalili, Hikmet Kocamaner, Baptiste Lanaspeze, Henri Lauzière, Marc Aziz Michael, Richard Nielsen, Golnar Nikpur, Edward Roger Owen, Laurence Ralph, Thomas Serres, Aaron Shakow, Ahmad Shokr, Bob Vitalis, Neha Vora, Larry Winnie, Malika Zeghal, and many others. I wrote this book while teaching at Brandeis University and I thank my colleagues at the Crown Center for Middle East Study and the Department of Anthropology for their feedback, in particular Elizabeth Ferry, Nader Habibi, David Patel, and Naghmeh Sohrabi. I also thank my students for their comments on the project, and, more essentially, for being the amazing interlocutors they are.

Research for this project was supported by a grant from the Centre Français d'Archéologie et de Sciences Sociales de Sanaa and by research funds from Princeton University, Harvard University, New York University Abu Dhabi, and Brandeis University. Writing took place in various locations—Boston, Milan, Lisbon, and Mexico City—often under the watchful eye of my husband, Bazil Lagerström, and of Rain the cat.

My mother, Anne-Marie Ménoret née Eger, died while I was writing this book. Born in Paris in 1936, World War II refugee, daughter of a Foreign Office administrator (grand-mère Fany) and of a mathematician (Max), she became a professor of mathematics and started teaching in Oran before the Algerian independence. She then came back to Marseille, where she taught at the Lycée Marcel Pagnol until she retired. Her intelligence and rigor gave me goose bumps as an adolescent. She was both terrifying and immensely loving, a true Mutter Courage. I have tried to avoid repeating her life patterns and can proudly say that I have failed so far. I miss her every day. This book is dedicated to her memory.

Notes

CHAPTER 1: GRAVEYARD OF CLERICS

1. Muhammad bin Ibrahim Al al-Shaykh, *Fatwa fi hukm sharb al-dukhan* (fatwa about smoking tobacco) (General presidency of scholarly research and ifta 2012), pp. 6, 17–18. All Arabic transliterations follow the transliteration system of the International Journal of Middle East Studies, simplified for the purpose of this book (long vowels are not signified by a macron, and emphatic consonants are not signified by an underdot).

2. *Al-sahwa al-islamiyya.*

3. Daniel Sargent, *A Superpower Transformed: The Remaking of American Foreign Relations in the 1970s* (Oxford University Press 2015), pp. 141–146, 154–155, 289.

4. Askar al-Enazy, *The Creation of Saudi Arabia: Ibn Saud and British Imperial Policy, 1914–1927* (Routledge 2013); Robert Vitalis, *America's Kingdom: Mythmaking on the Saudi Oil Frontier* (Verso 2009); Toby C. Jones, *Desert Kingdom: How Oil and Water Forged Saudi Arabia* (Harvard University Press 2010).

5. Alexei Vassiliev, *The History of Saudi Arabia* (Saqi Books 2000), pp. 282–283; Rosie Bsheer, "A Counter-Revolutionary State: Popular Movements and the Making of Saudi Arabia," *Past and Present* 238 (2018): 243–244.

6. Vitalis, *America's Kingdom*, pp. 92–98, 102–104, 145–162, 172–184; Bsheer, "A Counter-Revolutionary State," 255–268.

7. Mahmood Mamdani, *Good Muslim, Bad Muslim: America, the Cold War, and the Roots of Terror* (Pantheon Books 2004), pp. 84–87; Yaroslav Trofimov, *The Siege of Mecca: The Forgotten Uprising* (Allen Lane 2007), pp. 174–178. The leftist Egyptian singer Sheikh Imam parodied Valéry Giscard d'Estaing's alliance with repressive states in his 1975 eponym song, in which he sings, "We'll realize Arab Unity with London and the Vatican."

8.   Pascal Menoret, "Fighting for the Holy Mosque: The 1979 Mecca Insurgency," in C. Christine Fair and Sumit Ganguly (eds.), *Treading on Hallowed Ground: Counterinsurgency Operations in Sacred Spaces* (Oxford University Press 2008), pp. 117–139; International Archives, Caisse des Dépôts et Consignations, Paris: SCET COOP INTER, Assemblée Générale Ordinaire du 23 octobre 1980, Box 202.16; Interview with a French engineer, Paris, November 2013.

9.   Asma Alsharif, "Detainees Disappear into Black Hole of Saudi Jails," Reuters, August 25, 2011; Alastair Sloan, "Who Are the Political Prisoners in Saudi and Iran?" *Middle East Monitor*, May 3, 2014. See FBI Assistant Director of Public Affairs Cassandra Chandler's speech at the National Air and Space Intelligence Center, Wright-Patterson Air Force Base, Ohio, September 27, 2004, https://archives.fbi.gov/archives/news/speeches/fbi-intelligence-and-counterterrorism-program, and FBI Counterterrorism Division Deputy Assistant Director Thomas Harrington's testimony in front of the House Committee on International Relations, Washington, DC, March 24, 2004, https://archives.fbi.gov/archives/news/testimony/middle-east-and-central-asia-saudi-arabia-and-the-fight-against-terrorism-financing.

10.   "Saudi Arabia: New Terrorism Regulations Assault Rights: Campaign to Silence Peaceful Activists," Human Rights Watch, March 20, 2014. "Saudi Arabia Designates Muslim Brotherhood Terrorist Group," Reuters, March 7, 2014.

11.   "Jamal Khashoggi: Murder in the Consulate," *The Guardian*, October 21, 2018; "Credible Evidence Saudi Crown Prince Liable for Khashoggi Killing," *The Guardian*, June 19, 2019.

12.   *Al-Suʿudiyya maqbarat al-ʿulamaʾ wa sijn al-duʿa.*

13.   Joas Wagemakers, *A Quietist Jihadi: The Ideology and Influence of Abu Muhammad al-Maqdisi* (Cambridge University Press 2012), pp. 30–41.

14.   Abu Muhammad al-Maqdisi, *Al-Kawashif al-jaliya fi kufr al-dawla al-suʿudiyya* (The clear evidence of the irreligion of the Saudi state) (Minbar al-Tawhid wa-l-Jihad 2001 [1989]), pp. 214–224. All translations into English are mine, unless otherwise noted.

15.   Muqbil al-Wadiʿi, *Al-Musaraʿa* (The wrestle) (n.p. 1992), p. 475.

16.   François Burgat and Muʾhammad Sbitli, "Les Salafis au Yémen ou la modernisation malgré tout," *Chroniques Yéménites*, 10 (2002), https://journals.openedition.org/cy/137#article-137.

17.   Paul Dresch, *A History of Modern Yemen* (Cambridge University Press 2000), pp. 5–6.

18.   *Libiraliyun.*

19.   *ʿIlmaniyun.*

20.   *Al-shabab al-islami.*

21.   *Shabab al-sahwa.* Madawi Al-Rasheed, *Contesting the Saudi State: Islamic Voices from a New Generation* (Cambridge University Press 2007), p. 65.

22.   *Al-shabab.*

23.   Martin Kramer, "Coming to Terms: Fundamentalists or Islamists?" *Middle East Quarterly* 10, no. 2 (2003): 65–77; Voltaire, *Essai sur les moeurs et l'esprit des nations*

et sur les principaux faits de l'histoire depuis Charlemagne jusqu'à Louis XIII (Bordas 1990), vol. 1, ch. 7.

24.   Amélie Le Renard, *A Society of Young Women: Opportunities of Place, Power, and Reform in Saudi Arabia* (Stanford University Press 2014).

25.   Talal Asad, *Secular Translations: Nation-State, Modern Self, and Calculating Reason* (Columbia University Press 2018), p. 9.

26.   Asad, *Secular Translations*, p. 9. I thank Omer Shah for pointing me to this page.

27.   Saba Mahmood, *Politics of Piety: The Islamic Revival and the Feminist Subject* (Princeton University Press 2005), p. xi.

28.   *Al-ʿamal al-islami.*

29.   Talal Asad, "The Idea of an Anthropology of Islam," *Qui Parle* 17, no. 2 (2009): 1–30; Mahmood, *Politics of Piety*; Charles Hirschkind, *The Ethical Soundscape: Cassette Sermons and Islamic Counter-Publics* (Columbia University Press 2006).

30.   Samuli Schielke, "Second Thoughts about an Anthropology of Islam, or How to Make Sense of Grand Schemes in Everyday Life," ZMO Working Papers 2 (2010): 2, 10, 12.

31.   Engseng Ho, *The Graves of Tarim: Genealogy and Mobility Across the Indian Ocean* (University of California Press 2006), pp. 11–12.

32.   Eldon Rutter, *The Holy Cities of Arabia* (G. P. Putnam's Sons 1928), vol. 2, pp. 256–257, quoted in John Willis, "Governing the Living and the Dead: Mecca and the Emergence of the Saudi Biopolitical State," *American Historical Review* 122, no. 2 (2017): 362.

33.   Hussam Dakkak, "Makkah's Belongings," in *Mecca: The Lived City*, colloquium held at Harvard University's Center for Middle Eastern Studies, May 3, 2019.

34.   "Graves in Riyadh cemeteries to be specified electronically," *Arab News*, March 24, 2012.

35.   Achille Mbembe, "Necropolitics," *Public Culture* 15, no. 1 (2003): 39–40.

36.   Al-Rasheed, *Contesting the Saudi State*, p. 19. "Death-world" is an expression created by Mbembe in "Necropolitics," p. 40. The "death of the street" is an expression from Le Corbusier (see below, chapter 4).

CHAPTER 2: *LA MUBALA*

1.   To protect my interlocutors' confidentiality I have changed their names and any indication that could help identify them. All interlocutors' names are the product of my imagination. I have also changed the names of some of the places I write about and sometimes created fictional names.

2.   Frances F. Piven and Richard A. Cloward, *Poor People's Movements: Why They Succeed, How They Fail* (Vintage 1979), p. 14.

3.   Siegfried Kracauer, *The Mass Ornament: Weimar Essays* (Harvard University Press 1995 [1924]), pp. 331–334 (I thank Omer Shah for pointing me to this text); Francesca Polletta, "The Laws of Passion," *Law and Society Review* 35, no. 2 (2001): 480–481; Francesca Polletta, "Plotting Protest: Storytelling in the 1960 Student Sit-In Movement,"

in J. Davis (ed.), *Stories of Change: Narratives and Social Movements* (SUNY Press 2001). See also Guy Bajoit, "Exit, Voice, Loyalty . . . and Apathy. Les réactions individuelles au mécontentement," *Revue Française de Sociologie* 29, no. 2 (1988): 325–345.

4. Samuli Schielke, "Boredom and Despair in Rural Egypt," *Contemporary Islam* 2, no. 3: 251–270; Samuli Schielke, *Egypt in the Future Tense: Hope, Frustration, and Ambivalence Before and After 2011* (Indiana University Press 2015), pp. 27ff.

5. Pascal Menoret, *Joyriding in Riyadh: Oil, Urbanism, and Road Revolt* (Cambridge University Press 2014), pp. 57–60.

6. Mamoun Fandy, *Saudi Arabia and the Politics of Dissent* (St. Martin's Press 1999), pp. 149–175.

7. "Far From Home, a Saudi Opposition Makes Voice Heard," *New York Times*, October 27, 2003.

8. 'Abd al-'Aziz al-Khamis, "Umm Sa'ud tuqliqu Ibn Sa'ud wa taftahu bab al-taghyir al-kabir" (Umm Sa'ud upsets Ibn Sa'ud and opens the door to change), *Al-Quds al-'Arabi*, November 5, 2003.

9. *Ida'at al-islah*

10. *Ida'at al-qur'an.*

11. *Ma'qul al-an, ha-l-dawla da'ifa? Ha-tasqut mawqefat al-a'sa 'ala atraf asabi'ha?*

12. *'Endom ila majmu'a, tahmi nafsek. 'Indama 'andom 'ahmi al-thani.*

13. "Al-sultat al-su'udiyya tuwaqqifu afradan fi-l-Riyad bi-tuhmati kharqi al-qa-wanin" (The Saudi authorities arrest individuals in Riyadh for breaking the law), *Al-Sharq al-Awsat*, October 15, 2003.

14. "A Demonstration in Riyadh Ends in 150 Arrests," Kuwait News Agency, October 14, 2003; "Quwat al-'amn al-su'udiyya tamna'u al-tazahurat wa ta'taqilu al-'asharat" (The Saudi security forces ban demonstrations and arrest dozens), aljazeera.net, October 24, 2003; Human Rights Watch, "Saudi Arabia: Arrest of Protesters Belies Reform Pledges," October 28, 2003.

15. Al-Khamis, "Umm Sa'ud."

16. "Quwat al-'amn al-su'udiyya."

17. "Al-hasila al-niha'iya li-hariq al-ha'ir bi-l-riyad" (The final body count of the al-Hayer fire in Riyadh), *Al-Sharq al-Awsat*, September 18, 2003.

18. Al-Khamis, "Umm Sa'ud."

19. "Far From Home,", *New York Times*.

20. Al-Khamis, "Umm Sa'ud."

21. Al-Khamis, "Umm Sa'ud."

22. Al-Khamis, "Umm Sa'ud."

23. "Quwat al-'amn al-su'udiyya."

24. Amnesty International, "Saudi Arabia: Crackdown on Demonstrators Deals Another Blow to Human Rights," October 24, 2003.

25. Amnesty International, "Further Information on UA 301/03 (MDE 23/009/2003, 24 October 2003) and follow-ups (MDE 23/011/2003, 13 November 2003 and MDE 23/013/2003, 20 November 2003)—Possible prisoner of conscience/Torture and ill-treatment/Incommunicado detention/Medical concern," January 9, 2004.

CHAPTER 3: HOW CAN THE STATE TORTURE CLERICS?

1. Mamoun Fandy, *Saudi Arabia and the Politics of Dissent* (Palgrave Macmillan 2001), pp. 1–60; Mansoor Jassem Alshamsi, *Islam and Political Reform in Saudi Arabia: The Quest for Political Change and Reform* (Routledge 2011), pp. 78–136.

2. *Mishebb.*

3. *Mulhaq.*

4. *Majlis al-rajajil.*

5. *Jama'at al-taw'iya al-islamiyya.*

6. *Halaqat tahfiz al-qur'an.*

7. *Mu'askarat sayfiyya,* sometimes also *marakiz* or *andiya sayfiyya.*

8. *Al-taw'iya.*

9. Charles Kurzman, "Une déploration pour Mustafa: Les bases quotidiennes de l'activisme politique," in Mounia Bennani-Chraïbi and Olivier Fillieule (eds.), *Résistances et protestations dans les sociétés musulmanes* (Presses de Sciences Po 2003), pp. 184–186 and 193–194.

10. Khalid al-Shayi', "Ighlaq masajid al-Su'udiyya 'uqba kulli salatin li-asbabin 'amniyya" (Saudi mosques close after each prayer for security reasons), *Al-'Arabi al-Jadid,* January 16, 2017. This regulation, published in 2016–2017 by the Ministry of Islamic Affairs, made official a practice that had been commonplace for more than two decades.

11. Madawi Al-Rasheed, *Muted Modernists: The Struggle over Divine Politics in Saudi Arabia* (Oxford University Press 2016), in particular chapter 2.

12. *Mukashafa.*

13. Frances F. Piven and Richard A. Cloward, *Poor People's Movements: Why They Succeed, How They Fail* (Vintage 1979), p. 5.

14. Richard Nielsen, *Deadly Clerics: Blocked Ambition and the Path to Jihad* (Cambridge University Press 2017), pp. 1–26. For a conceptual introduction to the Salafi movement, see Michael Muhammad Knight, *Why I Am A Salafi* (Soft Skull Press 2015). For an introduction to the history of the Salafi movement, see Henri Lauzière, *The Making of Salafism: Islamic Reform in the Twentieth Century* (Columbia University Press 2016).

15. Yusef al-Qaradawi, *Ibn al-Qariya wa-l-Kuttab: Malamih Sira wa Masira* (Son of the village and of the Quranic school: an autobiography) (Dar al-Shuruq 2006), vol. 3, pp. 79–86.

16. Madawi Al-Rasheed, *Contesting the Saudi State: Islamic Voices from a New Generation* (Cambridge University Press 2007), pp. 64–65.

17. His website, www.almurabbi.com ("the educator"), is dedicated to pedagogical questions. (Accessed November 11, 2019.)

18. Philippe Ariès, *Centuries of Childhood: A Social History of Family Life* (Vintage 1965).

19. Stéphane Lacroix, "L'apport de Muhammad Nasir al-Din al-'Albani au salafisme contemporain," in Bernard Rougier (ed.), *Qu'est-ce que le salafisme?* (Presses Universitaires de France 2008), p. 55.

20. See Laurent Thévenot, "Une jeunesse difficile: Les fonctions sociales du flou et de la rigueur dans les classements," *Actes de la recherche en sciences sociales* 26, no. 1 (1979): 3–18; Pierre Bourdieu, "La jeunesse n'est qu'un mot," *Questions de sociologie* (Éditions de Minuit 1984), pp. 143–154; Ibrahim al-Juwayyir, *Ta'akhkhur al-Shabab al-Jami'i fi-l-Zawaj* (The delayed marriage of university students) ('Obeikan 1995); Khalid al-Salim, *Al-Dubt al-Ijtima'i wa-l-Tamasuk al-'Usari* (Social control and family cohesion) (n.p. 2000); 'Abd al-'Aziz al-Shithri, *Waqt al-Faragh wa Shaghluhu fi Madinat al-Riyad: Dirasa Maydaniyya* (Free time and its usage in Riyadh: a field study) (Imam Muhammad bin Sa'ud Islamic University 2001); Jon Savage, *Teenage: The Creation of Youth, 1875–1945* (Penguin 2007); Mounia Bennani-Chraïbi and Iman Farag (eds.), *Jeunesses des sociétés arabes par-delà les menaces et les promesses* (Aux lieux d'être 2007); Linda Herrera and Asef Bayat (eds.), *Being Young and Muslim: New Cultural Politics in the Global South and North* (Oxford University Press 2010); Laurent Bonnefoy and Myriam Catusse (eds.), *Jeunesses arabes du Maroc au Yémen: loisirs, cultures et politiques* (La Découverte 2013).

21. *Al-ri'asa al-'amma li-ri'ayat al-shabab.*

22. See 'Abd Allah 'Anas, *Wilada al-Afghan al-'Arab: Sirat 'Abd Allah 'Anas bayna Mas'ud wa 'Abd Allah 'Azzam* (The birth of the Arab Afghans: autobiography of 'Abd Allah Anas, between [Ahmad Shah] Mas'ud and 'Abd Allah 'Azzam) (Saqi Books 2002).

CHAPTER 4: GET IN YOUR CAR AND DRIVE

1. "Far from Home, a Saudi Opposition Makes Voice Heard," *The New York Times*, October 27, 2003.

2. Pascal Menoret, *Joyriding in Riyadh: Oil, Urbanism, and Road Revolt* (Cambridge University Press 2014), in particular chapters 5 and 6.

3. *Al-zahf al-kabir.*

4. *Fiqh al-muzaharat.*

5. Sa'id bin Zu'ayr "Al-Din al-Nasiha." See https://ar.islamway.net/lesson/1255/الدين-النصيحة?__ref=c-rel&__score=2.7 (Accessed November 11, 2019). Islamway is a popular online library of writings and audio recordings.

6. Quoted in Talal Asad, *Genealogies of Religion: Discipline and Reasons of Power in Christianity and Islam* (Johns Hopkins University Press 1993), p. 203.

7. *Nasiha.*

8. Quoted in Asad, *Genealogies of Religion*, p. 217.

9. *Mutashaddidin.*

10. *Mutatarrifin.*

11. Salman al-'Ouda, "Sultan al-'Ulama'", September 23, 1992: http://salmanalodah.com/main/1201-2-سلطان-العلماء.html. (Accessed November 11, 2019.) Salmanalodah.com is the digital encyclopedia of Sheikh Salman al-'Ouda's writings, sermons, and lectures.

12. Jorgen Nielsen, "Sultan al-Zahir Baybars and the Appointment of Four Chief Qadis, 663/1265," *Studia Islamica* 60 (1984): 172.

13. Sherman Jackson, *Islamic Law and the State: The Constitutional Jurisprudence of Shihab al-Din al-Qarafi* (Brill 1996), p. 10.

14. Pascal Menoret [Charles Pichegru, pseud.], "Les murs de Riyad: Islam et modernité urbaine en Arabie Saoudite," *Chroniques Yéménites* 9 (2001), https://journals.openedition.org/cy/72.

15. Teresa P.R. Caldeira, *City of Walls: Crime, Segregation, and Citizenship in São Paulo* (University of California Press 2000), pp. 4 and 213ff.

16. Le Corbusier, *La Ville radieuse: Éléments d'une doctrine d'urbanisme pour l'équipement de la civilisation machiniste* (Vincent, Fréal & Cie 1963), pp. 119–126; James Holston, *The Modernist City: An Anthropological Critique of Brasília* (The University of Chicago Press 1989), pp. 101–144.

17. *Al-'usra.*

18. *Mushrif.*

19. *Al-sayyara.*

CHAPTER 5: ARAMCO'S LEVITTOWN

1. *Istirahat.*

2. "Al-Suwaydi . . . akthar min hayy sakani . . . shahida al-sahwa fi-l-thamaniynat wa-l-irhab akhiran" (More than a residential suburb, Suwaydi witnessed the Islamic awakening in the 1980s and terrorism more recently), *Al-Sharq al-Awsat*, December 14, 2004.

3. Riyadh Development Authority, *Atlas Madinat al-Riyad* (Riyadh City Atlas), 1999, part 3.

4. Soraya Altorki and Donald P. Cole, *Arabian Oasis City: The Transformation of 'Unayzah* (University of Texas Press 1989), pp. 208–231; Amélie Le Renard, *A Society of Young Women: Opportunities of Place, Power, and Reform in Saudi Arabia* (Stanford University Press 2014).

5. Riyadh Development Authority, "Nahwi tatwir nizam naql 'am 'amin wa fa''al fi madinat al-riyad" (Toward the development of a safe and efficient public transit system in Riyadh), 2000.

6. Constantinos A. Doxiadis Archives, Archive File 23325, Final Master Plan of Riyadh, July 1971, p. 304.

7. Mike Featherstone, Nigel Thrift, and John Urry (eds.), *Automobilities* (Sage 2005), p. 2.

8. See Gordon Pirie, "Non-Urban Motoring in Colonial Africa in the 1920s and 1930s," *South African Historical Journal* 63, no. 1 (2011): 38–60; Georgine Clarsen and Lorenzo Veracini, "Settler Colonial Automobility: A Distinct Constellation of Automobile Cultures?" *History Compass* 10, no. 12 (2012): 889–900; Kristin V. Monroe, "Automobility and Citizenship in Interwar Lebanon," *Comparative Studies of South Asia, Africa and the Middle East* 34, no. 3 (2014): 518–531.

9. Alexei Vassiliev, *The History of Saudi Arabia* (Saqi Books 2000), p. 269.

10. Vassiliev, *The History of Saudi Arabia*, pp. 333 and 410–411.

11. Saleh al-Hathloul, "Tradition, Continuity, and Change in the Built Environment: The Arab-Muslim City" (PhD thesis, MIT 1981), p. 159.

12. Claudia Ghrawi, "Structural and Physical Violence in Saudi Arabian Oil Towns, 1953–56," in Ulrike Freitag, Nelida Fuccaro, Claudia Ghrawi, and Nora Lafi (eds.), *Urban Violence in the Middle East: Changing Cityscapes in the Transition from Empire to Nation State* (Berghahn 2015), p. 245.

13. Robert Vitalis, "Black Gold, White Crude: An Essay on American Exceptionalism, Hierarchy, and Hegemony in the Gulf," *Diplomatic History* 26, no. 2 (2002): 200ff.

14. Interview, al-Qatif, December 2006.

15. Interview, al-Khobar, December 2006.

16. Interview, al-Qatif, December 2006.

17. Robert Vitalis, *America's Kingdom: Mythmaking on the Saudi Oil Frontier* (Verso 2009), p. 94.

18. Quoted in Ghrawi, "Structural and Physical Violence," p. 252.

19. Ghrawi, "Structural and Physical Violence," p. 258.

20. Faisal Mubarak, "Urbanization, Urban Policy and City Form: Urban Development in Saudi Arabia," (PhD thesis, University of Washington 1992), p. 121.

21. Vitalis, *America's Kingdom*, p. 92.

22. Al-Hathloul, "Tradition, Continuity, and Change," pp. 144–154.

23. Ibrahim al-But'hie, "The Role of Citizens in Defining the Meaning and Quality of Traditional and Modern Built Environments: An Exploratory Study of Al-Riyad, Saudi Arabia," (PhD thesis, University of Texas at Austin 1996), p. 18.

24. Claudia Ghrawi, "A Tamed Urban Revolution: Saudi Arabia's Oil Conurbation and the 1967 Riots," in Nelida Fuccaro (ed.), *Violence and the City in the Modern Middle East* (Stanford University Press 2016), pp. 112–117.

25. Solon Kimball, "American Culture in Saudi Arabia," *Proceedings of the New York Academy of Science* 18, no. 5 (1956): 483.

26. Andrew Friedman, *Covert Capital: Landscapes of Denial and the Making of U.S. Empire in the Suburbs of Northern Virginia* (University of California Press 2013).

27. Nathan Citino, "Suburbia and Modernization: Community Building and America's Post-WWII Encounter with the Arab Middle East," *Arab Studies Journal* 13, no. 14 (2006): 43–45.

28. *Al-Riyad al-jadida.*

29. Fahad al-Said, "The Pattern of Structural Transformation of the Saudi Contemporary Neighborhood: The Case of Malaz, Riyadh, Saudi Arabia," 39th International Society of City and Regional Planners Congress, 2003.

30. Al-Hathloul, "Tradition, Continuity and Change," pp. 162–171.

31. Ghrawi, "A Tamed Urban Revolution," p. 122.

32. Constantinos A. Doxiadis Archives, Archive File 23305: *Riyadh—Existing Conditions (final report)*, DOX-SAU-A2, 1968, p. 287.

33. Constantinos A. Doxiadis Archives, Archive File 23354: C-SAU-A1143, April 17, 1973; Pascal Menoret, *Joyriding in Riyadh: Oil, Urbanism, and Road Revolt* (Cambridge University Press 2014), pp. 94–101.

34. Constantinos A. Doxiadis, *Architecture in Transition* (Oxford University Press 1963).

35. Rachel Kallus, "Patrick Geddes and the Evolution of a Housing Type in Tel-Aviv," *Planning Perspectives* 12 (1997): 281–320; Volker M. Welter, "The 1925 Master Plan for Tel-Aviv by Patrick Geddes," *Israel Studies* 14, no. 3 (2009): 94–119; Navida Khan, "Geddes in India: Town Planning, Plant Sentience, and Cooperative Evolution," *Environment and Planning* 29 (2011): 840–856.

36. Neal I. Payton, "The Machine in the Garden City: Patrick Geddes's Plan for Tel Aviv," *Planning Perspectives* 10 (1995): 366.

37. Ellen Shoshkes, "Jacqueline Tyrwhitt: A Founding Mother of Modern Urban Design," *Planning Perspectives* 21 (2006): 179–197.

CHAPTER 6: BLESSED ARE THE STRANGERS

1. Muhammad S. Makki, "Al-namu al-ʿomrani wa taghayyor malamih tarkib al-madina al-munawwara" (Urban growth and the changing structure of Medina), Symposium on the Arab City, The Arab Urban Development Institute, Medina, Feb. 28–Mar. 5, 1981, pp. 135–136.

2. *Al-salaf al-salih.*

3. Guido Steinberg, "The Wahhabi Ulama and the Saudi State: 1745 to the Present," in Paul Aarts and Gerd Nonneman (eds.), *Saudi Arabia in the Balance: Political Economy, Society, Foreign Affairs* (Hurst & Co. 2005), pp. 25–26.

4. *Al-jamaʿa al-salafiyya al-muhtasiba.*

5. Nasir al-Huzaymi, *Ayyam maʿ Juhayman: Kuntu maʿ al-jamaʿa al-salafiyya al-muhtasiba* (Days with Juhayman: I was with the Salafi group that commands virtue and combats vice) (al-Shabaka al-ʿarabiyya li-l-abhath wa-l-nashr 2010), pp. 42–44.

6. *Al-ikhwan.*

7. Al-Huzaymi, *Ayyam maʿ Juhayman*, pp. 45–46.

8. Nasir Al-Huzaymi, "Al-takfir wa-l-hijra kama ʿaraftuhum" (Excommunication and exodus as I knew them), *Al-Riyad*, May 19, 2003.

9. Al-Huzaymi, "Al-takfir wa-l-hijra."

10. Al-Huzaymi, *Ayyam maʿ Juhayman*, p. 23.

11. Yaroslav Trofimov, *The Siege of Mecca: The Forgotten Uprising* (Allen Lane 2007), pp. 37, 64.

12. Interview with a former member of the Salafi Group, Riyadh, March 2007.

13. Al-Huzaymi, *Ayyam maʿ Juhayman*, pp. 52–53.

14. Al-Huzaymi, *Ayyam maʿ Juhayman*, pp. 53–54.

15. Interview with a former member of the Salafi Group, Riyadh, March 2007.

16. Fahd Al-Qahtani, *Zilzal Juhayman fi Makka* (Juhayman's commotion in Mecca) (Munazzama al-thawra al-islamiya fi-l-jazira al-ʿarabiyya 1987), p. 53.

17. Al-Huzaymi, *Ayyam maʿ Juhayman*, p. 54.

18. Interview with a former member of the Salafi Group, Riyadh, March 2007.

19. Al-Qahtani, *Zilzal Juhayman*, p. 56.

20. Raf'at Sayyid Ahmad, *Rasa'il Juhayman al-'Otaybi, Qa'id al-muqtahamin li-l-masjid al-haram bi-Makka* (The letters of Juhayman al-'Otaybi, leader of the occupation of the Great Mosque of Mecca) (Madbouli 2004), pp. 67, 65.

21. Ahmad, *Rasa'il Juhayman*, pp. 75–77.

22. Al-Huzaymi, *Ayyam ma'Juhayman*, p. 63.

23. Al-Huzaymi, *Ayyam ma'Juhayman*, p. 65.

24. Interview of Nasir al-Huzaymi by Muhammad al-Qash'ami, Oral History of the Kingdom of Saudi Arabia, March 9, 2003.

25. Al-Qahtani, *Zilzal Juhayman*, 78.

26. Faisal Devji, *The Terrorist in Search of Humanity: Militant Islam and Global Politics* (Oxford University Press 2009), pp. 10–11.

27. Interview with a former member of the Salafi Group, March 2007.

28. Al-Qahtani, *Zilzal Juhayman*, p. 125.

29. Trofimov, *The Siege of Mecca*, pp. 191–197 and 207–212.

30. Pascal Menoret, "Fighting for the Holy Mosque: The 1979 Mecca Insurgency," in Christine Fair and Sumit Ganguly (eds.), *Treading on Hallowed Ground: Counterinsurgency Operations in Sacred Spaces* (Oxford University Press 2008), p. 130.

31. Al-Qahtani, *Zilzal Juhayman*, pp. 234–237.

CHAPTER 7: SUBDIVISION FRENZY

1. Faisal Mubarak, "Urban Growth Boundary Policy and Residential Suburbanization: Riyadh, Saudi Arabia," *Habitat International* 28 (2004): 582.

2. Lucille Haguenauer-Caceres, "Construire à l'étranger: le rôle de la SCET-Coopération en Côte d'Ivoire de 1959 à 1976," *Histoire Urbaine* 23, no. 3 (2008): 147–148; International Archives, Caisse des Dépôts et Consignations, Paris: SCET INTERNATIONAL, Box 040425-0231/DG, Folder 295-003: Témoignage de Léon-Paul Leroy, January 21, 1987.

3. International Archives, Caisse des Dépôts et Consignations, Paris: SCET INTERNATIONAL, Box 040425-0230/DG, Folder 294-001, Subfolder 294-004: SCET Inter Divers, New Year Speeches, Montparnasse, Speech by Jacques Bourdillon, ex-president of SCETI, 1983.

4. International Archives, Caisse des Dépôts et Consignations, Paris: SCET INTERNATIONAL, Politique générale and Conseils d'administration, Box 950350-0005/DABF, Conseil d'administration du lundi 6 juin 1977.

5. Interview with a former SCET development expert, Paris, November 2013.

6. Institut Français d'Architecture, *Architectures Françaises Outre-Mer* (Mardaga 1995), p. 216.

7. International Archives, Caisse des Dépôts et Consignations, Paris: A. de Roux, "Riyadh," in *CDC Panorama*, Numéro Spécial, December 1979: "SCET International, Vingt Ans d'Activité, 1959–1979," p. 144.

8. Interview with a former SCET development expert, Paris, November 2013.

9.   International Archives, Caisse des Dépôts et Consignations, Paris: A. de Roux, "Riyadh," p. 152.

10.   Paul Bonnenfant, "Real Estate and Political Power in 1970s Riyadh," *City: Analysis of Urban Trends, Culture, Theory, Policy, Action* 18, no. 6 (2014): 719.

11.   Mohammed al-Gabbani, "Population Density Pattern and Change in the City of Riyadh, Saudi Arabia," *GeoJournal* 24, no. 4 (1991): 376.

12.   Al-Gabbani, "Population Density," 385.

13.   Al-Gabbani, "Population Density," 379–382.

14.   Mubarak, "Urban Growth Boundary Policy," 583.

15.   Mubarak, "Urban Growth Boundary Policy," 584.

16.   Mubarak, "Urban Growth Boundary Policy," 589.

17.   Toby C. Jones, "Rebellion on the Saudi Periphery: Modernity, Marginalization, and the Shi'a Uprising of 1979," *International Journal of Middle East Studies* 38 (2006): 213–233.

18.   *Al-sabat.*

19.   Rosie Bsheer, "Choking Mecca in the Name of Beauty and Development," *Jadaliyya*, October 21, 2010; Ziauddin Sardar, "The Destruction of Mecca," *New York Times*, October 1, 2014; Rosie Bsheer, "The Property Regime: Mecca and the Politics of Redevelopment in Saudi Arabia," *Cairo Observer*, April 2015.

20.   Tahar Ledraa and Naser Abu-Anzeh, "Regeneration through Urban Megaprojects in Riyadh," in Libby Porter and Kate Shaw (eds.), *Whose Urban Renaissance? An International Comparison of Urban Regeneration Strategies* (Routledge 2008), pp. 43–62.

CHAPTER 8: THE GENIE WAS OUT OF THE BOTTLE

1.   *Dar al-ifta'*, now renamed the General Presidency of Scholarly Research and Ifta.

2.   Saddeka Arebi, *Women and Words in Saudi Arabia: The Politics of Literary Discourse* (Columbia University Press 1994), pp. 57–58.

3.   *Ma'rakat al-hadatha*. 'Abd Allah al-Ghadhdhami, *Hikayat al-hadatha fi-l-mamlaka al-'arabiyya al-su'udiyya* (The story of modernity in Saudi Arabia) (al-Markaz al-Thaqafi al-'Arabi 2004).

4.   Al-Ghadhdhami, *Hikayat al-hadatha*, pp. 16, 33n.

5.   John M. Willis, "Governing the Living and the Dead: Mecca and the Emergence of the Saudi Biopolitical State," *American Historical Review* 122, no. 2 (2017), pp. 359–362.

6.   Sa'd al-Faqih, "History of Dissent: The Rise and Evolution of the Modern Islamic Reform Movement in Saudi Arabia," in *Arabia Unveiled* (monthly newsletter of the Movement of Islamic Reform in Arabia), 1996–1997.

7.   Quran 3:110.

8.   Mamoun Fandy, *Saudi Arabia and the Politics of Dissent*, (St. Martin's Press 1999), pp. 61–114.

9. *Khitab al-matalib.*

10. *Muzakkirat al-nasiha.*

11. See Fandy, *Saudi Arabia and the Politics of Dissent,* pp. 115–148.

CHAPTER 9: WE COULD USE THE PORK RIND

1. Toby Matthiesen, "Centre-Periphery Relations and the Emergence of a Public Sphere in Saudi Arabia: The Municipal Elections in the Eastern Province, 1954–1960," *British Journal of Middle Eastern Studies* (2014): 17–18.

2. "Voters who cannot state their opinion by themselves on the ballot can express it orally only to members of the committee, and this opinion will be stated on paper and then deposed in the ballot box," La'iha al-intikhabat li-l-majalis al-mahaliyya fi-l-su'udiyya (Regulation about local elections in Saudi Arabia), 'Abd al-'Aziz al-Khudayri, *Idara al-hamlat al-intikhabiyya wa hamlat al-'alaqat al-'amma* (Dar Al-Sawlatiya li-l-Tarbiya 2007), p. 123.

3. "Quwat al-'amn tadakhkhalat li-tanzimi siri al-iqtira' fi-l-nazim" (The security forces intervened in Nazim to organize the vote), *Al-Riyad,* February 11, 2005.

4. "Fi i'lani nata'iji muraqabati al-intikhabat al-baladiya fi-l-sharqiyya: nakhibu hafr al-batin iqtahamu ba'd al-marakiz wa fatahu sanadiq al-iqtira'" (Results of the observation of the municipal elections in the Eastern Province: Hafr al-Batin voters attacked several stations and opened the ballot boxes), *Al-Jazira,* March 4, 2005.

5. "Al-fawda awqafat at-taswit wa yu'awwad al-yum fi markazin fi hafr al-batin" (Anarchy stopped the polls which resume today in a station in Hafr al-Batin), *Al-Hayat,* March 5, 2005.

6. "I'adat at-taswit fi hafr al-batin" (Elections reported in Hafr al-Batin), *Al-Riyad,* March 5, 2005.

7. *'Okaz,* March 12, 2005.

8. "Global Meet to Discuss Dirty Money, Terror Link," *Arab News,* January 29, 2005.

9. See Mishari al-Dhaydi, "Intikhabat al-riyad: al-dars al-awwal" (Riyadh elections: first lessons), *Al-Sharq al-Awsat,* Feb. 15, 2005.

10. "La'iha al-hamlat al-intikhabiyya" (Electoral campaign code), reproduced in al-Khudayri, *Idara al-hamlat al-intikhabiyya,* pp. 126–128.

11. Muhammad Rida Nasr Allah, "Nasihati li-l-murashshahin" (My advice to the candidates), *Al-Riyad,* February 2, 2005.

12. *Dharru ramad 'ala al-'uyun.*

13. *Sha'art 'an min jild al-khinzir fa'ida.*

14. *Ma 'indahum ma 'ind jiddati.*

CHAPTER 10: MAKE THE WAY NARROWER FOR THEM

1. "Murashshih iad'u aqriba' min al-kuwayt li-l-istifada min khibratihim fi-l-intikhabat" (Candidate invites Kuwaiti relatives to benefit from their electoral expertise), *Al-Riyad,* February 4, 2005.

2. *Muhadarat.*

3. Nasir al-ʿOmar, "Al-musharaka fi-l-intikhabat al-baladiya wa dawabituha" (Participation in the municipal elections and its rules), in "Al-jamiʿ li-fatawa al-intikhabat" (Anthology of Electoral Fatwas), http://www.saaid.net/fatwa/f49.htm.

4. Mansoor Jassem Alshamsi, *Islam and Political Reform in Saudi Arabia: The Quest for Political Change and Reform* (Routledge 2011), pp. 3–6, 161, 173.

5. Nasir al-ʿOmar, "Al-mujtamaʿ al-madani: al-riyad anmudhajan" (Civil society: the Riyadh model), public lecture, February 7, 2005.

6. *Dayyiqu ʿalayihim.*

7. Al-ʿOmar, "Al-mujtamaʿ al-madani."

8. *Shura.* ʿAwad al-Garni, "Al-intikhabat wa wazifatuha al-islahiyya" (The Elections and their Reformist Purpose), public lecture, April 16, 2005, Jeddah.

9. See Talal Asad, *Genealogies of Religion: Discipline and Reasons of Power in Christianity and Islam* (Johns Hopkins University Press 1993), pp. 214–223.

10. *Shura.*

11. "Murashshih iadʿu aqribaʾ."

12. "Al-tahqiq fi tajawuzat li-murashshahin aʿlanu wuʿudan kharij salahiyat al-majlis al-baladi" (Investigation into violations of candidates who made promises outside of the municipal council's competencies), *Al-Riyad*, February 4, 2005.

13. Electoral results in Riyadh, by ward:

Ward	Winner's name	Winner's vote count	Next candidate's vote count	Gap winner-next candidate
1st	ʿAbd Allah al-Suwaylim	21,405 (38%)	5,703 (10.1%)	15,702 (27.8%)
2nd	Sulayman al-Rushudi	14,868 (26.4%)	2,906 (5.1%)	11,962 (21.2%)
3rd	Tariq al-Qasabi	20,416 (36.2%)	3,199 (5.6%)	17,217 (30.5%)
4th	ʿAbd al-ʿAziz al-ʿOmari	14,311 (25.4%)	5,129 (9.1%)	9,182 (16.2%)
5th	ʿOmar Ba Sudan	12,237 (21.7%)	5,966 (10.5%)	6,271 (11.1%)
6th	Ibrahim al-Quʿayyid	12,808 (22.7%)	4,090 (7.2%)	8,718 (15.4%)
7th	Misfir al-Bawardi	13,411 (23.8%)	3,988 (7%)	9,423 (16.7%)

14. *Al-Watan*, April 6, 2005. "The commission of recourse summoned two candidates from the sheikhs' list and dismissed one of them after studying forty complaints."

15. *Al-Sahat*, online forums.

16. *Al-Madina*, April 25, 2005.

17. *Al-Sharq al-Qatariyya*, May 3, 2005.

18. *Islamiyun wa muslimun. Al-Hayat*, February 13, 2005.

CHAPTER 11: THE HARRY POTTER DISSENT

1. *Ra'id.*

2. This opinion was shared by the sheikhs Nasir al-'Omar and Muhammad al-Munajjid on their personal websites. See Nasir al-'Omar, "Hari butir wa iflas al-tarbiya al-gharbiya" (*Harry Potter* and the failure of Western education), http://almoslim.net/node/6746, December 4, 2007; Muhammad al-Munajjid, "Hari butir wa mufakkira al-mawt: fitnat al-sighar wa-l-kibar, kufr wa-ilhad" (*Harry Potter* and *Death Note*: Tempting young and old, unbelief and atheism), https://islamqa.info /ar/118258, July 7, 2008.

3. *Fitnat hari butir.*

4. *La tagra' al-ghayr 'arabi.*

5. On *Harry Potter*, see also Salman al-'Ouda, "Namazhij ma-min haqqaqu ahlama-hum" (Those successful people who realized their dreams), http://salmanalodah .com/main/15452-3-نماذج-ممن-حققوا-أحلامهم.html, December 25, 2009. Salmanalodah. com is the digital encyclopedia of Sheikh Salman al-'Ouda's writings, sermons, and lectures.

CHAPTER 12: ALL STREETS ARE JOYRIDING STREETS

1. Claire Beaugrand, *Stateless in the Gulf: Migration, Nationality, and Society in Kuwait* (I.B. Tauris 2018).

2. *Hinna 'iyal al-Tumya, ma ahad iahkumna.*

3. *Ahebbek ya mirweh; harat falluja; anik Abu Muhammad; ya majnun hezz al-hadid hobbek yazid.*

4. *Mabruk 'ala-l-boya al-jadida.*

5. *Salli qabla ma yusalla 'alayk; qul khayran wa usmud.*

6. Munira Al Sa'ud, *Idha' al-Atfal: Anwa'uhu wa asbabuhu wa khasa'is al-muta'rarridina lah* (Violence toward children: Typology, causes, and characteristics of the victims) (Dar al-Thaqafa al-Misriyya 2000), p. 41.

7. "*Al-wir'an, lazim tu'addibhum*"; "*Al-ma'ra la budda ann tustakhdam ma'ha al-'ayn al-hamra.*" Jibrin al-Jibrin, *Al-'Unf al-usari khilal marahil al-haya* (Familial violence across life periods) (King Khalid Charitable Foundation 2005), p. 79.

CHAPTER 13: MUSLIM BROTHERS AND SALAFIS

1. *Kalima ba'd al-sala.*

2. See for instance "Saudi Clergy and Scholars Petition for Change," *New York Times*, May 26, 1991.

3. Hossam Tammam, "The Salafization of the Muslim Brothers. The Erosion of the Fundamental Hypothesis and the Rising of Salafism within the Muslim Brotherhood: The Path and Repercussions of Change" (pamphlet, Bibliotheca Alexandrina 2011).

4. *Kuliyat al-shari'a wa usul al-din.*

CHAPTER 14: THE BEST AMONG YOU

1. *Rajul al-masjid.*

2. "Whether I shall turn out to be the hero of my own life, or whether that station will be held by somebody else, these pages must show" (Charles Dickens, *David Copperfield*, ch. 1). Published in Egypt in a series for young readers, the Arabic translation of Dickens's novel was widely available in Saudi Arabia.

3. *Jihad.*

4. ʿAbd al-Rahman Munif et al. (eds.), *ʿAwdat al-istiʿmar min al-ghazuw al-thaqafi ila harb al-khalij* (The return of colonization, from the cultural assault to the Gulf War) (Riyad al-Rayyis 1991).

5. *"Khayrukum man taʿallama al-Qurʾan wa ʿallamahu."*

CHAPTER 15: THE TALAL AFFAIR

1. Pascal Menoret, *Joyriding in Riyadh: Oil, Urbanism, and Road Revolt* (Cambridge University Press 2014), pp. 42–44.

CHAPTER 16: A STATE WITHIN THE STATE

1. *"Mamlaka al-insaniyya."* On humanitarianism, see Faisal Devji, *The Terrorist in Search of Humanity: Militant Islam and Global Politics* (Oxford University Press 2009).

2. See Carol Fleming al-Ajroush, "Siamese Twins and Separation: Saudi Arabia's Kingdom of Humanity," *American Bedu*, July 28, 2008, https://delhi4cats.wordpress.com/2008/07/28/siamese-twins-and-separation-the-kingdom-of-humanity/.

3. *Al-Jazira*, June 10, 2006.

4. *Multazimin.*

5. See Asef Bayat, "Islamism and the Politics of Fun," *Public Culture* 19, no. 3 (2007), pp. 433–459; Lara Deeb and Mona Harb, "Choosing Both Faith and Fun: Youth Negotiations of Moral Norms in South Beirut," *Journal of Anthropology* 78, no. 1 (2013).

CHAPTER 17: THE DOOR WHENCE THE WIND COMES

1. "Thoughts for the Summer Camps" (*Khawatir li-l-marakiz al-sayfiyya*), http://saaid.net/anshtah/mr/11.htm.

2. *Al-andiya' al-sayfiyya.*

3. Mansur al-Barrak, "Hubban li-l-watan wa riʿayatan li-thirwatih" (Out of love for the nation, out of care for its resources), *Al-Jazira*, June 10, 2006.

4. Saʿd al-ʿAqil, "333 andiyan sayfiyyan fi-l-mamlaka tastaqbilu 120 alf talib iʿtibaran min al-yum" (333 summer clubs in the Kingdom welcome 120,000 students from today on), *Al-Jazira, June 10, 2006.*

5. Salman al-ʿOuda, "Ha-hiya istiʾsaliya jadida?" (A new eradication campaign?), *Al-Jazira*, June 27, 2004.

6. *Al-bab elle yiji minnah al-rih siddah wa istirih.*

7. Muhammad al-Bishr, "'An al-marakiz al-sayfiyya, 'aydhan" (About the summer camps, once again), *Al-Jazira*, June 21, 2004.

8. *Hawamir.*

9. *Mutanaffis.*

10. On the similar notion of *tanfis* see Lisa Wedeen, *Ambiguities of Domination: Politics, Rhetoric, and Symbols in Contemporary Syria* (University of Chicago Press 1999), p. 90–92.

11. See 'Abd al-'Aziz al-Shithri, *Waqt al-Faragh wa Shaghluhu fi Madinat al-Riyad: Dirasa Maydaniyya* (Free time and its usage in Riyadh: a field study) (Imam Muhammad bin Saud Islamic University 2001).

12. *Nizam al-shilal.*

13. *Shudhudh.*

14. Stephen R. Covey, *The Seven Habits of Highly Effective People: Powerful Lessons in Personal Change* (Free Press 1989). Translated into Arabic as *Al-'adat al-sab' li-l-nas al-akthar fa'aliya: durus fa"ala hawla taghyir al-shakhsiya* (Maktabat Jarir 2000).

15. Husam Tammam and Patrick Haenni, "The management, nouvelle utopie islamiste. Une lecture managériale des textes," *Revue française de gestion* 33, no. 171 (2007): 178–179.

CHAPTER 18: FIERCE AND LOUD

1. Pascal Menoret, "L'Empire du dérisoire: Lecture d'une série televisée saoudienne de Ramadan: Tash Ma Tash" (MA thesis, Institut National d'Études Orientales, Paris 2004).

2. *Sakhin wa sakhib.*

CHAPTER 19: HOW WERE YOU FUCKED?

1. *"Amruhum shura baynahum,"* Quran 42:38.

2. *Hubb al-watan wa-l-qiyada.*

3. Abu 'Isa Muhammad bin 'Isa al-Tirmidhi, *Jami' al-Tirmidhi*, vol. 6 (Darussalam 2007), chapter 68, "Fi fadhli Makka," par. 3925, p. 520.

4. *Hubb al-watan.*

5. Pascal Menoret, "Al-Intikhabat al-baladiya fi-l-mamlaka al-'arabiyya al-su'udiyya 2005" (The 2005 Municipal Elections in Saudi Arabia) (Arab Reform Initiative 2005).

6. Pascal Menoret, *Joyriding in Riyadh: Oil, Urbanism, and Road Revolt* (Cambridge University Press 2014), pp. 46–47.

CHAPTER 20: THOSE DAMNED LIBERALS

1. *Ya mulabbis.*

2. *Al-jarh wa-l-ta'dil.*

3. *'Ilm al-rijal.*

4. François Burgat and Mu'hammed Sbitli, "Les Salafis au Yémen ou la modernisation malgré tout. 'Ils le disent . . . c'est donc qu'ils le sont!' ou les pièges du discours de l'objet," *Chroniques Yéménites* 10 (2002).

5. *Al-ikhwan al-muslimun.*

6. *Al-ikhwan al-muflisun.*

7. Burgat and Sbitli, "Les Salafis au Yémen."

8. Pascal Menoret, *Joyriding in Riyadh: Oil, Urbanism, and Road Revolt* (Cambridge University Press 2014), p. 21.

9. See Ahmed Dailami, "Militancy, Monarchy and the Struggle to Desacralize Kingship in Arabia," in Faisal Devji and Zaheer Kazmi (eds.), *Islam after Liberalism* (Oxford University Press 2017), pp. 203–218.

CHAPTER 21: THE STOREHOUSES OF THE LAND

1. For a similar development in 1990s Egypt, see Augustus Richard Norton, "Thwarted Politics: The Case of Egypt's Hizb al-Wasat," in Robert W. Hefner (ed.), *Remaking Muslim Politics* (Princeton University Press 2005), pp. 133–160; Carrie Rosefsky Wickham, *The Muslim Brotherhood: Evolution of an Islamist Movement* (Princeton University Press 2013), pp. 13–14 and 76ff.

2. See Hélène Thiollet, "Nationalisme d'État et nationalisme ordinaire en Arabie Saoudite: La nation saoudienne et ses immigrés," *Raisons Politiques* 37, no. 1 (2010): 89–101; Omar Saghi, *Paris-La Mecque: Sociologie d'un Pèlerinage* (Presses universitaires de France 2010); Thomas Hegghammer, *Jihad in Saudi Arabia: Violence and Pan-Islamism since 1979* (Cambridge University Press 2010); Amélie Le Renard, *A Society of Young Women: Opportunities of Place, Power, and Reform in Saudi Arabia* (Stanford University Press 2014); Stéphane Lacroix, *Awakening Islam: The Politics of Dissent in Contemporary Saudi Arabia* (Harvard University Press 2011); Nabil Mouline, *The Clerics of Islam: Religious Authority and Political Power in Saudi Arabia* (Yale University Press 2014).

3. *Amir al-rihla.*

4. "*Qala j'alni 'ala khaza'ini al-ardhi*" (Quran 12:55).

5. "*Qala ia bunayy la taqussus ru'yaka 'ala ikhwatika fa-yakidu laka kayda*" (Quran 12:5).

CHAPTER 22: PEOPLE DID NOT FALL FROM THE SKY

1. See 'Abd al-'Aziz Qasim, *Mukashafat* (Unveilings), vols. 1, 2, and 3 ('Obeikan 2007).

2. Carrie Rosefsky Wickham, *The Muslim Brotherhood: Evolution of an Islamist Movement* (Princeton University Press 2013), pp. 85–87.

3. *Tanzim.*

CHAPTER 23: BRATS AND BRAGGARTS

1.   Richard Bandler and John Grinder, *Frogs into Princes: Neuro Linguistic Programming* (Real People Press 1979). On NLP, see also Jane Bradley and Heinz-Joachim Biedermann, "Bandler and Grinder's Neurolinguistic Programming: Its Historical Context and Contribution," *Psychotherapy* 22, no. 1 (1985): 59–62; Barry Beyerstein, "Brainscams: Neuromythologies of the New Age," *International Journal of Mental Health* 19, no. 3 (1990): 27–36.

2.   Richard Nielsen, *Deadly Clerics: Blocked Ambition and the Path to Jihad* (Cambridge University Press 2017).

3.   *Qunbula mawquta.*

CHAPTER 24: DETAINED

1.   Jonathan Moyer, David Bohl, Taylor Hanna, Brendan Mapes, and Mickey Rafa, *Assessing the Impact of War on Development in Yemen* (United Nations Development Program 2019), pp. 21–22 and 37.

2.   "Sisi received $39.5 billion from Gulf, leaked recordings show," *Middle East Monitor*, February 13, 2015, https://www.middleeastmonitor.com/news/africa/16952-sisi-received-395bn-from-gulf-leaked-recordings-show.

3.   *Al-sha'biyyat.*

4.   On the story of the Swedish firm in Saudi Arabia, see Pascal Menoret, *Joyriding in Riyadh: Oil, Urbanism, and Road Revolt* (Cambridge University Press 2014), pp. 126–128.

5.   *Tarkib.*

6.   *"Ya Fahd ya himar bi't Makka bi-dular."*

7.   Jean-Michel Foulquier, *Arabie séoudite, la dictature protégée* (Albin Michel 1995).

8.   Rosie Bsheer, "A Counter-Revolutionary State: Popular Movements and the Making of Saudi Arabia," *Past and Present* 238 (2018), pp. 268–275.

9.   Hélène Thiollet, "Nationalisme d'État et nationalisme ordinaire en Arabie Saoudite: La nation saoudienne et ses immigrés," *Raisons Politiques* 37, no. 1 (2010): 89–101.

10.   "Saudi Arabia Arrests More Women's Rights Activists," Reuters, June 20, 2018.

11.   "Saudi Clerics Detained in Apparent Bid to Silence Dissent," Reuters, September 10, 2017.

12.   "Saudi Arabia Seeks Death Penalty for Preacher Awdah—Family, Friends," Reuters, September 4, 2018.

13.   *Jam'iyya al-huquq al-siyasiya wa-l-madaniya*, whose acronym is HASM.

14.   *'Asifa al-hazm.*

15.   Al-Rasheed, *Muted Modernists, op. cit.*, p. 40–55.

16.   *Jihad al-kalima.*

17.   *Jihad silmi.*

18.   Madawi Al-Rasheed, *Muted Modernists: The Struggle over Divine Politics in Saudi Arabia* (Oxford University Press 2016), pp. 69, 273.

19. *Al-munasirun.*

20. Al-Rasheed, *Muted Modernists*, p. 47.

21. Fishman, *Bourgeois Utopias: The Rise and Fall of Suburbia* (Basic Books 1987), pp. 34, 38.

22. Thomas Hegghammer, *Jihad in Saudi Arabia: Violence and Pan-Islamism since 1979* (Cambridge University Press 2010), pp. 89–90.

23. Madawi Al-Rasheed, *Contesting the Saudi State: Islamic Voices from a New Generation* (Cambridge University Press 2007), pp. 175–210.

24. Hasso Spode, "Fordism, Mass Tourism, and the Third Reich: The 'Strength Through Joy' Seaside Resorts as an Index Fossil," *Journal of Social History* 38, no. 1 (2004): 131.

25. Samuli Schielke, "Boredom and Despair in Rural Egypt," *Contemporary Islam* 2, no. 3: 251–270; Samuli Schielke, "Ambivalent Commitments: Troubles of Morality, Religiosity, and Aspiration among Young Egyptians," *Journal of Religion in Africa* 39 (2009): 158–185; Samuli Schielke, *Egypt in the Future Tense: Hope, Frustration, and Ambivalence Before and After 2011* (Indiana University Press 2015), in particular chapters 1, 3, and 6.

26. Achille Mbembe, *Politiques de l'inimitié* (La Découverte 2016), p. 55–56.

27. An exception to this metropolitan, elitist orientation is Marc Aziz Michael's "The Politics of Rurbanization and the Egyptian Society of the Muslim Brothers," *Political Geography* 72 (2019): 99–115.

28. Faisal Devji and Zaheer Kazmi (eds.), *Islam After Liberalism* (Oxford University Press 2017), p. 5.

29. Asad, *Genealogies of Religion: Discipline and Reasons of Power in Christianity and Islam* (Johns Hopkins University Press 1993), p. 233.

30. Clifford Geertz, *The Interpretation of Cultures: Selected Essays* (Basic Books 1973), pp. 219–229.

31. Faisal Devji, *Landscape of the Jihad: Militancy, Morality, Modernity* (Cornell University Press 2005).

32. Asad, *Genealogies of Religion*, p. 228.

References

ARCHIVES

Constantinos A. Doxiadis Archives, Benaki Museum, Athens.

Albert J. Meyer Papers, Pusey Library, Harvard University, Cambridge, MA.

Société Centrale pour l'Équipement du Territoire International Archives, Caisse des Dépôts et Consignations, Paris.

PUBLISHED SOURCES

Abu-Sulaiman, Abdulaziz Mahdi. "Learning to Plan: Jedda, 1959–87" (PhD thesis, University of Pennsylvania 1996).

Adelkhah, Fariba. *La révolution sous le voile. Femmes islamiques d'Iran* (Karthala 1991).

Adelkhah, Fariba, and François Georgeon (eds.). *Ramadan et politique* (CNRS Éditions 2000).

Adelson, Roger. "British and U.S. Use and Misuse of the Term 'Middle East,'" in Michael Bonine, Abbas Amanat, and Michael Gasper (eds.), *Is There a Middle East? The Evolution of a Geopolitical Concept* (Stanford University Press 2012).

Agamben, Giorgio. *State of Exception* (University of Chicago Press 2005).

Ahmad, Raf'at Sayyid. *Rasa'il Juhayman al-'Otaybi, Qa'id al-muqtahamin li-l-masjid al-haram bi-Makka* (The letters of Juhayman al-Utaybi, leader of the occupation of the Great Mosque of Mecca) (Madbouli 2004).

Al al-Shaykh, Muhammad bin Ibrahim. *Fatwa fi hukm sharb al-dukhan* (fatwa about smoking tobacco) (General presidency of scholarly research and ifta 2012).

Al-But'hie, Ibrahim. "The Role of Citizens in Defining the Meaning and Quality of Traditional and Modern Built Environments: An Exploratory Study of Al-Riyad, Saudi Arabia" (PhD thesis, University of Texas at Austin 1996).

Al-Enazy, Askar. *The Creation of Saudi Arabia: Ibn Saud and British Imperial Policy, 1914–1927* (Routledge 2013).

Al-Faqih, Sa'd. "History of Dissent: The Rise and Evolution of the Modern Islamic Reform Movement in Saudi Arabia," in *Arabia Unveiled* (monthly newsletter of the Movement of Islamic Reform in Arabia), 1996–1997.

Al-Gabbani, Mohammed. "Population Density Pattern and Change in the City of Riyadh, Saudi Arabia," *GeoJournal* 24, no. 4 (1991): 375–385.

Al-Ghadhdhami, 'Abd Allah. *Hikayat al-hadatha fi-l-mamlaka al-'arabiyya al-su'udiyya* (The story of modernity in Saudi Arabia) (al-Markaz al-Thaqafi al-'Arabi 2004).

Al-Hathloul, Saleh. "Tradition, Continuity, and Change in the Built Environment: The Arab-Muslim City" (PhD thesis, MIT 1981).

Al-Hemaidi, Waleed. "The Metamorphosis of the Urban Fabric in an Arab-Muslim City: Riyadh, Saudi Arabia," *Journal of Housing and the Built Environment* 16, no. 2 (2001).

Al-Hudayf, Muhammad. *Dima, hubbun awwal* (Dima, A first love) (Dar al-Bara' li-l-nashr wa-l-tawzi' 2003).

Al-Hudayf, Muhammad. *Guantánamo* (Dar al-Bara' li-l-nashr wa-l-tawzi' 2003).

Al-Hudayf, Muhammad. *Mudi, hilmun yamutu taht al-aqdam* (Mudi, a trampled dream) (Dar al-Bara' li-l-nashr wa-l-tawzi' 2003).

Al-Hudayf, Muhammad. *Nuqtatu taftish* (Checkpoint) (Dar al-Bara' li-l-nashr wa-l-tawzi' 2006).

Al-Hudayf, Muhammad. *Ramad 'adat bihi Sara* (The ashes Sara came back with) (Dar al-Bara' li-l-nashr wa-l-tawzi' 2010).

Al-Huzaymi, Nasir. *Ayyam ma' Juhayman: Kuntu ma' al-Jama'a al-salafiyya al-muhtasiba* (Days with Juhayman: I was with the Salafi group that commands virtue and combats vice) (al-Shabaka al-'arabiyya li-l-abhath wa-l-nashr 2010).

Al-Jibrin, Jibrin. *Al-'Unf al-'usari khilal marahil al-haya* (Familial violence across life periods) (King Khalid Charitable Foundation 2005).

Al-Juwayyir, Ibrahim. *Ta'akhkhur al-Shabab al-Jami'i fi-l-Zawaj* (The delayed marriage of university students) ('Obeikan 1995).

Al-Khudhayri, 'Abd al-'Aziz. *Idara al-hamlat al-intikhabiyya wa hamlat al-'alaqat al-'amma* (The management of electoral and public relation campaigns) (Dar Al-Sawlatiya li-l-Tarbiya 2007).

Al-Maqdisi, Abu Muhammad. *Al-Kawashif al-jaliya fi kufr al-dawla al-su'udiyya* (The clear evidence of the irreligion of the Saudi state) (Minbar al-Tawhid wa-l-Jihad 2001 [1989]).

Al-Mas'ari, Muhammad. *Al-'Adilla al-qat'iyya 'ala 'adam shar'iyya al-dawla al-su'udiyya* (The final evidence of the Saudi state's lack of legitimacy) (Al-Rafed 1996).

Al-Nakib, Farah. *Kuwait Transformed: A History of Oil and Urban Life* (Stanford University Press 2016).

Al-Qahtani, Fahd. *Zilzal Juhayman fi Makka* (Juhayman's earthquake in Mecca) (Munazzama al-thawra al-islamiya fi-l-jazira al-'arabiya 1987).

Al-Qaradawi, Yusef. *Ibn al-Qariya wa-l-Kuttab: Malamih Sira wa Masira* (Son of the village and of the Quranic school: an autobiography) (Dar al-Shuruq 2006).

Al-Rasheed, Madawi. *Contesting the Saudi State: Islamic Voices from a New Generation* (Cambridge University Press 2007).

Al-Rasheed, Madawi. *A History of Saudi Arabia* (Cambridge University Press 2002).

Al-Rasheed, Madawi. *A Most Masculine State: Gender, Politics, and Religion in Saudi Arabia* (Cambridge University Press 2013).

Al-Rasheed, Madawi. *Muted Modernists: The Struggle over Divine Politics in Saudi Arabia* (Oxford University Press 2016).

Al-Said, Fahad. "The Pattern of Structural Transformation of the Saudi Contemporary Neighborhood: The Case of Malaz, Riyadh, Saudi Arabia," 39th International Society of City and Regional Planners Congress, 2003.

Al-Salim, Khalid. *Al-Dubt al-Ijtima'i wa-l-Tamasuk al-Usari* (Social control and family cohesion) (n.p. 2000).

Al Sa'ud, Munira. *Idha' al-Atfal: Anwa'uhu wa asbabuhu wa khasa'is al-muta'rarridina lah* (Violence toward children: typology, causes, and characteristics of the victims) (Dar al-Thaqafa al-Misriyya 2000).

Alshamsi, Mansoor Jassem. *Islam and Political Reform in Saudi Arabia: The Quest for Political Change and Reform* (Routledge 2011).

Al-Shithri, 'Abd al-'Aziz. *Waqt al-Faragh wa Shaghluhu fi Madinat al-Riyad: Dirasa Maydaniyya* (Free time and its usage in Riyadh: a field study) (Imam Muhammad bin Saud Islamic University 2001).

Alskait, Khalid. "Impact of Increasing Building Density on Urban Roads: The Case of Riyadh," Paper presented at the World Planning Schools Congress, Perth, July 4–8, 2011.

Al-Tirmidhi, Abu 'Isa Muhammad bin 'Isa. *Jami' al-Tirmidhi*, vol. 6 (Darussalam 2007).

Altorki, Soraya, and Donald P. Cole, *Arabian Oasis City: The Transformation of 'Unayzah* (University of Texas Press 1989).

Al-Wadi'i, Muqbil. *Al-Musara'a* (The wrestle) (n.p. 1992).

Al-Yasini, Ayman. *Al-islam wa-l-'arsh: al-din wa-l-dawla fi-l-su'udiyya* (Islam and the throne: religion and state in Saudi Arabia) (Jaridat al-Ahali 1990).

Aminzade, Ron, Jack Goldstone, Doug McAdam, Elizabeth J. Perry, William H. Sewell Jr., Sidney Tarrow, and Charles Tilly (eds.). *Silence and Voice in the Study of Contentious Politics* (Cambridge University Press 2001).

Anas, 'Abd Allah. *Wilada al-Afghan al-'Arab: Sirat 'Abd Allah Anas bayna Mas'ud wa 'Abd Allah 'Azzam* (The birth of the Arab Afghans: autobiography of Abdullah Anas, between [Ahmad Shah] Mas'ud and Abdullah 'Azzam) (Saqi Books 2002).

Arebi, Saddeka. *Women and Words in Saudi Arabia: The Politics of Literary Discourse* (Columbia University Press 1994).

Ariès, Philippe. *Centuries of Childhood: A Social History of Family Life* (Vintage 1965).

Asad, Talal. *Genealogies of Religion: Discipline and Reasons of Power in Christianity and Islam* (Johns Hopkins University Press 1993).

Asad, Talal. "The Idea of an Anthropology of Islam," *Qui Parle* 17, no. 2 (2009): 1–30.

Asad, Talal. *Secular Translations: Nation-State, Modern Self, and Calculating Reason* (Columbia University Press 2018).

Auyero, Javier. *Poor People's Politics: Peronist Survival Networks and the Legacy of Evita* (Duke University Press 2000).

Babb, Florence. "'Managua Is Nicaragua': The Making of a Neoliberal City," *City & Society* 11, no. 1 (1999): 27–48.

Bajoit, Guy. "Exit, Voice, Loyalty . . . and Apathy. Les réactions individuelles au mécontentement." *Revue française de sociologie* 29, no. 2 (1988): 325–345.

Bandler, Richard, and John Grinder, *Frogs into Princes: Neuro Linguistic Programming* (Real People Press 1979).

Barnes, Trevor, and Claudio Minca, "Nazi Spatial Theory: The Dark Geographies of Carl Schmitt and Walter Christaller," *Annals of the Association of American Geographers* 103, no. 3 (2013): 669–687.

Bayat, Asef. "Islamism and the Politics of Fun," *Public Culture* 19, no. 3 (2007): 433–459.

Bayat, Asef. *Street Politics: Poor People's Movements in Iran* (Columbia University Press 1997).

Beaud, Stéphane. "L'usage de l'entretien en sciences sociales. Plaidoyer pour l'entretien ethnographique." *Politix* 35, (1996) 226–257.

Beaugrand, Claire. *Stateless in the Gulf: Migration, Nationality, and Society in Kuwait* (I.B. Tauris 2018).

Becker, Howard. *Outsiders: Studies in the Sociology of Deviance* (Free Press of Glencoe 1963).

Bennani-Chraïbi, Mounia, and Iman Farag (eds.). *Jeunesses des sociétés arabes par-delà les menaces et les promesses* (Aux lieux d'être 2007).

Bennani-Chraïbi, Mounia, and Olivier Fillieule (eds.). *Résistances et protestations dans les sociétés musulmanes* (Presses de Sciences Po 2003).

Beyerstein, Barry. "Brainscams: Neuromythologies of the New Age," *International Journal of Mental Health* 19, no. 3 (1990): 27–36.

Blondiaux, Loïc. "Faut-il se débarrasser de la notion de compétence politique? Retour critique sur un concept classique de la science politique," *Revue française de science politique* 57, no. 6 (2007): 759–774.

Bonnefoy, Laurent, and Myriam Catusse (eds.), *Jeunesses arabes du Maroc au Yémen: loisirs, cultures et politiques* (La Découverte 2013).

Bonnenfant, Paul. "L'Évolution de la vie bédouine en Arabie centrale. Notes sociologiques," *Revue de l'Occident musulman et de la Méditerranée* 23 (1977): 111–178.

Bonnenfant, Paul. "Real Estate and Political Power in 1970s Riyadh," *City: Analysis of Urban Trends, Culture, Theory, Policy, Action* 18, no. 6 (2014): 708–722.

Bourdieu, Pierre. "La jeunesse n'est qu'un mot," *Questions de sociologie* (Éditions de Minuit 1984), 143–154.

Bradley, Jane, and Heinz-Joachim Biedermann. "Bandler and Grinder's Neurolinguistic Programming: Its Historical Context and Contribution," *Psychotherapy* 22, no. 1 (1985): 59–62.

Bsheer, Rosie. "A Counter-Revolutionary State: Popular Movements and the Making of Saudi Arabia," *Past and Present* 238 (2018): 233–277.

Burgat, François. *L'islamisme en face* (La Découverte 2002). [English version: François Burgat. *Face to Face with Political Islam* (I.B. Tauris 2003).]

Burgat, François. *L'islamisme au Maghreb: La voix du Sud* (Payot 1995). [English version: François Burgat. *The Islamic Movement in North Africa* (Center for Middle Eastern Studies, University of Texas at Austin 1993).]

Burgat, François, and Muhammed Sbitli, "Les Salafis au Yémen ou la modernisation malgré tout. 'Ils le disent… c'est donc qu'ils le sont!' ou les pièges du discours de l'objet," *Chroniques Yéménites* 10 (2002), https://journals.openedition.org/cy/137#article -137.

Caldeira, Teresa P. R. *City of Walls: Crime, Segregation, and Citizenship in São Paulo* (University of California Press 2000).

Citino, Nathan. *From Arab Nationalism to OPEC: Eisenhower, Kind Saud, and the Making of U.S.-Saudi Relations* (Indiana University Press 2002).

Citino, Nathan. "Suburbia and Modernization: Community Building and America's Post-WWII Encounter with the Arab Middle East," *Arab Studies Journal* 13, no. 14 (2006): 39–64.

Clarsen, Georgine, and Lorenzo Veracini. "Settler Colonial Automobility: A Distinct Constellation of Automobile Cultures?" *History Compass* 10, no. 12 (2012): 889–900.

Cole, Donald P. *Nomads of the Nomads: The Al Murrah of the Empty Quarter* (Harlan Davidson 1975).

Cole, Donald P. "Where Have the Bedouin Gone?" *Anthropological Quarterly* 76, no. 2 (2003): 235–267.

Cooke, Miriam, and Bruce Lawrence (eds.). *Muslim Networks from Hajj to Hip Hop* (University of North Carolina Press 2005).

Covey, Stephen R. *The Seven Habits of Highly Effective People: Powerful Lessons in Personal Change* (Free Press 1989). [Translated into Arabic as *Al-'adat al-sab' li-l-nas al-akthar fa'aliya: durus fa''ala hawla taghyir al-shakhsiya* (Maktabat Jarir 2000).]

Dailami, Ahmed. "Militancy, Monarchy and the Struggle to Desacralize Kingship in Arabia," in Faisal Devji and Zaheer Kazmi (eds.), *Islam after Liberalism* (Oxford University Press 2017), 203–218.

Deeb, Lara, and Mona Harb. "Choosing Both Faith and Fun: Youth Negotiations of Moral Norms in South Beirut," *Journal of Anthropology* 78, no. 1 (2013): 1–22.

Déloye, Yves. *Les voix de Dieu. Pour une autre histoire du suffrage électoral: le clergé catholique français et le vote, 19e-20e siècles* (Fayard 2006).

Dercon, Chris. *Sculptures of Jeddah: Twentieth Century Sculpture in the Arabian Peninsula* (Booth-Clibborn Editions 2015).

Devji, Faisal. *Landscape of the Jihad: Militancy, Morality, Modernity* (Cornell University Press 2005).

Devji, Faisal. *The Terrorist in Search of Humanity: Militant Islam and Global Politics* (Oxford University Press 2009).

Devji, Faisal, and Zaheer Kazmi (eds.). *Islam After Liberalism* (Oxford University Press 2017).

Doxiadis, Constantinos A. *Architecture in Transition* (Oxford University Press 1963).

Dresch, Paul. *A History of Modern Yemen* (Cambridge University Press 2000).

Dunbar-Ortiz, Roxanne. *An Indigenous Peoples' History of the United States* (Beacon Press 2015).

Duncan, George Orr. "The Planning and Development of the City of Jeddah, 1970–1984" (PhD thesis, University of Durham 1987).

Ende, Werner. "The Nakhawila, a Shiite Community in Medina: Past and Present," *Die Welt des Islams* 37. no. 3 (1997): 263–348.

Fabietti, Hugo. *El Pueblo del Desierto. Historia, Economia, Estructura Familiar, Religion, etc., de un Pueblo Nomada* (Editorial Mitre 1985).

Facey, William. *Riyadh: The Old City* (Immel Publishing 1992).

Fandy, Mamoun. *Saudi Arabia and the Politics of Dissent* (St. Martin's Press 1999).

Farge, Arlette. *Dire et mal dire. L'opinion publique au 18eme siècle* (Le Seuil 1992).

Featherstone, Mike, Nigel Thrift, and John Urry (eds.), *Automobilities* (Sage 2005).

Fillieule, Olivier. *Stratégies de la rue. Les manifestations en France* (Presse de Sciences Po 1997).

Fishman, Robert. *Bourgeois Utopias: The Rise and Fall of Suburbia* (Basic Books 1987).

Foulquier, Jean-Michel. *Arabie séoudite, la dictature protégée* (Albin Michel 1995).

Freer, Courtney. *Rentier Islamism: The Influence of the Muslim Brotherhood in Gulf Monarchies* (Oxford University Press 2018).

Friedman, Andrew. *Covert Capital: Landscapes of Denial and the Making of U.S. Empire in the Suburbs of Northern Virginia* (University of California Press 2013).

Garrigou, Alain. *Histoire sociale du suffrage universel en France: 1848–2000* (Le Seuil 2002).

Geertz, Clifford. *The Interpretation of Cultures: Selected Essays* (Basic Books 1973).

Ghrawi, Claudia. "Structural and Physical Violence in Saudi Arabian Oil Towns, 1953–56," in Ulrike Freitag, Nelida Fuccaro, Claudia Ghrawi, and Nora Lafi (eds.), *Urban Violence in the Middle East: Changing Cityscapes in the Transition from Empire to Nation State* (Berghahn 2015): 243–264.

Ghrawi, Claudia. "A Tamed Urban Revolution: Saudi Arabia's Oil Conurbation and the 1967 Riots," in Nelida Fuccaro (ed.), *Violence and the City in the Modern Middle East* (Stanford University Press 2016): 109–126.

Graeber, David. *Direct Action: An Ethnography* (AK Press 2009).

Guionnet, Christine. *L'apprentissage de la politique moderne. Les élections municipales sous la monarchie de Juillet* (L'Harmattan 1997).

Haenni, Patrick. *L'islam de marché: L'autre révolution conservatrice* (Le Seuil 2005).

Haenni, Patrick. *L'ordre des caïds. Conjurer la dissidence urbaine au Caire* (Karthala 2005).

Hall, Peter. *Cities of Tomorrow: An Intellectual History of Urban Planning and Design since 1880* (Wiley Blackwell 2014).

Haguenauer-Caceres, Lucille. "Construire à l'étranger: le rôle de la SCET Coopération en Côte d'Ivoire de 1959 à 1976," *Histoire Urbaine* 23, no. 3 (2008): 145–159.

Hegghammer, Thomas. *Jihad in Saudi Arabia: Violence and Pan-Islamism since 1979* (Cambridge University Press 2010).

Herrera, Linda, and Asef Bayat (eds.), *Being Young and Muslim: New Cultural Politics in the Global South and North* (Oxford University Press 2010).

Hertzfeld, Michael. *The Social Production of Indifference: Exploring the Symbolic Roots of Western Bureaucracy* (University of Chicago Press 1993).

Hirschkind, Charles. *The Ethical Soundscape: Cassette Sermons and Islamic Counterpublics* (Columbia University Press 2006).

Hirschman, Albert O. *Exit, Voice, and Loyalty: Responses to Decline in Firms, Organizations, and States* (Harvard University Press 1970).

Ho, Engseng. *The Graves of Tarim: Genealogy and Mobility Across the Indian Ocean* (University of California Press 2006).

Hoggart, Richard. *The Uses of Literacy* (Essential Books 1957).

Holston, James. *The Modernist City: An Anthropological Critique of Brasília* (The University of Chicago Press 1989).

Institut Français d'Architecture. *Architectures Françaises Outre-Mer* (Mardaga 1995).

Jackson, Sherman. *Islamic Law and the State: The Constitutional Jurisprudence of Shihab al-Din al-Qarafi* (Brill 1996).

Jones, Toby C. *Desert Kingdom: How Oil and Water Forged Modern Saudi Arabia* (Harvard University Press 2010).

Jones, Toby C. "Rebellion on the Saudi Periphery: Modernity, Marginalization, and the Shiʿa Uprising of 1979," *International Journal of Middle East Studies* 38 (2006): 213–233.

Kallus, Rachel. "Patrick Geddes and the Evolution of a Housing Type in Tel-Aviv," *Planning Perspectives* 12 (1997): 281–320.

Khan, Navida. "Geddes in India: Town Planning, Plant Sentience, and Cooperative Evolution," *Environment and Planning* 29 (2011): 840–856.

Kimball, Solon. "American Culture in Saudi Arabia," *Proceedings of the New York Academy of Science* 18, no. 5 (1956): 469–484.

Knight, Michael Muhammad. *Why I Am A Salafi* (Soft Skull Press 2015).

Koolhaas, Rem, and Hans Ulrich Obrist, *Project Japan: Metabolism Talks* (Taschen 2009).

Kracauer, Siegfried. *The Mass Ornament: Weimar Essays* (Harvard University Press 1995 [1924]).

Kramer, Martin. "Coming to Terms: Fundamentalists or Islamists?" *Middle East Quarterly* 10, no. 2 (2003): 65–77.

Kurzman, Charles. "Une déploration pour Mustafa: Les bases quotidiennes de l'activisme politique," in Mounia Bennani-Chraïbi and Olivier Fillieule (eds.), *Résistances et protestations dans les sociétés musulmanes* (Presses de Sciences Po 2003): 177–196.

Kyrtsis, Alexandros-Andreas. *Constantinos A. Doxiadis: Texts, Design Drawings, Settlements* (Ikaros 2006).

Lacroix, Stéphane. "L'apport de Muhammad Nasser al-Din al-Albani au salafisme contemporain," in Bernard Rougier (ed.), *Qu'est-ce que le salafisme?* (Presses Universitaires de France 2008): 45–64.

Lacroix, Stéphane. *Awakening Islam: The Politics of Dissent in Contemporary Saudi Arabia* (Harvard University Press 2011).

Lacroix, Stéphane. "Between Revolution and Apoliticism: Nasser al-Din al-Albani and his Impact on the Shaping of Contemporary Salafism," in Roel Meijer (ed.), *Global Salafism: Islam's New Religious Movement* (Columbia University Press 2009), 58–80.

Lahr, Angela M. *Millennial Dreams and Apocalyptic Nightmares: The Cold War Origins of Political Evangelicalism* (Oxford University Press 2007).

Lauzière, Henri. *The Making of Salafism: Islamic Reform in the Twentieth Century* (Columbia University Press 2016).

Le Corbusier. *La Ville radieuse: Éléments d'une doctrine d'urbanisme pour l'équipement de la civilisation machiniste* (Vincent, Fréal & Cie 1963).

Ledraa, Tahar, and Naser Abu-Anzeh. "Regeneration through Urban Megaprojects in Riyadh," in Libby Porter and Kate Shaw (eds.), *Whose Urban Renaissance? An International Comparison of Urban Regeneration Strategies* (Routledge 2008), 43–62.

Lefebvre, Henri. *The Production of Space* (Wiley-Blackwell 1992).

Lefebvre, Henri. *The Urban Revolution* (University of Minnesota Press 2003).

Le Renard, Amélie. *A Society of Young Women: Opportunities of Place, Power, and Reform in Saudi Arabia* (Stanford University Press 2014).

Lewis, Bernard. *The Crisis of Islam: Holy War and Unholy Terror* (Random House 2003).

Losurdo, Domenico. *Liberalism: A Counter-History* (Verso 2011).

Mahmood, Saba. *Politics of Piety: The Islamic Revival and the Feminist Subject* (Princeton University Press 2005).

Makki, Muhammad S. "Al-namu al-'omrani wa taghayyur malamih tarkib al-Madina al-Munawwara" (Urban growth and the changing structure of Medina), Symposium on the Arab City, The Arab Urban Development Institute, Medina, Feb. 28–Mar. 5, 1981.

Mamdani, Mahmood. *Good Muslim, Bad Muslim: America, the Cold War, and the Roots of Terror* (Pantheon Books 2004).

Mandaville, Peter. *Global Political Islam* (Routledge 2007).

March, Andrew F. *Islam and Liberal Citizenship: The Search for an Overlapping Consensus* (Oxford University Press 2009).

Marx, Karl. *Zur Kritik der Hegelschen Rechtsphilosophie* (Karl Dietz Verlag 1976).

Matthiesen, Toby. "Centre-Periphery Relations and the Emergence of a Public Sphere in Saudi Arabia: The Municipal Elections in the Eastern Province, 1954–1960," *British Journal of Middle Eastern Studies* (2014): 320–338.

Mbembe, Achille. "Necropolitics," *Public Culture* 15, no. 1 (2003): 11–40.

Mbembe, Achille. *Politiques de l'inimitié* (La Decouverte 2016).

McAdam, Doug. *Freedom Summer* (Oxford University Press 1988).

McAdam, Doug. "Recruitment to High Risk Activism: The Case of Freedom Summer," *American Journal of Sociology* 92 (1986): 64–90.

McFarquhar, Michael. *Circuits of Faith: Migration, Education, and the Wahhabi Mission* (Stanford University Press 2016).

Menoret, Pascal. "L'Empire du dérisoire: Lecture d'une série televisée saoudienne de Ramadan: Tash Ma Tash" (MA thesis, Institut National d'Études Orientales, Paris 2004).

Menoret, Pascal. "Al-Intikhabat al-baladiya fi-l-mamlaka al-ʿarabiya al-suʿudiyya 2005" (The 2005 municipal elections in Saudi Arabia) (Policy Brief, Arab Reform Initiative 2005).

Menoret, Pascal. "Fighting for the Holy Mosque: The 1979 Mecca Insurgency," in Christine Fair and Sumit Ganguly (eds.), *Treading on Hallowed Ground: Counterinsurgency Operations in Sacred Spaces* (Oxford University Press 2008), 117–139.

Menoret, Pascal. *Joyriding in Riyadh: Oil, Urbanism, and Road Revolt* (Cambridge University Press 2014).

Menoret, Pascal [Charles Pichegru, pseud.]. "Les murs de Riyad: Islam et modernité urbaine en Arabie Saoudite," *Chroniques Yéménites* 9 (2001), https://journals .openedition.org/cy/72.

Michael, Marc Aziz. "The Politics of Rurbanization and the Egyptian Society of the Muslim Brothers," *Political Geography* 72 (2019): 99–115. Meyer, Albert J. *Middle Eastern Capitalism: Nine Essays* (Harvard University Press 1959).

Mitchell, Sandy. *Saudi Babylon: Torture, Corruption, and Cover-Up Inside the House of Saud* (Mainstream Publishing 2006).

Monroe, Kristin V. "Automobility and Citizenship in Interwar Lebanon," *Comparative Studies of South Asia, Africa and the Middle East* 34, no. 3 (2014): 518–531.

Mouline, Nabil. *The Clerics of Islam: Religious Authority and Political Power in Saudi Arabia* (Yale University Press 2014).

Moyer, Jonathan, David Bohl, Taylor Hanna, Brendan Mapes, and Mickey Rafa. *Assessing the Impact of War on Development in Yemen* (United Nations Development Program 2019).

Mubarak, Faisal. "Urban Growth Boundary Policy and Residential Suburbanization: Riyadh, Saudi Arabia," *Habitat International* 28 (2004): 567–591.

Mubarak, Faisal. "Urbanization, Urban Policy and City Form: Urban Development in Saudi Arabia" (PhD thesis, University of Washington 1992).

Mumford, Lewis. *The City in History: Its Origins, its Transformations, and its Prospects* (Harcourt 1968).

Munif, ʿAbd al-Rahman. *Mudun al-milh*, vol. 1: *al-Tih* (al-Muʾassasa al-ʿarabiya li-l-dirasat wa-l-nashr 1984). [English version: Abdelrahman Munif, *Cities of Salt* (Random House 1987).]

Munif, ʿAbd al-Rahman, et al. (eds.), *ʿAwdat al-istiʿmar min al-ghazuw al-thaqafi ila harb al-khalij* (The return of colonization, from the cultural assault to the Gulf War) (Riyad al-Rayyis 1991).

Nielsen, Jorgen. "Sultan al-Zahir Baybars and the Appointment of Four Chief Qadis, 663/1265," *Studia Islamica* 60 (1984).

Nielsen, Richard. *Deadly Clerics: Blocked Ambition and the Path to Jihad* (Cambridge University Press 2017).

Norton, Augustus Richard. "Thwarted Politics: The Case of Egypt's Hizb al-Wasat," in Robert W. Hefner (ed.), *Remaking Muslim Politics* (Princeton University Press 2005), 133–160.

Payton, Neal I. "The Machine in the Garden City: Patrick Geddes' Plan for Tel Aviv," *Planning Perspectives* 10 (1995): 359–381.

Pine, Jason. *The Art of Making Do in Naples* (University of Minnesota Press 2012).

Pirie, Gordon. "Non-Urban Motoring in Colonial Africa in the 1920s and 1930s," *South African Historical Journal* 63, no. 1 (2011): 38–60.

Piven, Frances F. and Richard A. Clowen. *Poor People's Movements: Why They Succeed, How They Fail* (Vintage 1979).

Polletta, Francesca. "The Laws of Passion," *Law & Society Review* 35, no. 2 (2001): 480–481.

Polletta, Francesca. "Plotting Protest: Storytelling in the 1960 Student Sit-In Movement," in J. Davis (ed.), *Stories of Change: Narratives and Social Movements* (SUNY Press 2001): 31–52.

Pouillon, François. "Un État contre les Bédouins, l'Arabie Saoudite," *Monde Arabe Maghreb-Machrek* 147 (1995): 132–148.

Qasim, 'Abd al-'Aziz. *Mukashafat* (Unveilings), vols. 1, 2, and 3 ('Ubaykan 2007).

Ralph, Laurence. *Renegade Dreams: Living Through Injury in Gangland Chicago* (University of Chicago Press 2014).

Renner, Andrea. "The American Way: IBEC Housing Projects in Latin America" (Research Report, The Rockefeller Archive Center 2010).

Renner, Andrea. "Housing Diplomacy: U.S. Housing Aid to Latin America, 1949–1973" (PhD thesis, Columbia University 2011).

Riyadh Development Authority, *Atlas Madinat al-Riyad* (Riyadh City Atlas), 1999.

Riyadh Development Authority, "Nahwi tatwir nizam naql 'am 'amin wa fa''al fi madinat al-riyad" (Toward the development of a safe and efficient public transit system in Riyadh), 2000.

Robin, Corey. *The Reactionary Mind: Conservatism from Edmund Burke to Sarah Palin* (Oxford University Press 2011).

Roy, Olivier. *Globalized Islam: The Search for a New Oumma* (Columbia University Press 2006).

Rutter, Eldon. *The Holy Cities of Arabia* (G. P. Putnam's Sons 1928).

Saghi, Omar. *Paris-La Mecque: Sociologie d'un Pèlerinage* (Presses universitaires de France 2010).

Sampson, William. *Confessions of an Innocent Man: Torture and Survival in a Saudi Prison* (McClelland & Steward 2006).

Sargent, Daniel. *A Superpower Transformed: The Remaking of American Foreign Relations in the 1970s* (Oxford University Press 2015).

Savage, Jon. *Teenage: The Creation of Youth, 1875–1945* (Penguin 2007).

Schielke, Samuli. "Ambivalent Commitments: Troubles of Morality, Religiosity, and Aspiration among Young Egyptians," *Journal of Religion in Africa* 39 (2009): 158–185.

Schielke, Samuli. "Boredom and Despair in Rural Egypt," *Contemporary Islam* 2, no. 3 (2008): 251–270.

Schielke, Samuli. *Egypt in the Future Tense: Hope, Frustration, and Ambivalence Before and After 2011* (Indiana University Press 2015).

Schielke, Samuli. "Second Thoughts about an Anthropology of Islam, or How to Make Sense of Grand Schemes in Everyday Life," ZMO Working Papers 2 (2010).

Schielke, Samuli, and Lisa Debevec (eds), *Ordinary Lives and Grand Schemes: An Anthropology of Everyday Religion* (Berghahn Books 2012).

Schwedler, Jillian. *Faith in Moderation: Islamist Parties in Jordan and Yemen* (Cambridge University Press 2007).

Scott, James C. *Domination and the Arts of Resistance: Hidden Transcript* (Yale University Press 1990).

Scott, James C. *Seeing Like a State* (Yale University Press 1998).

Seiler, Cotton. *Republic of Drivers: A Cultural History of Automobility in America* (The University of Chicago Press 2008).

Seurat, Michel. *L'État de barbarie* (Le Seuil 1989).

Shoshkes, Ellen. "Jacqueline Tyrwhitt: A Founding Mother of Modern Urban Design," *Planning Perspectives* 21 (2006): 179–197.

Singerman, Diane. *Avenues of Participation: Family, Politics and Networks in Urban Quarters of Cairo* (Princeton University Press 1995).

Spode, Hasso. "Fordism, Mass Tourism, and the Third Reich: The 'Strength Through Joy' Seaside Resorts as an Index Fossil," *Journal of Social History* 38, no. 1 (2004): 127–155.

Steinberg, Guido. *Religion und Staat in Saudi-Arabien: Die Wahhabitischen Gelehrten 1902–1953* (Ergon Verlag 2002).

Steinberg, Guido. "The Wahhabi Ulama and the Saudi State: 1745 to the Present," in Paul Aarts and Gerd Nonneman (eds.), *Saudi Arabia in the Balance: Political Economy, Society, Foreign Affairs* (Hurst & Co. 2005): 11–34.

Tammam, Hossam. "The Salafization of the Muslim Brothers. The Erosion of the Fundamental Hypothesis and the Rising of Salafism within the Muslim Brotherhood: The Path and Repercussions of Change" (pamphlet, Bibliotheca Alexandrina 2011).

Tammam, Husam, and Patrick Haenni, "Le management, nouvelle utopie islamiste. Une lecture managériale des textes," *Revue française de gestion* 33, no. 171 (2007), 175–193.

Tarrow, Sidney. *Power in Movement: Social Movements, Collective Action and Politics* (Cambridge University Press 1994).

Taylor, Verta. "Social Movement Continuity: The Women's Movement in Abeyance," *American Sociological Review* 54 (1989): 761–775.

Thévenot, Laurent. "Une jeunesse difficile: Les fonctions sociales du flou et de la rigueur dans les classements," *Actes de la recherche en sciences sociales* 26, no. 1 (1979): 3–18.

Thiollet, Hélène. "Nationalisme d'État et nationalisme ordinaire en Arabie Saoudite: La nation saoudienne et ses immigrés," *Raisons Politiques* 37, no. 1 (2010): 89–101.

Thompson, Edward P. *The Making of the English Working Class* (Penguin 1982).

Tilly, Charles, and Sidney Tarrow. *Contentious Politics* (Paradigm Publishers 2007).

Trofimov, Yaroslav. *The Siege of Mecca: The Forgotten Uprising* (Allen Lane 2007).

Vassiliev, Alexei. *The History of Saudi Arabia* (Saqi Books 2000).

Veyne, Paul. *Comment on écrit l'histoire* (Le Seuil 1971).

Vitalis, Robert. *America's Kingdom: Mythmaking on the Saudi Oil Frontier* (Verso 2009).

Vitalis, Robert. "Black Gold, White Crude: An Essay on American Exceptionalism, Hierarchy, and Hegemony in the Gulf," *Diplomatic History* 26, no. 2 (2002): 185–213.

Voltaire (François-Marie Arouet). *Essai sur les moeurs et l'esprit des nations et sur les principaux faits de l'histoire depuis Charlemagne jusqu'à Louis XIII* (Bordas 1990).

Wagemakers, Joas. *A Quietist Jihadi: The Ideology and Influence of Abu Muhammad al-Maqdisi* (Cambridge University Press 2012).

Wedeen, Lisa. *Ambiguities of Domination: Politics, Rhetorics, and Symbols in Contemporary Syria* (University of Chicago Press 1999).

Welter, Volker M. "The 1925 Master Plan for Tel-Aviv by Patrick Geddes," *Israel Studies* 14, no. 3 (2009): 94–119.

Wickham, Carrie Rosefsky. *The Muslim Brotherhood: Evolution of an Islamist Movement* (Princeton University Press 2013).

Wiktorowicz, Quentin. *The Management of Islamic Activism: Salafis, the Muslim Brotherhood, and State Power in Jordan* (SUNY Press 2001).

Wilford, Justin G. *Sacred Subdivisions: The Postsuburban Transformation of American Evangelicalism* (New York University Press 2012).

Willis, John. "Governing the Living and the Dead: Mecca and the Emergence of the Saudi Biopolitical State," *American Historical Review* 122, no. 2 (2017): 346–370.

Index

Stanford Studies *in* Middle Eastern
and Islamic Societies *and* Cultures

Joel Beinin and Laleh Khalili, editors

EDITORIAL BOARD
Asef Bayat, Marilyn Booth, Laurie Brand, Timothy Mitchell,
Jillian Schwedler, Rebecca L. Stein, Max Weiss